TIME SERIES ANALYSIS AND APPLICATIONS

Edited by **Nawaz Mohamudally**

Time Series Analysis and Applications
http://dx.doi.org/10.5772/intechopen.68262
Edited by Nawaz Mohamudally

Contributors

Mahmoud Ghofrani, Musaad Alolayan, Ali Babikir, Mohammed Hassan, Henry Mwambi, Toru Yazawa, Jiancheng Jiang, Sha Yu, Renata Ribeiro Do Valle Goncalves, Jurandir Zullo Junior, Bruno Ferraz Do Amaral, Elaine Parros Machado Sousa, Luciana Alvim Santos Romani, Wiston Risso, Antonio Pepe, Joseph Cavanaugh, Fan Tang, Milan Cisty, Veronika Soldanova, Nawaz Mohamudally

Published by InTech

Janeza Trdine 9, 51000 Rijeka, Croatia

Publishing Process Manager Dajana Pemac
Technical Editor SPi Global
Cover InTech Design team

First published January, 2018
Printed in Croatia
Legal deposit, Croatia: National and University Library in Zagreb

Additional hard copies can be obtained from orders@intechopen.com

Time Series Analysis and Applications, Edited by Nawaz Mohamudally
p. cm.
Print ISBN 978-953-51-3742-9
Online ISBN 978-953-51-3743-6

For EU product safety concerns:
IN TECH d.o.o., Prolaz Marije Krucifikse Kozulić 3, 51000 Rijeka, Croatia,
info@intechopen.com or visit our website at intechopen.com.

Meet the editor

Dr. Nawaz Mohamudally graduated in telecommunications from the University of Science and Technology of Lille I in France and is currently an associate professor and chairman of the Research Degrees Committee at the University of Technology, Mauritius, where he had been the head of the School of Software Engineering and Business Informatics and the School of Innovative Technologies and Engineering. He was the chairman of the Internet Management Committee, an advisory unit to the Mauritian authority from 2010 to 2014. His core research areas are mobile and pervasive computing and data science. He has successfully supervised 6 PhD students and published 150+ refereed research articles and papers, co-authored 1 book and authored 6 book chapters. Dr. Mohamudally was awarded the "Best Professor in Industrial Systems Engineering" by Africa Education Leadership Award in 2015. His current research focuses on anomaly detection engine development in IoT using time series analysis.

Contents

Preface

Time series analysis initially applied in financial analysis, statistics and forecasting has gained huge momentum in data science. This book presents a cross section of the time series applications in diverse fields such as agriculture, biostatistics, geospatial, renewable energy and others. Common issues as well as specific ones, for instance, nonlinear time series, are hereby addressed. Ten chapters including an introductory one from the editor compose the book to enlighten the readers about latest trends and developments in time series across the globe.

The possibilities offered by time series analysis are by far more efficient than traditional transform like Fourier transform in electromagnetic fields modelling, for example. However, just by representing data points in time domain does not make it spontaneous for analysis. The choice of algorithms and methodologies in itself is quite complex, and there is actually a panoply of time series analysis techniques. Readers will discover different techniques in every chapter and hopefully would be more confident about time series after reading the whole book. Moreover, a mix of general knowledge and specialised content on time series can be found. Although the mathematical intricacies are generally present in the content, the manuscripts are well described for early career researchers or university students.

It is worth mentioning that authors representing institutions from Brazil, Japan, Slovak Republic, the United States, Italy, Uruguay, Sudan and South Africa participated in this book project. Nevertheless, we expect to disseminate the knowledge compiled globally.

This book would not be possible without the support of the InTechOpen team, namely, the Publishing Process Manager Ms. Dajana Pemac and the technical editors. The chapters retained for publishing are of very high standard indeed. We wish to congratulate the authors for their efforts and contributions in this endeavour. We would like to express a note of thanks to the InTechOpen Editorial Board through the commissioning editor for this initiative and opportunity.

Associate Professor (Dr.) Nawaz Mohamudally
University of Technology,
Mauritius

Chapter 1

Introductory Chapter: Time Series Analysis (TSA) for Anomaly Detection in IoT

Nawaz Mohamudally

Additional information is available at the end of the chapter

http://dx.doi.org/10.5772/intechopen.72669

1. Introduction

Observing data points over time with proper transform may reveal valuable information about systems behaviours and trends. This book entitled "Time Series Analysis (TSA) and Applications" comes at a very opportune period where business enterprises are overloaded with data and looking for swift analytics and on the other hand have not yet trusted the powerful algorithms such as deep learning and AI. Academics prefer simple tools like Matlab or Mathematica to run TSA. However, statistics and probabilistic instruments have gained wide acceptance for decades. Time Series Analysis had been often assimilated to finance and forecasting. The chapters presented here prove the contrary and show how far TSA is being applied across an array of disciplines and how efficient and effective this technique could be if it is fittingly utilised. In the same spirit, this chapter provides an overview of time series as applied to detect anomalies in Internet of Things (IoT) networks. Specific attention is paid to anomalies that occur in smart cities IoT use cases. The final aim of this research work partly described here is to mount plug n play anomaly detection engine (ADE).

The Internet has evolved from its original aim of providing access to web resources globally to what is commonly called today Internet of Things, where it is expected that objects will internetwork and have a presence on the Internet just with an IPv6 address for example. The objects market is estimated in billions and trillions, very far from the global human population. This has led to new business models with development of dedicated IoT networks such as SigFox, LoRa, Symphony Link, and NB-IoT, and production of IoT compliant devices from microcontrollers' manufacturers such as Microchip, Intel, and Raspberry PI. Software companies have come up with virtual machines and statistical tools for big data analytics whereas network devices constructors like Cisco and Juniper for instance have come up with network

Figure 1. IoT Value Chain.

gateways and routers to accommodate devices connection, routing, and IoT data transit. The myriad of technologies involved within the IoT ecosystem should empower smart environments as it happens likewise in smart cities. The next section introduces the IoT value chain and then lists some use cases of IoT in smart environments whereby anomalies arouse, followed by the classification of anomalies in the time domain, the time series models applicable and finally problematics in applying TSA to anomaly detection in IoT.

2. IoT value chain

The IoT value chain in **Figure 1** shows that the value added services to IoT & key differentiator is the data analytics part which comprises the anomaly detection component with the help of TSA. Data analytics in IoT could be a higher income generator than key technology enablers like SDN, IPv6, and 5G, even more than machine automation. We are talking about Analytics as a Service (AaaS). According to Cisco's annual Visual Networking Index, machine-to-machine (M2M) connections that support IoT applications will account for more than half of the world's 27.1 billion devices and connections by 2021.

2.1. Anomalies categories

Table 1 illustrates the anomalies descriptions in selected smart cities IoT use cases.

Let us now classify the anomalies in the time domain.

i. *Static vs. dynamic*: anomalies are defined as data points not following current patterns; static means in the same direction but with different characteristics whereas dynamic refers to opposite direction.

Smart	***Anomalies description***	***Benefits***
Water	Water leakages	To prevent water waste
Lighting	Broken bulbs	Save time and fuel for maintenance
Home	Gas leakage	Alert home users on the incident
Building	Electricity peak and pipe leakage	Energy monitoring
Farm	Anomalies in farm data and weather	Monitor growth
Goods	Traffic congestion spots	Optimize route and delivery

Table 1. Benefits of Anomaly Detection in Smart City Applications.

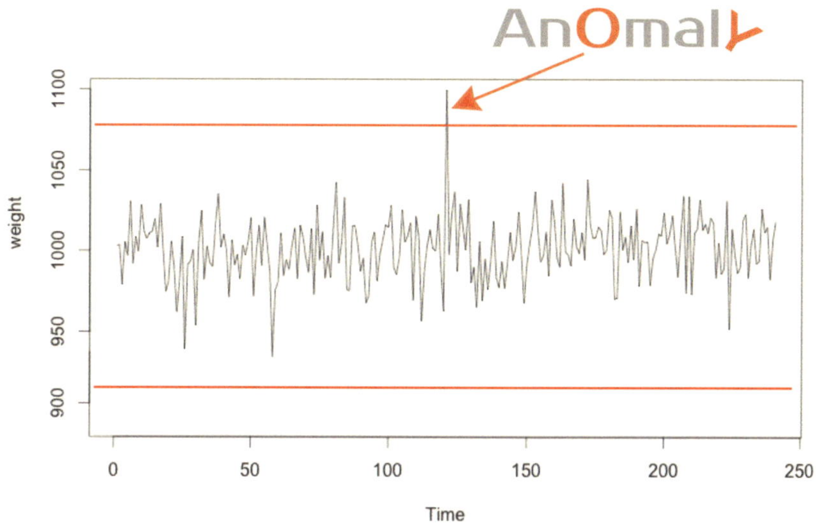

Figure 2. Outlier anomaly (https://anomaly.io/anomaly-detection-normal-distribution/).

ii. *Outlier*: an outlier is not necessarily an anomaly; it all depends on the defined threshold, for instance in the example in **Figure 2** showing sugar bags weight with respect to time, any bag <920 g or >1080 g is considered as an anomaly.

iii. *Contextual*: a data point could be an anomaly in one context but not in another. For example, a temperature of 35°C in January is an anomaly in a northern European country but normal in a southern hemisphere island for the same month.

iv. *Collective*: this happens when there is elongation in time of a particular anomaly like it happens in telecom transmission; there are accumulation of delays that result in jitters.

2.2. Time series models

There is actually no one size fit all solution for the development of an ADE as well as no de facto time series model that suits the ADE. Below are some of the popular time series models adopted for ADE in IoT.

i. *Autoregressive models*: an autoregressive model specifies that the output variable depends linearly on its own previous values. It is based on an approach that several points from the past generate a forecast of the next point with the addition of some random variable, which is usually white noise. The autoregressive integrated moving average (ARIMA) is applicable to stationary time series only.

ii. *Symbolic TSA*: data points are converted to bits and bytes 10100111001; then, Information Theory; Shannon, FFT, DFT, DWT is applied.

iii. *Seasonal-trend-Loess* (*STL*) *decomposition*: data points together with the noise or multiple data sets over a period are decomposed and analyzed to detect eventual anomalies.

iv. *Machine learning*: there are two main branches of machine learning namely supervised learning whereby the pattern for the anomaly is learnt and known, whereas in supervised mode, detection is done by inference or featuring. The latter is more challenging as the anomaly pattern is unknown and the algorithm learnt from the data points is to be analyzed. The supervised mode comprises the following methods: Decision Table, Random Forest, K-nearest Neighbor, SVMs, Deep Learning, Naive Bayes. The popular *"unsupervised"* algorithms are K-means clustering, DBSCAN, N-SVM, Stream Clustering, and LDA (Latent Dirichlet Allocation).

2.3. Problematics

Below listed are the 10 main issues, in which some are inherent to the IoT network and others to the time series properties.

i. Missing data points/holes: missing data can happen due to device malfunctioning, for instance, or issues related to device identification for example. "Potent, climate warming gases are being emitted into the atmosphere but are not being recorded in official inventories," a BBC (http://www.bbc.com/news/science-environment-40669449) investigation has found.

ii. Data corruption: for instance, data can be corrupted due to external factors or device malfunctioning; thus, it is important to ensure that the data points analyzed are accurate and come from the system under investigation.

iii. Encrypted data: in most IoT networks, data are encrypted during transmission and normally decrypted for customer usage. If detection is to be performed on encrypted data, anomaly detection might not be straightforward.

iv. Sensor fusion: data points from different sensors can be aggregated for a specific function. For example, different parameters like temperature, carbon footprint, wind speed can be captured from different sensors and merged for modelling on a server for environmental impact study. In such cases, the TSA needs to deal with multiple datasets. Sensor fusion is also assimilated to evolving sources.

v. Real-time detection: this is probably more inherent to the network itself, but the processing and programming aspects of the TSA are also determinants.

vi. Seasonality: also called as periodic time series, arrives when the time series is influenced by the seasonal factors such as day, night, month, and so on.

vii. Heteroscedasticity: it involves frequent changes in variances that can render the transformation of the time series more complex.

viii. Noisy data: data points with very low amplitude can be drowned into the intrinsic transmission electronic noise. Network equipment vendors are proposing edge computing routers that would actually clean the IoT device data in a closer location prior to run the complete analytics on the cloud.

ix. Traffic surge: at times, there could be excessive throughput like number SMS on the eve of New Year that could bring an overload on the ADE.

x. Non-linearity: date points that are not stationary and changing with time would require multivariate analysis.

3. Conclusion

This chapter highlights the challenges relevant to core elements involved in the development of an anomaly detection engine (ADE). It was found that an accurate and reliable ADE relies on three main selection factors namely, the quality of the data points, the time series transformation, and where analytics are executed. Moreover, due to the heterogeneous nature of networking environments, the convergence of communication and data protocols in IoT requires special attention when it comes to anomaly detection software development. For instance, raw data points from a smart water application are surely completely different from that from a health care IoT application; hence, the domain of application is another determinant factor in the construction of an efficient ADE. Machine learning in the unsupervised mode is indeed very efficient in situations where datasets are unpredictable. Moreover, cases where data points show nonlinear time series require multivariate analysis that makes the process more computing intensive. This property is not favorable to real-time anomaly detection as more computation at the ADE level will affect the accuracy of the ADE. From a software development perspective, the trend is similar to data mining tools embedded in popular database servers. Once the dataset is compiled, the user can choose the most appropriate statistical tool. In a near future, ERP solution providers will probably propose the ADE as a customizable module that would best fit the customers' requirements. Future work will investigate into the challenges from empirical experimentations and how anomaly detection can be translated as a service in cloud computing.

Author details

Nawaz Mohamudally

Address all correspondence to: alimohamudally@umail.utm.ac.mu

University of Technology, Mauritius, Port Louis, Mauritius

Chapter 2

Anxiety, Worry and Fear: Quantifying the Mind Using EKG Time Series Analysis

Toru Yazawa

Additional information is available at the end of the chapter

http://dx.doi.org/10.5772/intechopen.71041

Abstract

We analyse the heartbeat interval time series in this chapter. Our time series analysis concepts and techniques have been reported previously, for example, in the Intech Book chapter. Here, we would like to introduce how it works by presenting typical examples. The techniques can distinguish between healthy, sick and stressful hearts. All data were obtained by us from natural heartbeat data. Therefore, we have notes behind data, especially about behavioural psychological observations. Results of analysis are the following: healthy hearts exhibit a healthy scaling exponent (SI), which is near 1.0, stressful hearts exhibit a lower SI, such as 0.7, dying heart's SI approaches to 0.5, and so forth.

Keywords: cardiovascular system, EKG, electrocardiogram, heartbeat-interval time series, modified detrended fluctuation analysis, mDFA, scaling exponent

1. Introduction

The cardiovascular control system (CVCS) – the heart, the vessels and the brain – executes optimum performance of the blood circulation if it works under a healthy condition. If CVCS is defective, the heart contractions lose any useful rhythm, for example, like as patient who is suffering from sinus node dysfunction. It is ideal to identify the causes of defectiveness by existing diagnostic methods.

The discovery of the circulation of the blood (William Harvey in 1628) was a long time ago. But until recently, we do not know about what is the proper behaviour of CVCS. In 1982, Kobayashi and Musha reported and determined that a healthy heart exhibits a 1/f spectrum-like fluctuation [1]. 1/f fluctuations are widely found in nature (beginning, Johnson and Nyquist noise, 1920s). Until now, 1/f rhythm of healthy hearts has become a widely held notion [2, 3]. We consider that 1/f spectrum is a state where, mathematically, scaling exponent (SI) is 1.0. We have, therefore, made a time series analysis programme in order to check the heartbeat wellness: computing whether or not a time series exhibits SI = 1.0. Our technique is a random-walk analysis, which calculates 'the number of steps proceeded within a box, i.e., increased or decreased' [4, 5]. The name of the method is mDFA (abbreviated name, modified detrended fluctuation analysis). We have explained it elsewhere, about the box, steps and entrance and the exit of a box, and so on [4, 5]. As a result, our method showed that SI can quantify the condition of CVCS [4, 5]. This quantification is like the thermometer. It has a baseline value. If the body condition is normal, it is 37°.

In particular, as far as we know, the association of high SI with unpredictable cessation of heart pumping has been discovered. It has not been shown empirically before us. We first observed it in the crustacean heart; thereafter, we confirmed the same phenomena (high SI) on humans with ischaemic disease and a person who underwent a surgery that made an incision of the heart [4, 5].

By the way, our heart rhythm is apparently not regular. Cardiac rhythmicity is continuously changing, because CVCS is responding to stimulus from the internal and outer world. Therefore, marked irregularity and/or over-regularity might be a deficient state. At least mDFA seems to detect defect/problem that derives from an injury of the myocardial cells caused by either ischaemic reasons or artificial/synthetic reasons. It seems that mDFA is a better way to compute this correlation between an SI value and a poor condition of CVCS.

Lower animals such as crustaceans have a heart. Crustacean CVCS has been well studied over 100 years. For example, the English comparative biologist-anatomist Tomas Henry Huxley published about crayfish zoology in ca. 1900s [6]. And Swedish American physiologist Anton Julius Carlson has already documented detailed morphology and physiology of the heart of horseshoe crabs (*Limulus polyphemus*), in 1904 [7]. It is worth noting that Carlson already considered invertebrate hearts as a model of our heart.

Until now, the anatomy of cardiac nerve of crustaceans is well documented. The crustacean animal has autonomic nervous system that controls the heart (see Cooper et al., e.g. [8], and legendary articles [9, 10]). Typically, crustacean heart is innervated by two acceleratory nerves and one inhibitory nerve (**Figure 1**, see [11]). **Figure 2** shows a diagrammatical view of cardiac nerves in both vertebrates and crustaceans. Crustacean diagram is based on our publication [11]. In summary, the cardiac inhibitory nerve innervates pacemaker cells (P in **Figure 2**) in both crustaceans and humans. In turn, the cardiac acceleratory nerve innervates not only P cells but also myocardial cells (ventricle cells). As shown in **Figure 2**, it is important to acknowledge that nerve fibres of accelerator (CA) proceed deep inside the heart. This fact presents evidence that CA nerve regulates not only the rhythm of the heart but also the strength of heart contraction. **Figure 2** highlights an important issue in terms of evolution: the heart and its controller system resemble in both invertebrate and vertebrate. Further discussions about the resemblance are shown in Ref. [4]. Thus, we strongly expect that a basic finding obtained from invertebrate animals is applicable to humans, according to an evolutional view [4].

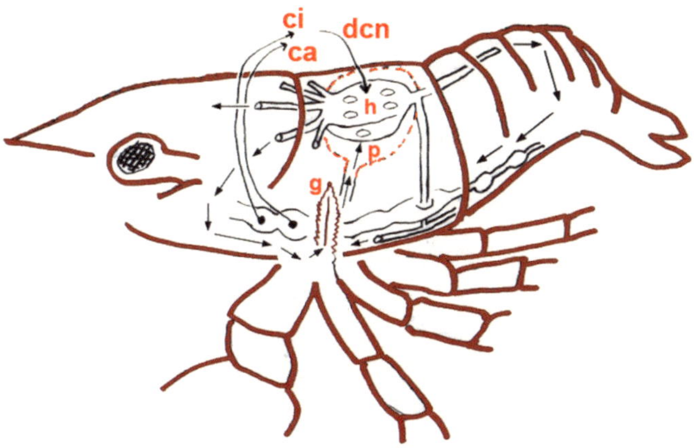

Figure 1. Crustacean CVCS. Autonomic-like regulation of the heart. Cardio-regulatory nerves are the following: ci, cardio-inhibitory nerve, ca, cardio-acceleratory nerve, dcn, bilateral dorsal cardiac nerves. A dcn carries only three nerve axons, one ci and two ca nerves. Arrows, the direction of blood flow. Blood is pumped out from the heart (h), all meeting at the gill (g) where blood is oxygenated. After leaving from the gill, blood enters the pericardial sinus (p) and finally withdrawn into the heart through ostium. Therefore, this is a system constituted of a pump and a controller.

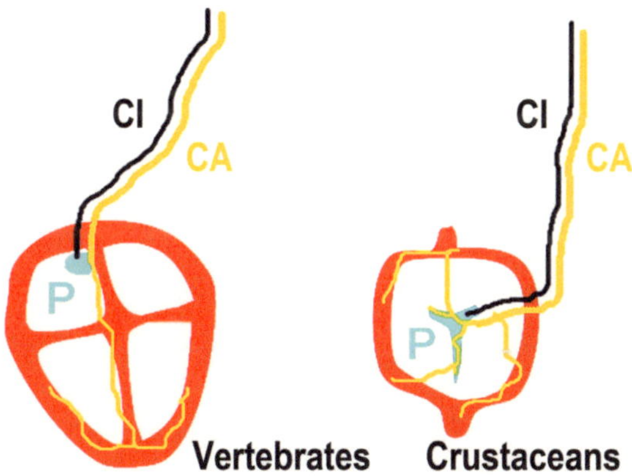

Figure 2. Resemblance of a wiring design in CVCSs between evolutionarily distinct two different animals, vertebrates (four chambered) and crustaceans (single chambered). The cardioinhibitory (CI) and cardioacceleratory (CA) nerves, P, pacemaker cells.

2. EKG: crustaceans

Therefore, we have been studied crustacean heart as a model of human heart [4, 11, 12]. Crab's electrocardiograms (EKGs) were analysed by a random-walk analysis technique that we innovated by our group [4, 5] and discovered that dying crab hearts (**Figure 3**) show a low scaling exponent [scaling index (SI)], and healthy crab hearts show a normal SI, near 1.0. Experiments on several animal species (crabs, lobsters, isopod Ligia, crayfish and insects) revealed that natural death processes decrease SI, falling towards a low level, that is, SI ≒ 0.5 [4, 5] (**Figure 4**). Then, we encountered strange specimens that exhibited a high SI, such as ~1.5. Their hearts

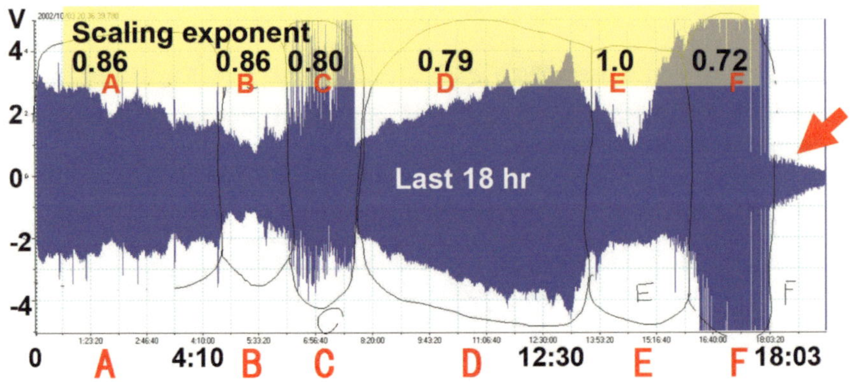

Figure 3. A natural death EKG recorded from a dying coconut crab (*Birgus latro*). From A to F, decrements in scaling exponents. Immediately after F, the heart stops pumping and fibrillation-like electrical signal remained (an arrow).

Figure 4. EKG test arena (sea water) and some specimens engaged in the tests. After mounting electrodes, EKGs were continuously recorded for the rest of their life. These specimens were terminally inconvenienced after a period of time, for example, from 2 weeks to 2 years.

stopped suddenly, meaning that they died unpredictably (**Figure 5**): we noticed that high-SI specimens are unique and of rare case. A key observation was that unpredictable death crab always had myocardial injury that was caused by the mounting of artificial EKG electrodes (**Figure 6**).

Figure 5 shows EKG data taken during the unexpected dying process. We normally put two EKG electrodes into crustacean dorsal carapace. However, this crab (**Figure 6**) received three, an excess electrode. As EKG electrodes have no good contact with the surface of heart muscles, they make EKG signal weak. We never want to damage the heart. However, this insufficient condition sometimes occurred. Any electrode can cause this unwished outcome: damaging local myocardial cells. From this unexpected outcome, we 'accidentally' obtained data that prove that myocardial damage increases SI. Then, we had an idea from this crustacean phenomenon that human ischaemic myocardium damage might be the same in terms of physiological nature, and damaged human heart might be able to be analysed with mDFA (see subsequent text).

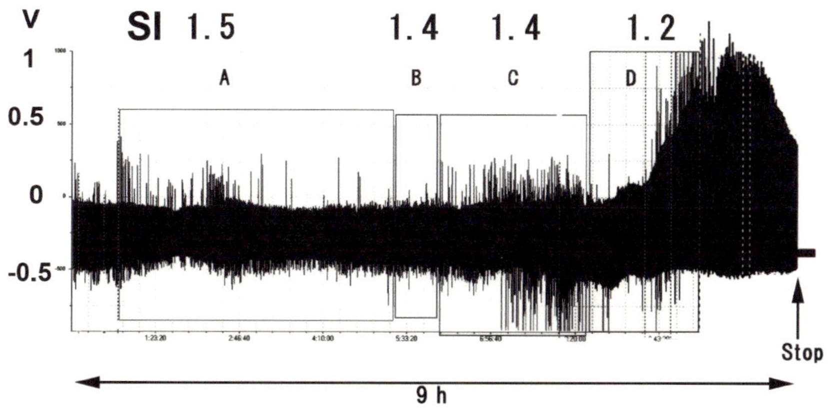

Figure 5. Unpredictable death. EKG from a crab (*Portunus* sp.). A similar experiment as shown in **Figure 3**, but this specimen's heart suddenly ceased at an arrow. Note, scaling exponents (SI) are always very high, from A to D.

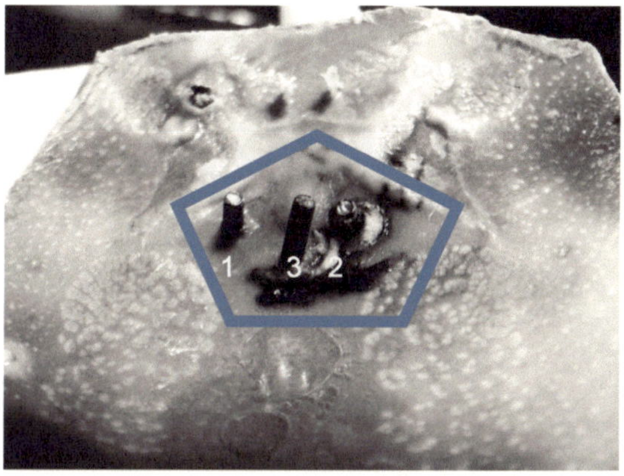

Figure 6. Inside view of a crab carapace. Gazami crab, *Portunus* sp. the approximate size of the heart is shown, pentagon-shaped diagram. This picture was taken after the crab's death. Electrode-1, -2, and -3, for EKG. Diameter of electrodes: 1 mm. One can see that electrode-3 is too long in size to damage the heart being located immediately beneath the carapace. Myocardial damage caused unpredictable cessation of heartbeat. It took 2 weeks before this crab stopped her heart pumping, which was unpredictable (see **Figure 5**).

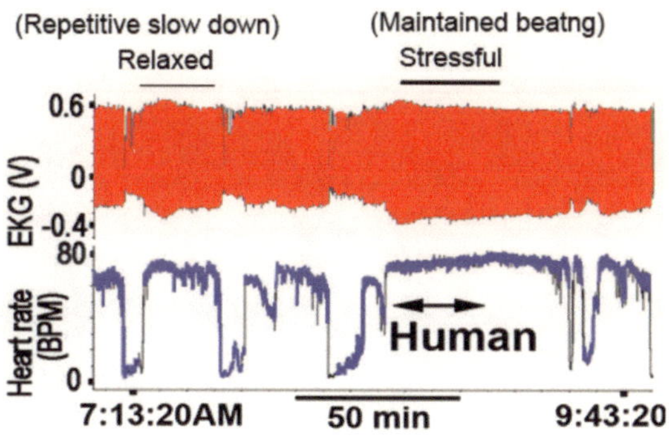

Figure 7. Intermittent-stopping manner of heartbeat. Lobster (*Panulirus japonicus*). The intermittency ceased when a human approached the lobster tank. Note: An increasing tendency of heart rate during the presence of a human (between arrows).

We believed that crustacean heartbeat continuously persists beating, that is, their hearts beat like the human heart does. But it was not the case (**Figure 7**). With EKGs from freely moving lobsters/crabs, we found that the heartbeat pattern is not continuous but intermittent if animals are not disturbed (**Figure 7**). This intermittency is induced by the activity of cardio-inhibitory nerve (**Figure 8**, [12]). Then, EKG analysis revealed that a relaxed lobster exhibits an SI near 1.0 and a nervous lobster exhibits an SI near 0.5 (**Figure 9**). These results suggested

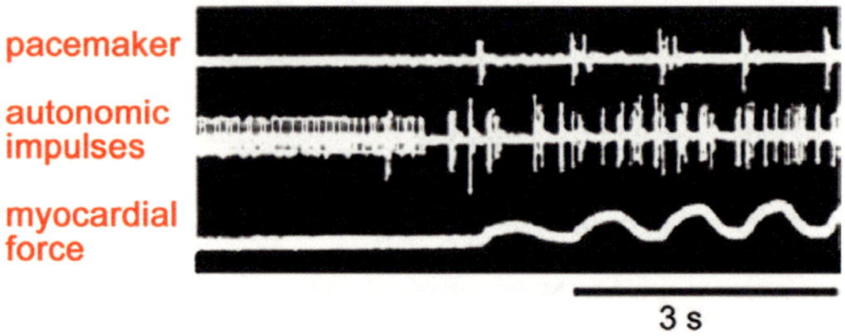

Figure 8. Simultaneous electro-physiological recording: heart (pacemaker, largest spike size, approximately 3 mV), cardio-regulatory nerve (autonomic impulses, largest spike size, approximately 500 micro-V), and mechanical transducer (myocardial force, the largest peak force of contraction is approximately 1 mg). An increase of a nerve activity corresponds to a complete stop of heartbeat. The smallest spikes in amplitude are the cardio-inhibitory impulses. The other two include the cardio-acceleratory impulses. Hermit crab (*Aniculus aniculus)* (modified from Yazawa and Kuwasawa [12]).

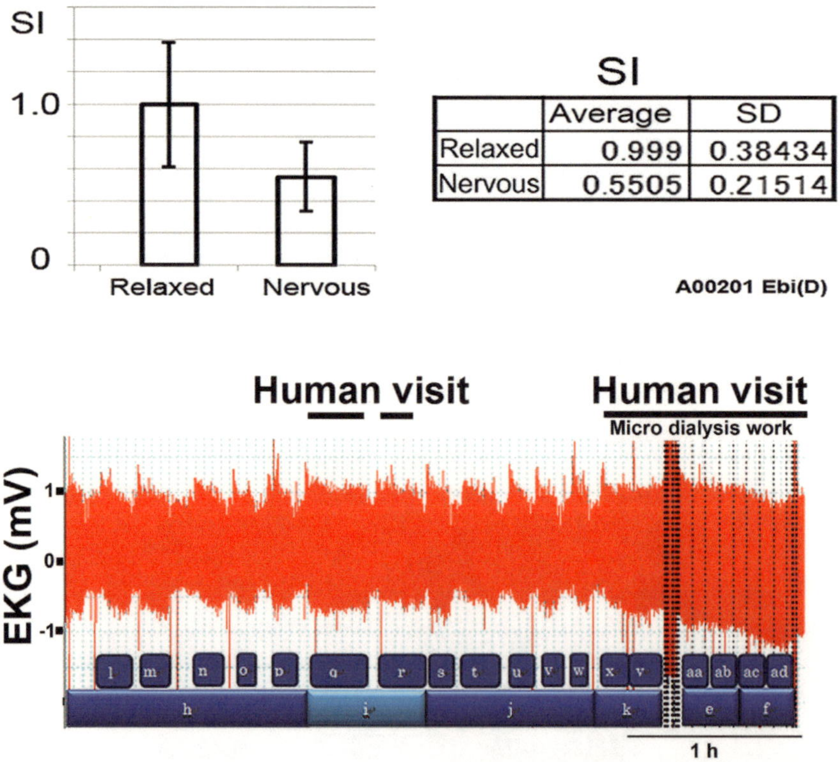

Figure 9. A long EKG recording. Lobster, *Panulirus japonicus*. A human visit (thick lines) changes the heartbeat pattern. In relaxed and nervous conditions: SI ≒ 1 and SI ≒ 0.6, respectively (upper inset). SI distinguishes lobster's psychology.

to us that SI might be useful to quantify the psychology of lobster. Indeed, stressful stimuli decrease lobster's SI significantly, and electro-physiologically the nervous/stressful state is a state of acceleration dominant and lost-inhibition controls of the heart (**Figure 7**).

We have long been specifically studying the neurobiology of crustaceans [11]. However, the crustacean experiments opened our eyes bigger, and our viewpoint was extended to human hearts. SI measures could be applicable not only to crustaceans but also to humans at least applying to their time series signal obtained from the heartbeat. According to our guideline, the normal SI ranges approximately 0.8–0.9 < SI < 1.1–1.2 [5].

3. EKG: humans

All experimental subjects were treated as per the ethical control regulations of universities (Tokyo Metropolitan University; Tokyo Women's Medical University; Universitas Advent Indonesia, Bandung; Universitas Airlangga, Surabaya, Indonesia).

We have tested so far over 500 human individuals [5]. We have learned that SI is a useful indicator for job-related stress and/or contentment of everyday life, as well as for heart disease. Typical results from them are shown in **Table 1** (modified from Ref. [4]). When subjects reply to an interview that stress level is fairly low, the person's SI is near 1.0. In turn, subjects who have stress exhibit a low SI such as 0.7–0.8 (**Table 1**). Subjects who have ischaemic heart disease, that is, having damaged myocardium, have a high SI such as 1.2–1.4 (**Table 1**). It is worth noting that we found a correlation between a high SI and myocardial damage, when we conducted crustacean experiments (**Figures 5** and **6**).

Subject	Categories cardiac disease	Age	Stress level (interview)/daily life	SI
1	Business owner (a company)	50s, male	Fairy low	1.03
2	Business owner (a company)	50s, male	High	0.72
3	Top management, President of a Univ.	60s, male	High	0.84
4	Top management, Vice President of a Univ.	40s, female	High	0.84
5	Middle management, Dean	40s, male	High	0.72
6	Middle management, Secretary of president	40s, female	High	0.76
7	Ordinary employee, Teaching only professor	50s, male	Fairly low	1
8	Ordinary employee, Teaching only professor	50s, female	Fairly low	0.98
9	Patient with stent-placement	60, male	Daily life OK	1.26
10	Patient with bypass-surgery	45, male	Daily life OK	1.38
11	Patient with implantable cardioverter	53, male	Daily life OK	1.22
12	Ventricular septal defect (20 years ago operation)	48, female	Daily life OK	1.41
13	Healthy representative, housewife	46, female	Daily life OK	1.03

Table 1. Typical mDFA results.

4. EKG-mDFA gadget

Health wellness monitoring has been advancing in health care and medical applications [14]. We focus our attention to heartbeat checking. **Figure 10** shows lab-made data logging and mDFA computing devices for a real-time detection and measurement. **Figure 10A** shows electrodes for EKG, commercially available, in-hospital use, using for a prematurely born baby in an incubator, Vitrode V, Nihon Koden, Tokyo, Japan. **Figure 10** shows an EKG amplifier, heartbeat-interval calculator and Bluetooth radio transmitter. This EKG amplifier (**Figure 10B**) receives live-body EKG signal from the two terminals (**Figure 10A** and **B**, any two electrodes, the third one is a spare electrode). **Figure 10C** shows an iPod (Apple, USA), which has a computation program mDFA [4, 5]: We incorporated mDFA into an iPod (not for sale). This system (**Figure 10**) is commercially available except for two items: (1) mDFA program and (2) modified electrode attachment (**Figure 10B**). To us, ready-made goods (**Figure 10B**) have the inconvenience for precision recording of the heartbeat signal, because it often fails to detect R-peaks of EKG.

Figure 12 shows a practical view of iPod touch screen. To start recording, an operator can touch the button (Rec), and then after completing capture of 2000 beats, it automatically

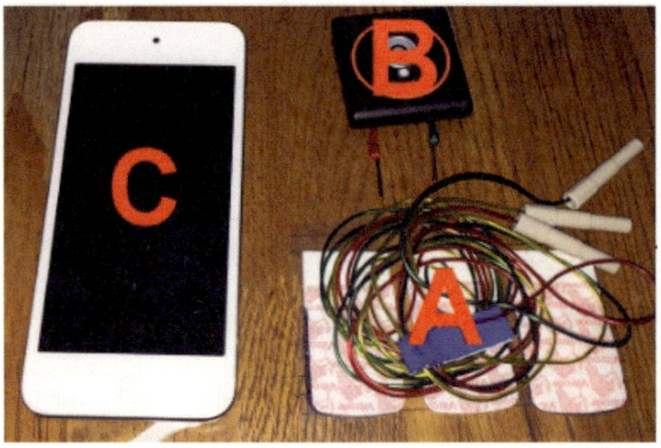

Figure 10. EKG logging and mDFA calculation, a real-time detection and measurement.

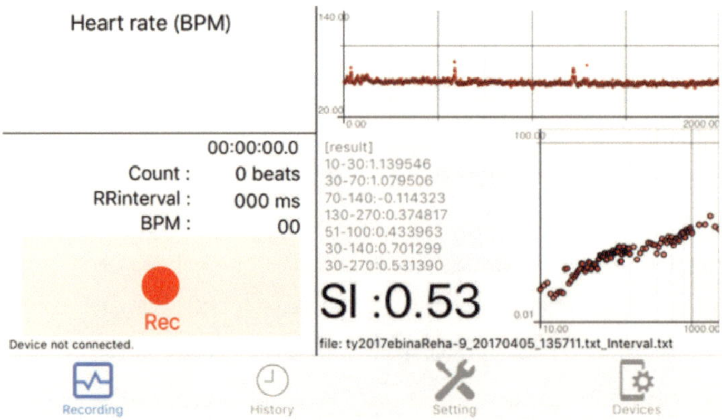

Figure 11. An example of a screen view of an iPod (lab-made, not for sale).

computes SI. As can be seen in the figure, SI is 0.53 (**Figure 11**). Generally, SIs are computed from various box size ranges: [10; 30], [30; 70], [70; 140], [130; 270], [51; 100], [30; 140] and [30; 270] (see [4, 5] in detail). For the final best SI, we take the last one, here, it is 0.531390 [30; 270], as explained in [4, 5]. Computational and mathematical explanations about mDFA are presented in [4, 5].

5. Case study 1: driving safely

Figure 12–14 show 14 results of consecutive and automated mDFA computation. A volunteer (a male aged 66) drove a car from his home to a town 150 km away to visit his mother-in-law who is hospitalised. He has been driving the road a number of times; thus he is familiar with the road conditions every corner. Furthermore, he drove safely as possible as he can by obeying the speed limit. We recorded his EKGs while driving and computed the scaling exponents (SI) using the device shown in **Figure 10**.

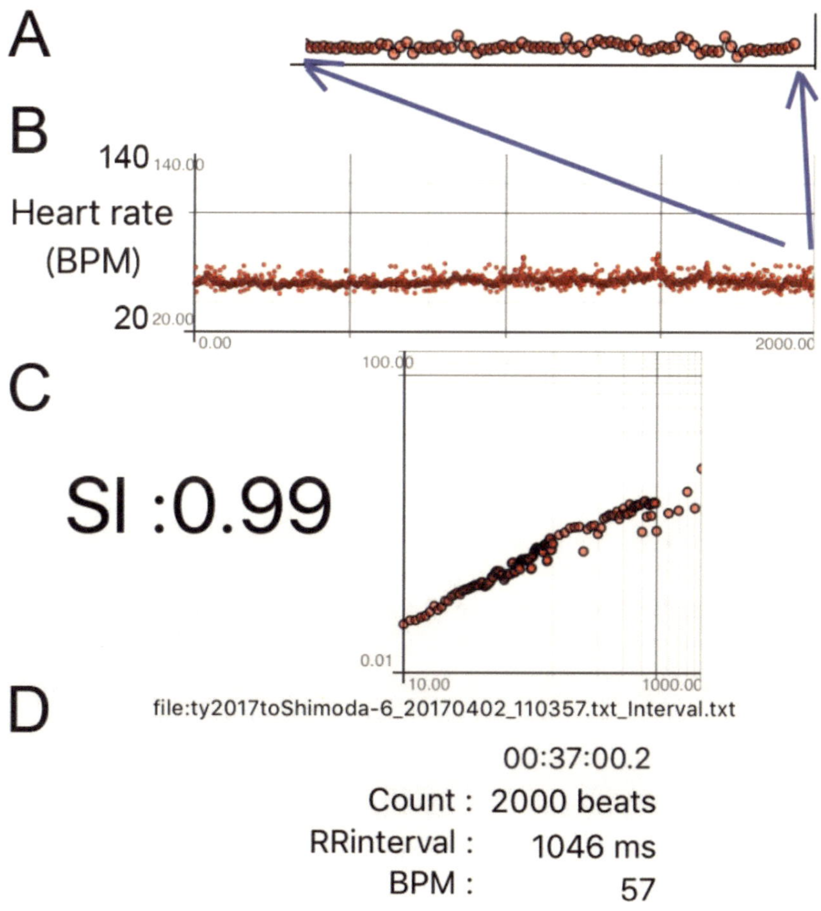

Figure 12. An example for EKG monitoring and mDFA results.

	2017Apr2, Driving a car to see relatives		SI
1	Talk about Gas, driving route, etc., before the express way		0.84
2	Express way, driving at about 70km by legal speed		1.03
3	Ordinary road, driving at about 40km by legal speed		1.09
4	Ordinary road, driving at about 40km by legal speed		1
5	Ordinary road, driving at about 40km by legal speed		1.03
6	Ordinary road, driving at about 40km by legal speed	*	0.99
7	Ordinary road, driving at about 40km by legal speed		1.04
8	Ordinary road, driving at about 40km by legal speed		1
9	Lunch, Chinease restaulant, sweet-sour pork, special black vineger		0.61
10	Visit hospital, meeting elderly mom-in-low, nervous		0.64
11	In the hospital, nervous		0.53
12	Ordinary road, driving safely, super market		0.84
13	Super market, driving safely ordinary road		0.99
14	Meeting/greeting brother-in-law, nervous conversation		0.77

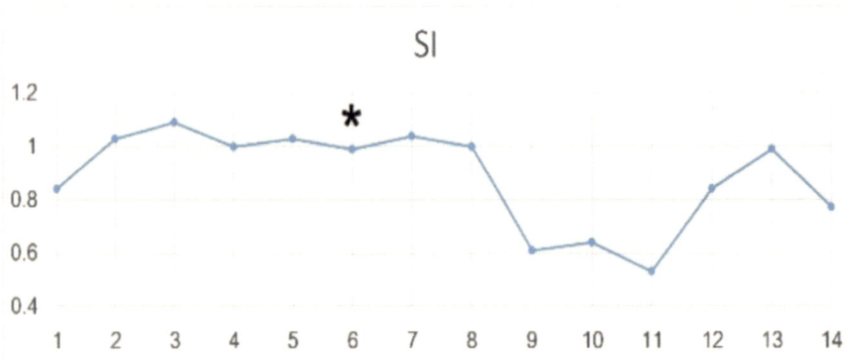

Figure 13. Fourteen consecutive EKG monitoring and resulting SIs.

The driver's heart rate was monitored by the aforementioned device (**Figure 10**). **Figure 12** shows an example result of mDFA computation. **Figure 12B** represents a 2000-beat recording, that is, an example time series. **Figure 12A** shows an expanded time series of heart rate recording (arrows). Interval signals were transferred to an iPod and stored in it. The iPod has our mDFA program [4, 5]. The program instantaneously computed the scaling exponent (SI) from the heart rate time series, immediately after capturing 2000 heartbeats (**Figure 12C**). **Figure 12D** shows a summary of the characteristics of the data (i.e. the file-name (interval. txt), 37 min and 0.2 s in total recording time for the 2000 beats, R-R interval value and heart rate (beat per min, BPM) for the last heartbeat, i.e. 1046 ms.). **Figure 12C** indicates that driving safely gives a perfect healthy scaling exponent near 1.0. Here, the SI is 0.99.

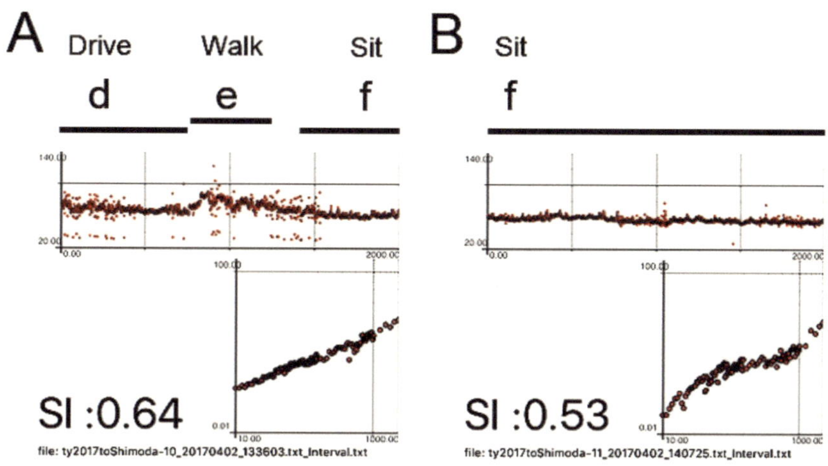

Figure 14. Two examples of iPod-mDFA. A, corresponding to **Figure 13**, number 10. B, corresponding to **Figure 13**, number 11. A 5-min break of recording between A and B. Driving the car (d), walking into the hospital (e), sitting in the room of the patient (f).

Figure 13 summarises results of driving-mDFA test. At first, SI showed a low value (SI = 0.84, **Figure 13**, number 1). This can be explained that the driver handled many worries about fuel gas, driving route and so force. After taking the express way, the driver maintained a speed limit (70 km/h) and enjoyed the blue sky of a spring morning day (SI = 1.03, **Figure 13**, number 2). Many vehicles overtook his car one right after the other although some law-abiding cars followed his car. He continued driving safely (**Figure 13**). One can see that his safe driving gave good values of SI, that is, near 1.0 as can be seen in the SI values from 2 to 8 (**Figure 13**).

It is very unique result that a specific behaviour, eating lunch, decreased the SI value (SI = 0.61, **Figure 13**, number 9). We can explain these results as the following: the mind (his brain function, i.e. autonomic nerve function) concentrated to enjoying foods, digesting them in the stomach and even pay less attention to environment. It seems that a dynamic CVCS response to environment is not dominant when eating lunch.

One can see that SI decreased when the subject walked into the hospital and visited/stayed in the room of his mother-in-law (see **Figure 13**, numbers 10 and 11, SI = 0.64 and 0.53, respectively). After going out from the hospital, SI recovered: during driving and shopping at the super market (see **Figure 13**, numbers 12 and 13). We would like to conclude that mDFA can capture anxiety/worry of a subject.

The last result (**Figure 13**, number 14, SI = 0.77) is interesting. When meeting a new person (the driver's brother-in-law) in order to greet him, SI decreased again to a very low value (**Figure 13**, number 14, SI = 0.77), which indicates that the volunteer subject is very nervous. He said that he tried NOT to display an ungentlemanly attitude to the son of mother-in-law.

Figure 14 shows two examples of iPod-mDFA screen view. This might give convincing evidence for the idea that 'stressfulness decreases SI'. We would like to emphasise that iPod-mDFA is beneficial more than we have expected.

In conclusion, stress decreases SI down to a lower value. We would like to emphasise that three examples, SI = 0.64, and SI = 0.53, SI = 0.77, are great results of iPod-mDFA gadget, and read-out time after 2000 heartbeat detections is only 1–2 s. All SI monitoring were instantaneously computed by iPod-mDFA system as shown in **Figure 13**.

6. Case study 2: overseas flight

A volunteer (a male aged 66) travelled by air from the Narita-Tokyo Airport to the Washington Dulles International Airport in order to attend a conference held in the USA. Using the iPod device, we recorded his EKGs and computed the scaling exponents as shown in **Figure 15**. Twenty-four SI measurements during the flight were documented and plotted, from which we found that mDFA accomplished understandable results similar to that shown in **Figure 13**.

We confirmed that the SI values can represent the internal world of the subject (see **Figure 15**). For example, when the subject was at an aroused state such as in the waiting lounge (see 1 in **Figure 15**), watching an exciting documentary (note: highly personalised expression), and preparing for landing (see 24 in **Figure 15**), the SI is near 1.0. In turn, when watching a movie which has an emotional involvement (note: highly personalised expression), the heartbeat of subject shows a lower SI values (see 18–20 in **Figure 15**). Finally, when the subject is at asleep condition, the SI decreases significantly (see 7–9 in **Figure 15**).

In conclusion, a happy life could fundamentally guarantee a healthy exponent. Anxiety and stress lowered the scaling exponent. mDFA might reflect psychological and physical internal bodily state. mDFA might look at the internal state through the heart. The heart is the window of the mind.

7. Uncertainty and accuracy of mDFA computation

7.1. Physics/mathematics

Readers of this article might have questions about the uncertainty and accuracy when it comes to the acquisition of the data points.

We must identify all R-peaks (R-peak within a single heartbeat of EKG trace) to construct a heartbeat-interval time series. Firstly, we put a red-mark sign on top of each and every R-peak. Unfortunately, our computer does miss some R-peaks due to the movement of subjects (animals). There are two major reasons for that. One is inevitable drift of baseline of EKG trace. The other is electric-originated or muscle-movement-originated spike-like noises. Therefore, secondly in our study, we always check/repair each and every R-peak by eyes on a PC screen. This is NOT easy tasks but must-do tasks for us; we decided so in the beginning of

http://dx.doi.org/10.5772/intechopen.71041

2017 3/20 NRT-WDC		SI
1	Waiting lounge, embarkation	1.06
2	Taxi, take-off, a disturbing kid next seat	0.74
3	Climbing flight, a disturbing kid next seat	0.86
4	Red wine service	0.91
5	Meal service, talked to the neibour thus feeling less stress	0.93
6	Meal, coffee, feeling sleepy	0.91
7	Fall asleep	0.67
8	Fall asleep	0.57
9	Fall asleep	0.54
10	Feeling sleepy	0.76
11	A long yawn, drowsy but watch a video, Mr. W. Disney	0.83
12	W. Disney history	0.89
13	W. Disney history, watch a documentary, Stars	0.86
14	Feel half awake	0.78
15	Stars, then a documentary, Petra	1.05
16	Petra, talk to a flight attendant, drinks	0.84
17	A yawn, a movie Asia, then a movie, Mr. Church, Eddy Murphy	0.9
18	Mr. Church, emotional involvement	0.76
19	Mr. Church, emotional involvement	0.77
20	Mr. Church, emotional involvement	0.77
21	Mr. Church, next movie, not so interesting	0.79
22	Movie, sleepy	0.73
23	Fall asleep	0.6
24	Sleepy but announcement "approacing WD airport"	0.95
	low battery condition	

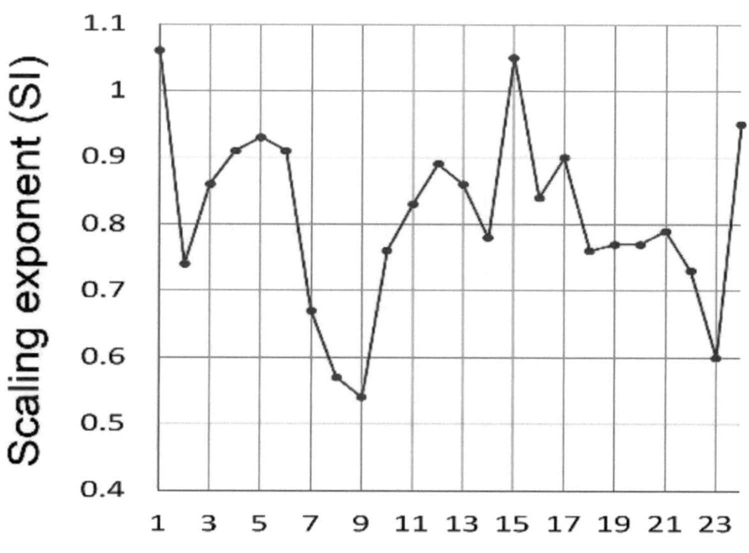

Figure 15. mDFA results during **a** 13-h overseas flight.

this study. As a result, our time series obtained from any subjects are a 100% accurate. It is a perfectly captured R-R interval data: prematured ventricular contractions, atrial fibrillations, whatever it is.

mDFA computes SI values. For a given time series data, mDFA returns only one SI. If you repeat this procedure for a given time series, you get an exactly the same SI value. Readers can imagine an artificial time series that is, for example, a white noise-like fluctuation data, it gives a scaling exponent of 0.5. A random-walk-like time series data give a scaling exponent of 1.5. However, 1/f time series (SI = 1.0) is very difficult to make artificially, definitely because 1/f-spectrum-like fluctuation is an outcome from natural dynamic phenomena. In short, a structure of a time series gives a single SI. It is mathematically accurate.

7.2. Biology/medicine

The uncertainty derives from the uncertainty of BioMedicine. The problem to be solved is how we interpret the meaning of SI. We agree that it could be a controversial issue for the people who read this article without doing experiments. Diagnosis/interpretation of data is never perfect, but SI calculation is accurate and perfect.

I recall my childhood: cicadas sing during the day of sunny summer days. It is like under perfect condition they sing. At night, I hear insects most of them were a cricket or a katydid. Whenever 'a boy of a curious nature' tried to capture them, he experienced, the insects stop singing if he approached too closer to them. Typically, animals do not love human approaching.

A few people have asked me if lobsters/crabs feel stress. My answer is 'yes' although there is a problem regarding the uncertainty and accuracy (see earlier text). The truth is not known yet, because animals never tell us how they feel. But they indeed sense a human. At least, the truth that we found is SI changes when they sense a human (**Figures 7** and **9**).

We can explain that SI measure is like temperature measure (Celsius, C degree). SI has a criterion value as temperature does. If C is 37°, our healthiness is fine as far as temperature is of concern. In the same way, if SI is one (1.0), healthiness is fine. 1/f is comparable to SI = 1. It has been shown by Kobayashi and Musha in 1982 [1] and Peng et al. in 1990s [2, 3]. In those days, when Kobayashi et al. worked, their computer never had enough power to quickly calculate/handle the time series data.

In short, the scaling exponent (SI) is accurate. The uncertainty derives from our interpretation. For our guide line, believe it or not, you may have no problem for the heart if you have SI, ranging $0.8 < SI < 1.2$.

8. Conclusion

This study suggests that the scaling exponents (SI) computed by mDFA can quantify stress. Furthermore, mDFA results were intriguing: cardiac muscle injury can be detected using mDFA. An ischaemic heart has a high SI. Before these findings, we already have proven in animal models that injured crustacean hearts exhibited a high exponent [4, 5].

http://dx.doi.org/10.5772/intechopen.71041

Although we need much more comprehensive examples, we propose that mDFA is a helpful and beneficial computation tool in the research on emotion, particularly fear and anxiety disorders, understanding how emotion is encoded in the heartbeat time series, in animal models and humans.

If the body is tortured by stimuli from environment, and/or if some stimuli would harm us internally, which is invisible from outside, we would be upsetting for the nervous system. If we use mDFA, we can realise that stimuli is distorting the autonomic nerve function, little of which has been understood by a human being until today [13], although we spend everyday under advanced science and technology. We would like to emphasise that, using mDFA computation, we can numerically evaluate/quantify the state of our body, even if it is invisible to us.

Although we (basic scientists, biologists) cannot make by ourselves, making a gadget is very rewarding. It is the right time to start making it. The gadget can work: (1) recording 2000 consecutive heartbeats without missing even a single pulse, (2) computing automatically the scaling exponent that can check the scaling exponent = 1.0, which is perfectly healthy state [4, 5], and finally (3) the gadget would capture what is going on in front of, around, and inside our mind. It gives us health information, for example, each time we use it on an everyday basis.

In the present paper, we would suggest that we have entered the world experiencing seeing inside without sight. Sometimes, a new technology does not have to be supercomplicated. mDFA computation is a kind of high school-level mathematics instead of sophisticated nonlinear measures and/or linear complex computation like the HRV, the heart rate variability. mDFA looks at how the brain communicates with the heart and also with the world. mDFA is a tool that enables us to explore previously uncharted territories. For both preventive and post-diagnostic health wellness monitoring [14], we hope that the market might find this beneficial nature of mDFA.

Acknowledgements

This work was supported by JSPS Grant No. 17 K01364.

Author details

Toru Yazawa

Address all correspondence to: yazawa-tohru@tmu.ac.jp

Biological Science, Tokyo Metropolitan University, Hachioji, Tokyo, Japan

References

[1] Kobayashi M, Musha T. 1/f fluctuation of heartbeat period. IEEE Transactions on Biomedical Engineering. 1982;**29**:456-457

[2] Goldberger AL et al. PhysioBank, PhysioToolkit, and PhysioNet. Components of a new research resource for complex physiologic signals. Circulation. 2000;**101**:e215-e220

[3] Goldberger AL et al. Application of nonlinear dynamics to clinical cardiology. Annals of the New York Academy of Sciences. 1987;**504**:195-231

[4] Yazawa T. Quantifying stress in crabs and humans using modified DFA. In: Serra PA, editor. Advances in Bioengineering. Rijeka, Croatia – European Union: Intech; 2015, Chap. 13, pp. 359-382. ISBN 978-953-51-2141-1

[5] Yazawa T. mDFA. New York, USA: ASME; monograph. 2015. ISBN 978-0-7918-6038-0

[6] Huxley TH. The crayfish: An introduction to the study of zoology. In: , International Scientific Series. Vol. XXVIII. New York: D. Appleton and Company; 1880 (Reprinted 1973, 1974, 1977, MIT Press, Cambridge, MA (1880))

[7] Carlson AJ. The nervous origin of the heart-beat in limulus, and the nervous nature of co-ordination or conduction in the heart. The American Journal of Physiology. 1904;**12**:67-74

[8] Cooper RM, Finucane HS, Adami M, Cooper RL. Heart and ventilatory measures in crayfish during copulation. Open Journal of Molecular and Integrative Physiology. 2011;**1**:36-42

[9] Alexandrowicz JS. The innervation of the heart of the crustacea. I. Decapoda. Quaternary Journal of Microscopic Science. 1932;**75**:181-249

[10] Maynard DM. Circulation and heart function. In: , The Physiology of Crustacea. Vol. 1. New York: Academic Press; 1961. p. 161-226

[11] Yazawa T, Kuwasawa K. The cardio-regulator nerves of the hermit crabs: Anatomical and electrophysiological identification of their distribution inside the heart. Journal of Comparative Physiology. 1984;**154**:871-881

[12] Yazawa T, Kuwasawa K. Intrinsic and extrinsic neural and neurohunorl control of the decpod heart. Experientia. 1992;**48**:832-840

[13] Hu K, Ivanov PC, Hilton MF, Chen Z, Ayers RT, Stanley HE, Shea SA. Endogenous circadian rhythm in an index of cardiac vulnerability of changes in behavior. Proceedings of the National Academy of Sciences. 2004;**101**(52):18223-18227

[14] Frost and Sullivan, Biosensors in Health and Wellness Monitoring. 2016. Available from: https://www.frost.com/frost-perspectives/biosensors-transforms-health-wellness-monitoring/ [Accessed: Aug 14, 2017]

Chapter 3

Agricultural Monitoring in Regional Scale Using Clustering on Satellite Image Time Series

Renata Ribeiro do Valle Gonçalves,
Jurandir Zullo Junior, Bruno Ferraz do Amaral,
Elaine Parros Machado Sousa and
Luciana Alvim Santos Romani

Additional information is available at the end of the chapter

http://dx.doi.org/10.5772/intechopen.71148

Abstract

The remote sensing images are more accessible nowadays and there are proper technologies to receive, distribute, manipulate and process long satellite image time series that can be used to improve traditional methods for harvest monitoring and forecasting. The potential of the satellite multi-temporal images to support research of agricultural monitoring has increased according to improvements in technological development, especially in analysis of large volume of data available for knowledge discovery. In Brazil, sugarcane is cultivated on extensive fields and is the main agriculture crop used to produce ethanol. The main objective of this chapter is to monitor the sugarcane crop by clustering analysis with multi-temporal satellite images having low spatial resolution. A large database of this kind of image and specific software were used to perform the image pre-processing phase, extract time series, apply clustering method and enable the data visualization on several steps during the whole analysis process. According to the analysis done, our methodology allows to identify land areas with similar development patterns, also considering different growing seasons for the crops, covering monthly and annual periods. Results confirm that satellite images of low spatial resolution can indeed be satisfactorily used in agricultural crop monitoring in regional scale.

Keywords: time series, AVHRR/NOAA, NDVI, k-means, sugarcane

1. Introduction

With the current challenge to improve the agricultural monitoring, forecast and planning, which are strategic for a country with continental dimensions and great diversity of land uses, the importance of the time series of digital images acquired by low-spatial-resolution satellites (such as the AVHRR/NOAA and MODIS/Terra) to monitor the expansion and production of agricultural crops (such as the sugarcane) in tropical regions (such as the southeastern region of Brazil) that have a huge amount of clouds during the growing season making the operational use of remote sensing data difficult is an essential highlight.

The AVHRR/NOAA is a meteorological remote sensor that has been widely used also as source of spectral information for environmental and agricultural purposes. Since the sugarcane is cultivated on large and extensive fields, medium- and low-spatial-resolution satellites such as the AVHRR/NOAA can be used to properly monitor this agricultural crop. Sugarcane production has expanded in the last years in southeastern Brazil making this agricultural product strategic for its economy and environment since it is the main renewable source of energy used to replace fossil fuels and reduce the emissions of greenhouse gases that cause the global warming.

Remote sensing images have been efficient to evaluate important characteristics of the sugarcane cultivation, providing relevant results to the debate of sustainable ethanol production from sugarcane [1]. The accuracy of the thematic mapping of sugarcane through satellite images was assessed [2], and a methodology for contributing in the automation of sugarcane mapping over large areas, with time series of remotely sensed imagery [3], was developed.

In addition, researchers have conducted studies to assess social and economic impacts in sugarcane cultivation [4], as well as to predict its yield [5]. An alternative masking technique for satellite image time series, called yield-correlation masking, can be used for the development and implementation of regional crop yield forecasting models eliminating the need for a land cover map [6].

In fact, this agricultural commodity has an increasing economic importance especially due to the increasing demand for ethanol (one of its derivative) used as renewable energy source to replace fossil fuels. Although there is a consensus about the benefits from a temperature increase for the sugarcane production, its expansion to the warmest regions can be negatively impacted whether the water deficit becomes more severe in consequence of climate changing scenarios in those areas. Thus, researchers have been dedicated to more detailed studies regarding expansion and productivity of sugarcane fields to find innovative and optimized methods in order to understand the impact of global warming in this crop production [7].

Even being more accessible and available nowadays, many users still have difficulties to deal with satellite images due to different and more sophisticated demands as well as the fast-growing quantity and complexity of this kind of data [8]. In this context, knowledge discovery technologies are an important alternative to explore and find relevant information on this huge volume of data. Some initiatives involving data and image mining have been accomplished through different techniques with reasonable results [9–13].

In this context, we focus on computational methods that allow analysis at regional scale with the purpose of improving agricultural crop monitoring and increasing the sustainable usage of the soil, taking into account that climate changes are in course. Even so, we show a clustering-based approach to analyze time series extracted from multi-temporal NDVI images and visualization. The main objective of this chapter is to monitor the sugarcane crop by clustering analysis through multi-temporal satellite images of low spatial resolution.

2. Material and methods

2.1. Study area

The study area is located in São Paulo, an important state of southeastern macro-region of Brazil (54°00′ to 43°30′W and 25°30′ to 19°30′S), which is responsible for 60% of the national production and 25% of the global production of sugarcane (**Figure 1**).

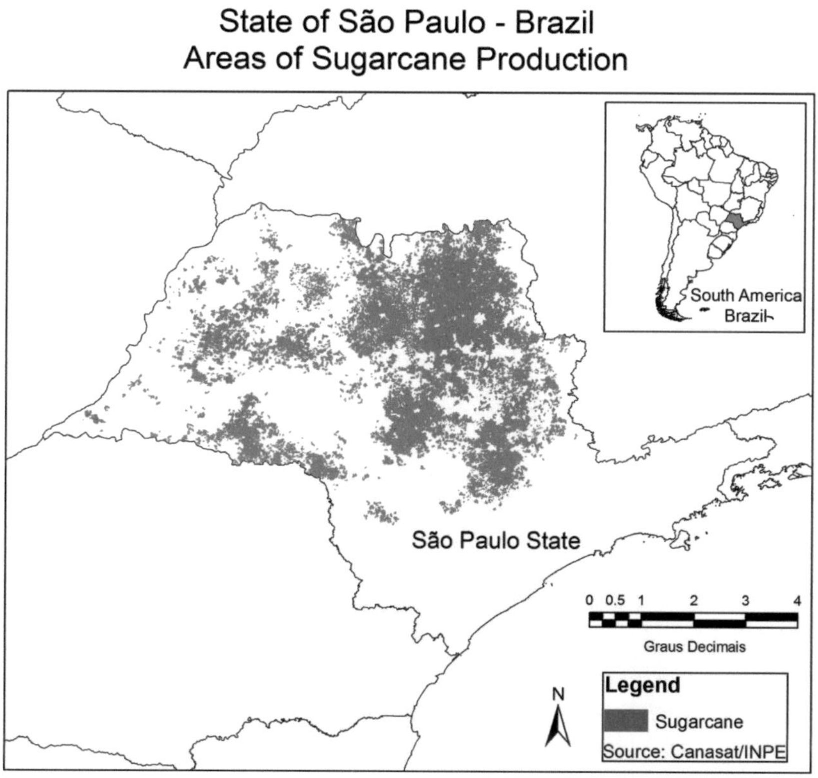

Figure 1. Location of study area, state of São Paulo in Brazil. The areas shown in gray are sugarcane production area.

2.2. Proposed approach

The knowledge discovery process comprehends three main steps: (1) data preparation of satellite image time series, (2) extraction of the NDVI profiles, and (3) clustering analysis. **Figure 2** presents a flowchart of the proposed process to assess multi-temporal satellite images.

2.2.1. Satellite image time series (SITS)

The database of multi-temporal NDVI/NOAA/AVHRR images used in this chapter is available at the Centre for Meteorological and Climatic Research Applied to Agriculture (Cepagri) at the University of Campinas (Unicamp), Brazil, having AVHRR/NOAA images recorded since April 1995 with approximately 6 terabytes of data. It was used in the analysis AVHRR/NOAA-16 and AVHRR/NOAA-17 images gathered from April 2001 to March 2010.

It is necessary to preprocess the images, since the AVHRR/NOAA images often have geometric distortions caused by the Earth curvature and rotation, attitude errors and imprecise orbits of the satellite [14]. These distortions must be corrected specially for land applications that require

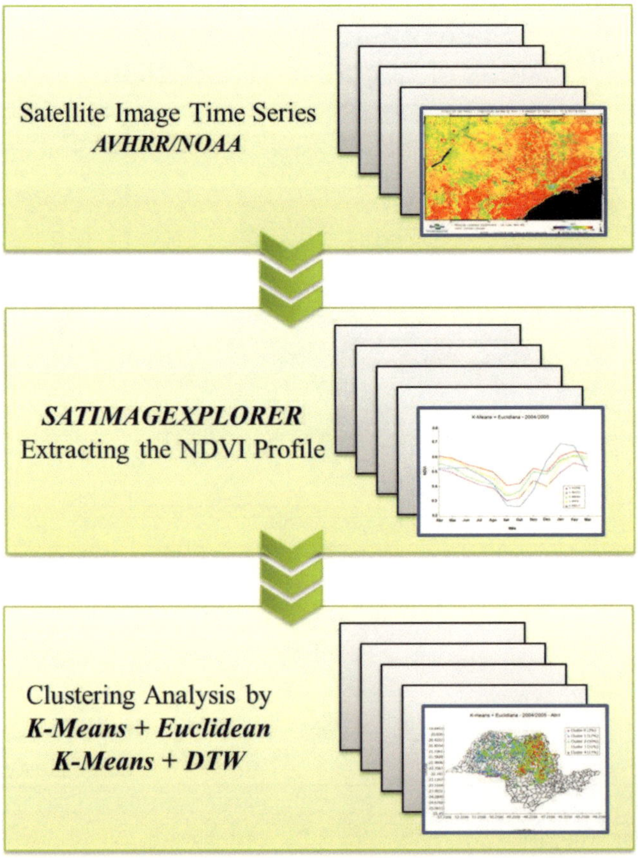

Figure 2. Flowchart with the main steps of proposed approach employed in this chapter.

a highly accurate geometric matching, with one pixel accuracy (1.1 km) in the Equidistant Cylindrical Projection. To perform accurate geometric, the maximum cross-correlation (MCC) method is applied. The MCC method compares a target image to a base image (one for each year season), geometrically accurate and cloudless [15]. The first step to be executed corresponds to the image georeferencing process, which is executed in batch mode by the NAVPRO system [16, 17] to accomplish the necessary tasks, such as:

- Conversion from a raw to an intermediary format
- Radiometric calibration
- Geometric correction
- Identification of pixels classified as cloud

To attenuate the effect of the atmosphere on the images, maximum-value composite (MVC) of NDVI images was generated. Following the recommendations [18], it is important to mask out the inappropriate pixels, such as cloud-contaminated pixels. The georeferencing module allows users to generate NDVI images for a specific region. As the volume of images is huge, it was used the SatImagExplorer system [19]. This system is interactive and allows the user to specify regions of interest (ROIs), using as input basis a satellite image time series. SatImagExplorer extrapolates the region indication for all images in the sequence, generating time series of the ROIs corresponding to that indicated for all available images. This tool allows the user to focus their analysis on strategic points of interest, as well as facilitates the analysis of a long series of data. Time series extracted from multi-temporal images using SatImagExplorer are one of the data to be mined by the clustering method.

2.2.2. Clustering analysis

The clustering task is defined as a process of grouping similar objects, following a given criterion [20]. In this step, NDVI time series are analyzed by clustering method implemented in the SatImagExplorer system. We have used the partition-based method named k-means.

k-Means divide n objects from the input dataset into k partitions. Initially, the algorithm randomly determines k objects as initial centroids and associates each remaining object to the partition represented by the most similar (closest) centroid. In the end of each iteration, centroids that correspond to the average values of the cluster objects are recalculated to define the new order of n objects in the clusters during the next iteration. The k-means algorithm converges when there are no more changes in the clusters. Although simple and computationally efficient (O(nk)), as k-means considers average values, it is more sensitive to errors when noise and outliers appear in time series [21].

The k-means method uses a distance function to perform similarity search operations to find the series most similar to a given time series that is being analyzed. A distance function or metric can be defined as a similarity measure between two data elements that are, in this case, two time series. The most widely used distance functions are those from the Minkowski family (or Lp norm). The Euclidean distance corresponds to L2, which is commonly used to calculate the distance between multidimensional arrays and vectors. The dynamic time warping (DTW) is a very efficient distance function to compare time series [22]. Its main objective is to keep close time series that have similar behavior but are delayed or distorted along the time axis. Thus, this technique presents a proper way of working to warping, because the comparisons between corresponding points are not rigid. DTW is a tool with two of the main issues raised by high-temporal-resolution satellite image time series, namely, the irregular sampling in the temporal dimension and the need for comparison of pairs of time series having different numbers of samples [23].

We will show next the three clustering analyses performed:

First: k-Means used with Euclidean distance, when we considered only monthly NDVI values. These values of sugarcane fields were extracted using geographical coordinates (latitude and longitude) provided by the Canasat/INPE Project (www.canasat.inpe.br). In this approach, each element of the dataset corresponds to one NDVI value, which refers to a month value in a given location (pixel), in order to obtain monthly analysis of the region of interest. Considering similarity among NDVI values, elements were assigned to different clusters. Five clusters were generated for each month of the crop season (2004–2005), being able to follow the development stage of the crop per month. For example, whether crop is in maturing phase, it has already been harvested, and there are not spectral mixing with other crops or vegetation;

Second: k-Means used with DTW distance function, when we have generated series of NDVI values corresponding to one or more sugarcane crop series. The clustering was determined by five clusters for each crop season (2001–2010) for annual crop monitoring according to the type of planting in each crop season, for example, sugarcane ratoon, sugarcane expansion, sugarcane renewed, sugarcane under renewing and not defined [13, 24].

Third: k-Means used with DTW distance function of three dimensional (multivariate) time series database, extracted from 324 monthly images of NDVI, albedo and surface temperature. Since DTW calculates the distance between pairs of data points using Euclidean distance, DTW method can be applied to multivariate time series. The whole dataset had 220,238 data series, being each observation a triplet of NDVI, albedo and surface temperature values of study area in a given month, with 108 values per time series [25].

3. Results and discussion

In this section, we present the results and discuss the three analyses performed in this chapter described above.

3.1. k-Means used with Euclidean distance

In this section we present how results of appliance of k-means clustering with Euclidean distance function over NDVI monthly values extracted from the study area can assist the monitoring of sugarcane fields.

Months from December to May correspond to the period of maximum vegetative growth of sugarcane. In **Figure 3J**, **L** and **B**, pixels that appear in yellow and red colors correspond to the maximum NDVI values, being included in the clusters 3 and 4, respectively. On the other hand,

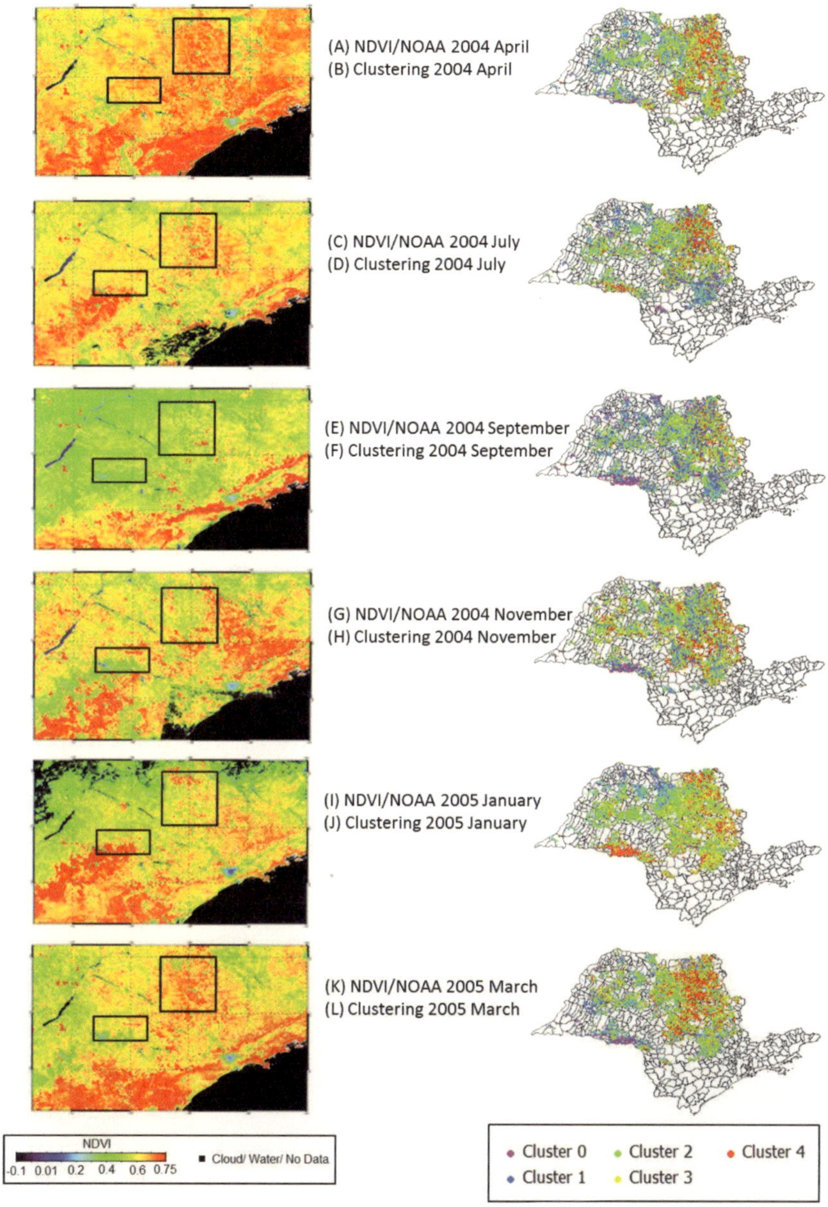

Figure 3. Monthly MVC NDVI images and clustering of NDVI (five clusters) of sugarcane planting area in the state of São Paulo for months from April 2004 to march 2005. (A) NDVI/NOAA 2004 April; (B) Clustering 2004 April; (C) NDVI/NOAA 2004 July; (D) Clustering 2004 July; (E) NDVI/NOAA 2004 September; (F) Clustering 2004 September; (G) NDVI/NOAA 2004 November; (H) Clustering 2004 November; (I) NDVI/NOAA 2005 January; (J) Clustering 2005 January; (K) NDVI/NOAA 2005 March; (L) Clustering 2005 March.

months of August, September and October correspond to harvest season. In these months (**Figure 3F**), pixels in magenta and blue, with minimum NDVI values, correspond to clusters 0 and 1, respectively. Cluster 2 (green) corresponds to sugarcane intermediate stage of growth.

These clusters can be validated in the MVC NDVI images. The black squares over the satellite images in the left correspond to the main sugarcane planting areas. Analyzing the MVC NDVI images in the northeastern region of São Paulo, the evolution of the sugarcane vegetative growth cycle can be seen (**Figure 3**). Planting begins in August represented in the images by pixels in shades of green and blue located in the northeastern region of the state. These colors represent low NDVI values (around 0.2) characterizing areas with exposed soil and sparse vegetation. Similar pattern also occurs in the months from September to November. From December, when sugarcane begins to grow up and acquire more biomass, these regions are shades of yellow, orange and red. Months from January to May show shades of dark red, when sugarcane reaches the highest stage of growth with maximum NDVI values (between 0.7 and 0.8). The dark areas in images represent pixels covered by clouds and water.

There is no predominance of one or two clusters in all producing regions if we consider all months of the crop season. As we can observe, both plant and ratoon sugarcane are grown throughout the state, and the five clusters appear in all months. There is a higher percentage of pixels in the clusters with higher NDVI during some months. However, in other months, the largest number of pixels is included in clusters with lower NDVI (**Figure 3**).

Figure 4 has the temporal profile of clusters showing dynamics of crop planting and harvesting throughout the growing season. Analyzing the temporal profile of **Figure 4**, we can observe that in months from December to May, the NDVI values are higher and represent a larger percentage of pixels for clusters 2, 3 and 4 (from 20 to 40% of the pixels). For the months from August to November, the NDVI values are lower, representing higher percentages for clusters 0 and 1 (around 30% of the pixels). Each month features a sugarcane planting area at a certain stage of growth, appearing in clusters 0 or 1 (harvested or bare soil) and in clusters 2, 3 and 4 (in growth or ready to be harvested) (**Figure 3**).

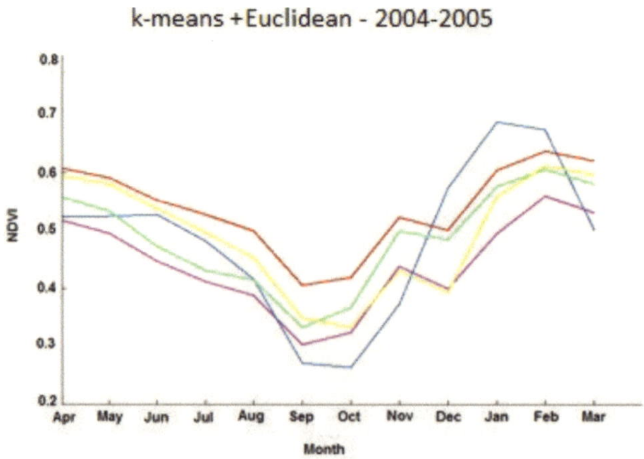

Figure 4. Temporal profile of five NDVI clusters of sugarcane fields for the months from April 2004 to March 2005.

Although the k-means method is simpler and more widely used, their application in satellite image time series of low spatial resolution allows the regional study of crop, even with the difficulty in the analysis due to the possibility of spectral mixing in pixels.

3.2. k-Means was used with DTW distance

Results of the MVC NDVI image time series analysis about the period 2001–2010 for the state of São Paulo are presented hereafter. Maps and temporal profiles correspond to results of clusters (k-means with DTW distance function), pixels with NDVI values from year to year. In general, clusters that were identified as sugarcane may be (i) related to the type of planting carried out each year, for example, identifying areas of sugarcane ratoon (the sugarcane available for harvest after one or more cuts), sugarcane expansion (the sugarcane planted in new areas that will be harvested for the first time), sugarcane renewed (the year-and-half sugarcane plant that has undergone renovation during the previous crop year and will be available for harvest in the current crop year), sugarcane under renewing (the sugarcane area is not harvested due to renovation, not available for that specific crop year) and not defined area, and (ii) related to the quantity produced. Clusters, which were determined by clustering analysis, do not remain constant from year to year as the sugarcane planting is dynamic along the time series.

Thus, applying the k-means clustering analysis, we can verify sugarcane planting type from the years analyzed. Cluster 4 (red) indicates the maximum NDVI values in the month, corresponding to areas with higher biomass. Cluster 0 (magenta) shows the lower NDVI values, corresponding to bare soil. The k-means method showed more homogeneous temporal profiles (**Figure 5**). Low peaks in NDVI profiles during the months of December and January (**Figure 5**) match NDVI values related to clouds, because this period of year is the rainy season in the state.

Analyzing every year, we found that each cluster corresponds to different types of sugarcane planting (**Table 1**). For example, in crop season 2001–2002, 2003–2004, 2006–2007 and 2008–2009, cluster 2 (green; **Figure 6A**, **C**, **F** and **H**) corresponds to the type of sugarcane ratoon, and this cluster (29–47% of the pixels) is correlated (between R = 0.74 and R = 0.87) with the crop production (**Figure 7**). In crop seasons 2002–2003 and 2009–2010 (**Figure 6B** and **I**), sugarcane ratoon corresponds to cluster 1 (blue), with a correlation of R = 0.84 and R = 0.73 with the production and 36 and 33% of the sugarcane pixels (**Figure 7**). Crop season 2004–2005 (**Figure 6D**) corresponds to cluster 3 (yellow), with correlation

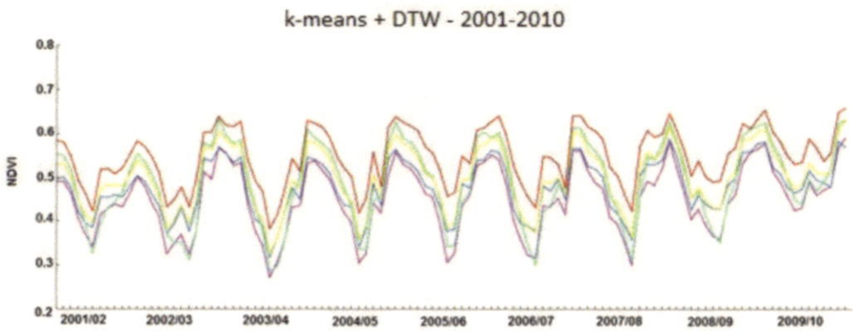

Figure 5. Temporal profiles of each cluster for each crop season in the period 2001–2002 to 2009–2010.

Cluster	2001–2002	2002–2003	2003–2004	2004–2005	2005–2006	2006–2007	2007–2008	2008–2009	2009–2010
0	Expansion 9%	Under renewing 18%	Expansion 7%	Expansion 4%	Renovated 3%	Not defined 14%	Under renewing 12%	Renewed 11%	Renewed 21%
1	Renewed 17%	Ratoon 36%	Under renewing 27%	Not defined 17%	Ratoon 21%	Expansion 20%	Not defined 7%	Under renewing 11%	Ratoon 33%
2	Ratoon 29%	Expansion 13%	Ratoon 41%	Under renewing 20%	Under renewing 18%	Ratoon 29%	Renewed 21%	Ratoon 47%	Expansion 18%
3	Not defined 19%	Renewed 15%	Not defined 13%	Ratoon 32%	Expansion 35%	Under renewing 21%	Expansion 28%	Expansion 22%	Under renewing 19%
4	Under renewing 24%	Not defined 15%	Renewed 9%	Renewed 24%	Not defined 20%	Renewed 14%	Ratoon 29%	Not defined 7%	Not defined 6%

Table 1. Type of sugarcane planting in each crop season and pixels number percentage for each cluster by k-means with DTW.

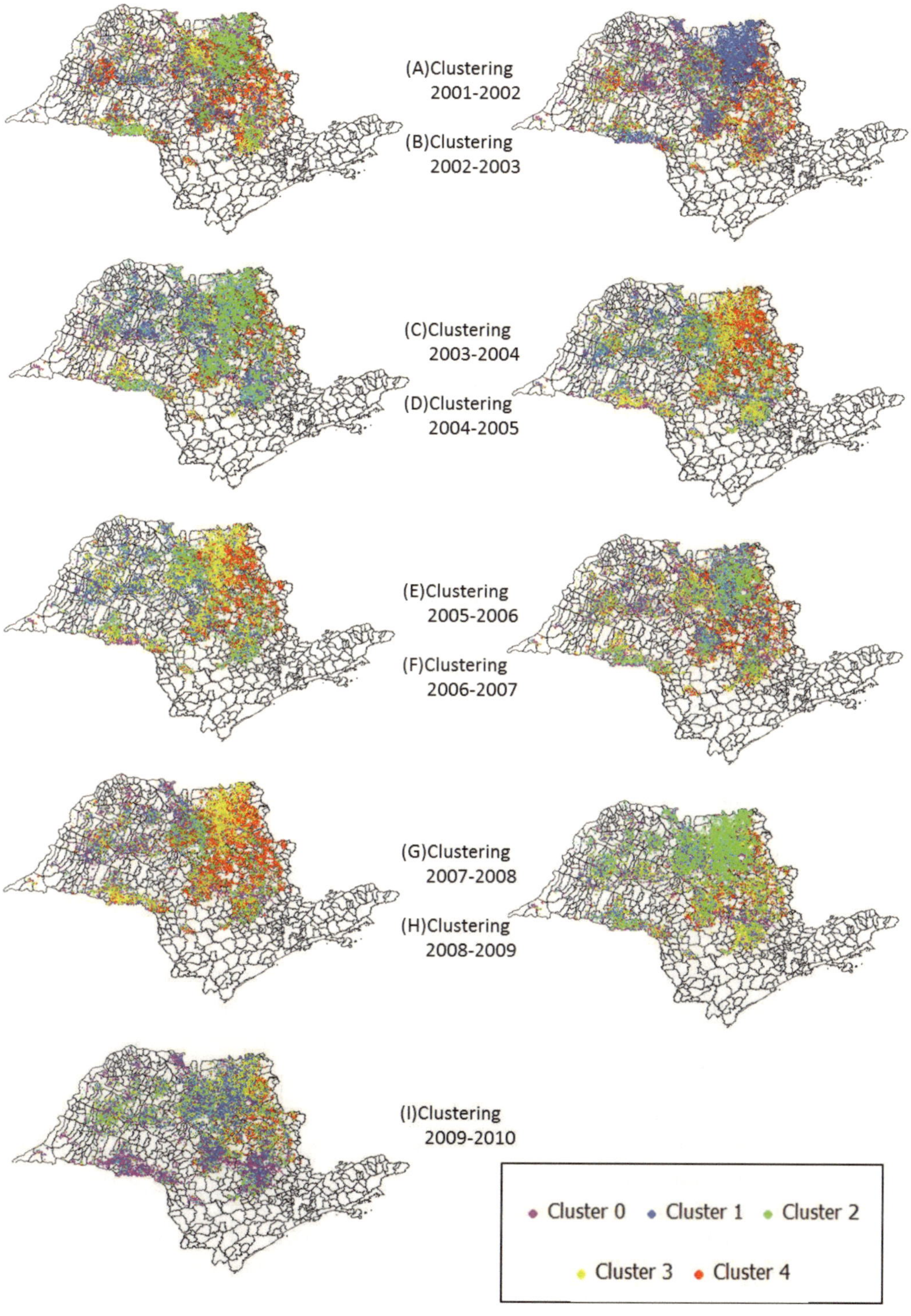

Figure 6. k-Means clustering with DTW distance function for each crop season in the period 2001–2002 to 2009–2010. (A) Clustering 2001–2002; (B) Clustering 2002–2003; (C) Clustering 2003–2004; (D) Clustering 2004–2005; (E) Clustering 2005–2006; (F) Clustering 2006–2007; (G) Clustering 2007–2008; (H) Clustering 2008–2009; (I) Clustering 2009–2010.

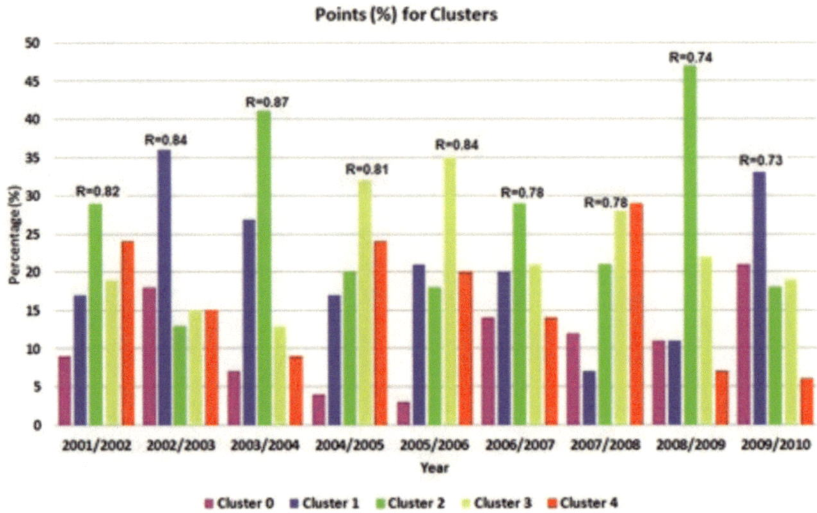

Figure 7. Graph of pixels' number percentage for each cluster regarding each crop seasons in the period 2001–2002 to 2009–2010. Correlation values of the clusters with the sugarcane production.

index R = 0.81 and 32% of the sugarcane pixels (**Figure 7**). In most crop seasons, sugarcane ratoon is strongly correlated with the sugarcane production. Only in crop seasons 2005–2006 and 2007–2008 (**Figure 6E** and **G**), the sugarcane expansion is correlated with crop production.

3.3. k-Means was used with DTW distance function of three dimensional (multivariate) time series database

Dataset with more than 220,000 series in the state of São Paulo were clustered into five clusters (0–4) by k-means method with DTW distance function. Each cluster was formed according to the characteristics of NDVI, surface temperature and albedo extracted from AVHRR/NOAA images in the period 2001–2010. The identified areas were cluster 0 (magenta), which corresponds to water; cluster 1 (blue), which to the urban area and areas where the soil is exposed or have low vegetation and pasture; cluster 2 (green), which represents areas of agricultural crops; cluster 3 (yellow), which corresponds to sugarcane; and cluster 4 (red), which represents forest areas (**Figure 8A** and **B**).

NDVI was useful to separate vegetation areas from other targets, for example, forests present high values of NDVI during the whole season (have high concentration of vegetation and biomass), and these areas are normally shown by red-colored representative time series, in profile visualization (**Figure 9A**). On the other hand, albedo variable was useful to separate water areas from other targets, but was not enough to distinguish areas having different levels of vegetation cover (**Figure 9B**). The water represented by cluster 0 was well clustered, since the NDVI values and especially the albedo values were different from other clusters, as shown in the temporal

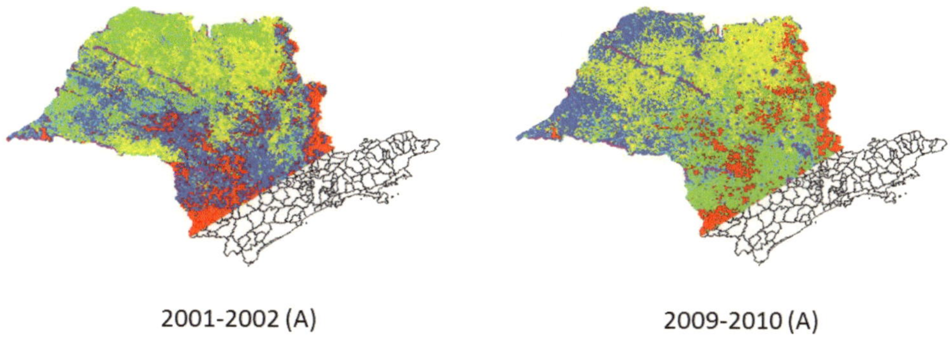

Figure 8. Geographic spatial of 2001–2002 (A) and 2009–2010 (B) of clustering results; yellow represents sugarcane.

profile of NDVI (**Figure 9A**) and albedo (**Figure 9B**). The albedo and NDVI values are lower (less than 0.1), since there is no presence of vegetation in the water or when there is minimal.

Clustering results for agricultural crops and grassland were less accurate, probably because different crops present similar NDVI values in some phenological phase during vegetative crop cycle, but are useful to separate agricultural from nonagricultural areas, such as water,

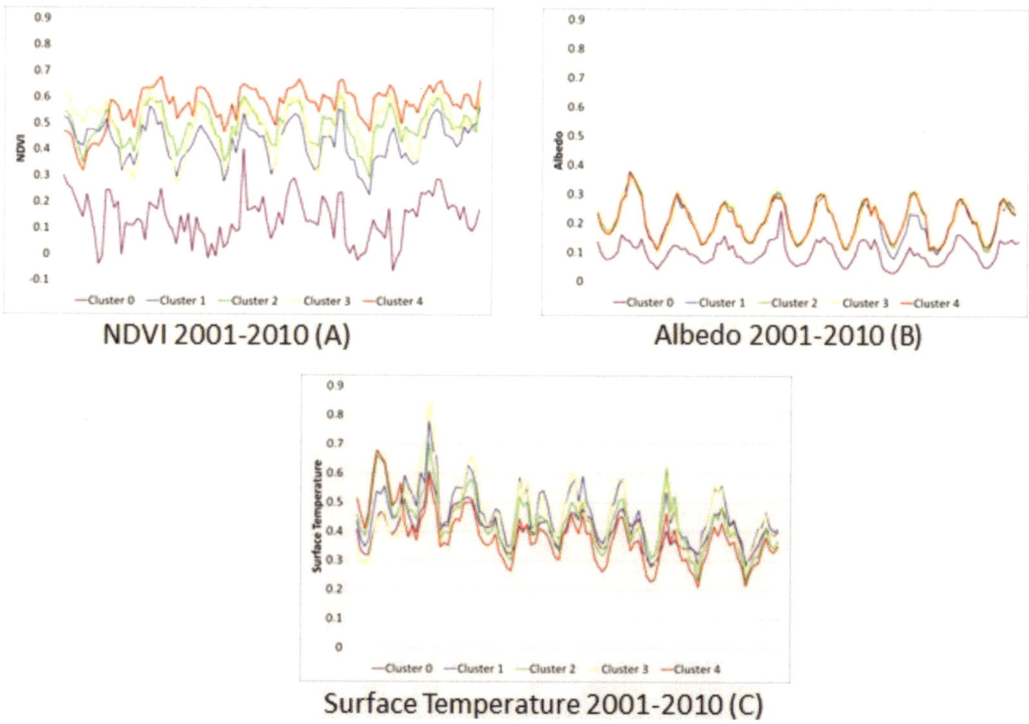

Figure 9. Profile visualization (2001–2010) of NDVI (A), albedo (B) and surface temperature (C) of clustering results.

urban areas and forest. Clustering of these areas was defined mainly by surface temperature, being higher for targets with lower canopy, such as urban areas and exposed soil, and lower for woodland (**Figure 9A** and **C**). For example, the forest areas represented by cluster 4, in **Figure 8A** and **B**, have high NDVI values (**Figure 9A**) and lower surface temperature values (**Figure 9C**), as they are very shady and dense vegetation coverage areas.

However, sugarcane fields were well clustered over the crop seasons because the sugarcane has a typical behavior (long seasonal cycle) than other crops. In **Figure 8A** and **B**, it is possible to observe the dynamic of this agricultural crop, represented by cluster 3 (yellow), throughout the decade in which in the crop years 2001–2002 the acreage was low, with higher production, and planted in the northeast area of the state, and in the end of the crop years 2009–2010, there was a significant increase in the planted area toward the western of the state. This technique of clustering in three dimensional (multivariate) time series database was efficient to perform temporal analysis of land use, indicating that this methodology can be used to identify and analyze the dynamics of land use and cover.

4. Conclusions

This chapter presented a new approach to boost the agricultural monitoring including the expansion of crops to different regions, through techniques of time series mining. We used clustering analysis associated with the Euclidean and the DTW distance functions. We demonstrated that it is possible to take advantage of off-the-shelf computational methods to support agricultural monitoring as well as to automatically determine sugarcane fields' expansion that is a valuable contribution of this work.

Moreover, we also showed the potential use of time series of satellite images with low spatial resolution in agricultural monitoring although spectral mixtures can occur. The main advantage of this approach is the high temporal resolution, low cost and global coverage of the remote sensing system used (AVHRR/NOAA). The performance analysis of a simple clustering technique based on a time series of satellite images is in providing a further step in the researches on the use of renewable energy sources, such as the sugarcane ethanol. The impact of such approach becomes even stronger, and it increases the need for researching on new ways to reduce greenhouse gas emissions, mainly in the trail of the recent occurrences of extreme events in different locations of the planet.

Acknowledgements

The authors thank FAPESP/AlcScens and CNPq for funding and Cepagri/Unicamp for the database of remote sensing imagery.

Author details

Renata Ribeiro do Valle Gonçalves[1]*, Jurandir Zullo Junior[1], Bruno Ferraz do Amaral[2], Elaine Parros Machado Sousa[2] and Luciana Alvim Santos Romani[3]

*Address all correspondence to: renata@cpa.unicamp.br

1 Center of Meteorological and Climate Researches Applied to Agriculture (Cepagri), University of Campinas (Unicamp), Cidade Universitária Zeferino Vaz, Campinas, SP, Brazil

2 Department of Computer Science, University of São Paulo (USP), São Carlos, SP, Brazil

3 Embrapa Agriculture Informatics, Campinas, SP, Brazil

References

[1] Rudorff BFT, Aguiar DA, Silva WF, Sugawara LM, Adami M, Moreira MA. Studies on the rapid expansion of sugarcane for ethanol production in São Paulo State (Brazil) using Landsat data. Remote sensing. 2010;**2**:1057-1076. DOI: 10.3390/rs2041057

[2] Adami M, Mello MP, Aguiar DA, Rudorff BFT, Souza AF. A web platform development to perform thematic accuracy assessment of sugarcane mapping in South-Central Brazil. Remote Sensing. 2012;**4**:3201-3214. DOI: 10.3390/rs4103201

[3] Vieira MA, Formaggio AR, Rennó CD, Atzberger C, Aguiar AA, Mello MP. Object based image analysis and data mining applied to a remotely sensed Landsat time-series to map sugarcane over large areas. Remote Sensing of Environment. 2012;**123**:553-562. DOI: 10.1016/j.rse.2012.04.011

[4] Martinelli LA, Filoso S. Expansion of sugarcane ethanol production in brazil: Environmental and social challenges. Ecological Applications. 2008;**18**:885-898. DOI: 10.1890/07-1813.1

[5] Nascimento CR, Gonçalves RRV, Zullo J Jr, Romani LAS. Estimation of sugar cane productivity using a time series of AVHRR/NOAA-17 images and a phenology-spectral model. In: MultiTemp 2009 – The Fifth International Workshop on the Analysis of Multi-Temporal Remote Sensing Images; Connecticut, Groton. 2009. p. 365-372

[6] Kastens JH, Kastens TL, Kastens DLA, Price KP, Martinko EA, Lee RY. Image masking for crop yield forecasting using AVHRR NDVI time series imagery. Remote Sensing of Environment. 2005;**99**:341-356. DOI: 10.1016/j.rse.2005.09.010

[7] Loarie SR, Lobell DB, Asner GP, Field CB. Direct impacts on local climate of sugar-cane expansion in Brazil. Nature Climate Change Letter. Vol 1, pp. 105-109. 2011. DOI: 10.1038/nclimate1067

[8] Datcu M, Pelizzari A, Daschiel H, Quartulli M, Seidel K. Advanced value adding to metric resolution SAR data: Information mining. In 4th European Conference on Synthetic Aperture Radar (EUSAR 2002), Cologne, Germany; 2002. p. 1-14

[9] Datcu M, Daschiel H, Pelizzari A, Quartulli M, Galoppo A, Colapicchioni A, Pastori M, Seidel K, Marchetti PG, D'Elia S. Information mining in remote sensing image archives: System concepts. IEEE Transactions on Geoscience and Remote Sensing. 2003;**41**:2923-2936. DOI: 10.1109/TGRS.2003.817197

[10] Li J, Narayanan RM. Integrated spectral and spatial information mining in remote sensing imagery. IEEE Transactions on Geoscience and Remote Sensing. 2004;**42**:673-685. DOI: 10.1109/TGRS.2004.824221

[11] Daschiel H, Datcu M. Information mining in remote sensing image archives: System evaluation. IEEE Transactions on Geoscience and Remote Sensing. 2005;**43**:188-199. DOI: 10.1109/TGRS.2004.838374

[12] Romani LAS, Avila AMH, Zullo J Jr, Chbeir R, Traina C Jr, Traina AJM. Clearminer: A new algorithm for mining association patterns on heterogeneous time series from climate data. In: Association for Computing Machinery (ACM) Symposium on Applied Computing – SAC' 2010; Sierre, Switzerland. 2010. p. 900-905. DOI: 10.1145/1774088.1774275

[13] Romani LAS, Gonçalves RRV, Amaral BF, Chino DYT, Zullo J Jr, Traina C Jr, Sousa EPM, Traina AJM. Clustering analysis applied to NDVI/NOAA multitemporal images to improve the monitoring process of sugarcane crops. In: MultiTemp 2011 – The Sixth International Workshop on the Analysis of Multi-Temporal Remote Sensing Images; Trento, Italy. 2011. p. 33-36. DOI: 10.1109/Multi-Temp.2011.6005040

[14] Rosborough DGEWJ, Baldwin GW. Precise AVHRR image navigation. IEEE Transactions on Geoscience and Remote Sensing. 1994;**32**:644-657. DOI: 10.1109/36.297982

[15] Emery W, Baldwin DG, Matthews D. Maximum cross correlation automatic satellite image navigation and attitude corrections for open ocean image navigation. IEEE Transactions on Geoscience and Remote Sensing. 2003;**41**:33-42. DOI: 10.1109/TGRS.2002.808061

[16] Emery WJ, Brown J, Novak ZP. AVHRR image navigation: Summary and review. Photogrammetric Engineering and Remote Sensing. 1989;**55**:1175-1183. DOI: 19890064704

[17] Esquerdo JCDM, Antunes JFG, Baldwin DG, Emery WJ, Zullo J Jr. An automatic system for AVHRR land surface product generation. International Journal of Remote Sensing. 2006;**27**:3925-3942. DOI: 10.1080/01431160600763956

[18] Chen PY, Srinivasan R, Fedosejevs G, Kinitry JR. Evaluating different NDVI composites techniques using NOAA-14 AVHRR data. International Journal of Remote Sensing. 2003;**24**:3403-3412 DOI: 10.1080/0143116021000021279

[19] Chino DYT, Romani LAS, Traina AJM. Constructing satellite image time series for climate data summarization and monitoring agricultural crops. In: Electronic Journal of Scientific Initiation (REIC); 2010: 1-16

[20] Han J, Kamber M. Data Mining - Concepts and Techniques. 2nd ed. New York: Morgan Kaufmann Publishers; 2006. p. 770

[21] Kaufman L, Rousseeuw PJ. Finding Groups in Data: An Introduction to Cluster Analysis. John Wiley and Sons, Wiley Online Library; 1990. p. 342. DOI: 10.1002/9780470316801

[22] Berndt DJ, Clifford J. Using dynamic time warping to find patterns in time series. In: Proceedings of the Knowledge Discovery in Databases – KDD Workshop (KDD' 1994) Seattle, Washington, USA. 1994. p. 359-370

[23] Petitjean F, Inglada J, Gançarski P. Satellite image time series analysis under time warping. IEEE Transactions on Geoscience and Remote Sensing. 2012;**50**:3081-3095. DOI: 10.1109/TGRS.2011.2179050

[24] Gonçalves RRV, Zullo J Jr, Romani LAS, Amaral BF, Sousa EPM. Agricultural monitoring using clustering techniques on satellite image time series of low spatial resolution. In: MultiTemp 2017 – The Ninth International Workshop on the Analysis of Multi-Temporal Remote Sensing Images; Bruges, Belgium. 2017. p. 1-4

[25] Gonçalves RRV, Zullo J Jr, Amaral BF, Coltri PP, Sousa EPM, Romani LAS. Land use temporal analysis through clustering techniques on satellite image time series. In: IGARSS 2014 – IEEE International Geoscience and Remote Sensing Symposium; Quebec, Canada. 2014. p. 2173-2176.

Chapter 4

Volatility Parameters Estimation and Forecasting of GARCH(1,1) Models with Johnson's SU Distributed Errors

Mohammed Elamin Hassan, Henry Mwambi and
Ali Babikir

Additional information is available at the end of the chapter

http://dx.doi.org/10.5772/intechopen.70506

Abstract

This paper proposes a GARCH-type model allowing for time-varying volatility, skewness, and kurtosis assuming a Johnson's SU distribution for the error term. This distribution has two shape parameters and allows a wide range of skewness and kurtosis. We then impose dynamics on both shape parameters to obtain autoregressive conditional density (ARCD) models, allowing time-varying skewness and kurtosis. ARCD models with this distribution are applied to the daily returns of a variety of stock indices and exchange rates. Models with time-varying shape parameters are found to give better fit than models with constant shape parameters. Also, a weighted forecasting scheme is introduced to generate the sequence of the forecasts by computing a weighted average of the three alternative methods suggested in the literature. The results showed that the weighted average scheme did not show clear superiority to the other three methods.

Keywords: GARCH models, conditional volatility, skewness and kurtosis

1. Introduction

Many papers deal with the departures from normality of asset return distributions. It is well known that the distributions of stock return exhibit negative skewness and excess kurtosis; see among others [2, 9, 14, 15]. The higher moments of the return specifically, excess kurtosis (the fourth moment of the distribution) makes extreme observations more likely than in the normal case, which means that the market gives higher probability to extreme observations than in normal distribution. However, the existence of negative skewness (the third moment of the distribution) has the effect of accentuating the left-hand side of the distribution, which means that a higher probability of decreases given to asset pricing than increases in the market.

The generalized autoregressive conditional heteroscedasticity (GARCH) models, introduced by Engle [5] and Bollerslev [1], allow for time-varying volatility[1] but not for time-varying skewness or time-varying kurtosis. Different GARCH models have been developed in the literature to capture dependencies in higher order moments, starting with Hansen [7] who proposed a skew-Student distribution to account for both time-varying excess kurtosis and skewness. A significant evidence of time-varying skewness found [9]. Others [11, 12] found a significant time varying in both skewness and kurtosis, while [3, 15, 16] found little evidence of either. With regard to the frequency of observation, Jondeau and Rockinger [11] found the presence of time-varying skewness and kurtosis in daily but not weekly data, while others including [2, 7, 9] found an evidence of time-varying skewness and kurtosis in weekly and even monthly data. Regarding daily data [4, 12, 18] found an evidence of time-varying skewness and kurtosis in daily data. The chapter employed GARCH(1,1) model as the performance of the model proved compared large number of volatility models; for more details, see Hansen and Lunde [8].

This paper contributes to the literature of volatility modeling in two aspects. First, we jointly estimate time-varying volatility, skewness, and kurtosis assuming Johnson SU distribution for the error term. The method is applied to two different daily returns: stock indices and exchange rates. Second, a new alternative scheme is introduced to generate the sequence of the forecasts.

The rest of the paper is organized as follows. Following this introduction, Section 2 presents the empirical results regarding the estimation of the model. Section 3 compares the models. In Section 4, the new forecasting scheme is presented, while Section 5 gives concluding remarks.

2. Empirical results and methodology

2.1. Data and preliminary findings

The time series data used for modeling volatility in this paper consists of two sets of financial data. The first set includes daily returns of five stock indices: NASDAQ100 (US), Germany (DAX30), Ishares MSCI South Africa index (EZA), Shanghai stock exchange composite index (SSE), and Ishares MSCI Canada index (EWC).[2] The second data set includes daily returns of five exchange rates series: British Pound (USD/GBP), Australian Dollar (USD/AUD), Italian Lira (USD/ITL), South Africa Rand (USD/ZAR), and Brazilian Real (USD/BRL).[3] The two data

---

[1]In general terms, volatility refers to the fluctuations observed in some phenomenon overtime. In terms of modeling and forecasting literature, it means "the conditional variance of the underlying asset return" [17].

[2]Some of the closing price indices were put into US-dollar and some were put into other currencies. For unification of foreign exchange rates, all closing price indices were converted into American US dollar. These closing price indices are obtained from Yahoo Finance (http://finance.yahoo.com).

[3]The exchange rates have been retrieved from the website (http://www.oanda.com).

sets include daily closing prices from August 6, 2001, through December 10, 2013, for all stock indices and from July 1, 2005, to September 17, 2013, for all exchange rate series with a total of 3001 observations for each data set. The estimation process for the two sets of data was run using 2001 observations as in-sample, while the remaining 1000 observations were used for the out-of-sample forecast. Based on the empirical evidence, it is common to assume that the logarithmic return series $r_t = 100 * [\ln(p_t) - \ln(p_{t-1})]$ (where P_t and P_{t-1} are the price at the current day and previous day, respectively) is weakly stationary. **Table 1** reports the descriptive statistics for all return series. It shows that all data exhibit excess kurtosis (leptokurtosis) and skewness, which represents the nature of departure from normality. The Jarque-Bera (JB) statistics for normality test show that the null hypotheses of normality are strongly rejected for all daily returns of stock and exchange rate series.

2.2. Methodology

Preliminary results in the preceding section provided evidence of a significant deviation from normality and obvious leptokurtosis in all daily return series. This suggests specifying GARCH models that capture these characteristics. In presenting these models, there are two distinct equations or specifications, one for the conditional mean and the other for the conditional variance. For the models employed in this paper, the mean equation for all stock return series is the AR(1) model with a constant, and for all exchange rate return series, we used the MA(1) model without a constant. After estimating the mean equation, the next step was to identify whether there is substantial evidence of heteroscedasticity for the daily returns of stock and exchange rate series. **Table 2** provides the Ljung-Box statistics of order 20 for ε_t^2, ε_t^3 and ε_t^4, where ε_t is the error term from the mean equation. The results show that the Ljung-Box

Assets	N	Mean	S.D.	Skewness	Kurtosis	Jarque-Bera
Stock indices						
NASDAQ100	2000	0.011	1.789	0.084	7.139	1429.85*
DAX30	2000	0.032	1.795	0.053	6.473	1929.78*
SSE	2000	0.048	1.764	−0.078	6.929	1292.92*
EZA	2000	0.076	2.403	−0.354	14.436	10968.85*
EWC	2000	0.049	1.673	−0.473	9.327	3420.18*
Exchange rates						
USD/GBP	2000	0.007	0.485	0.658	11.419	6066.76*
USD/AUD	2000	−0.013	0.702	0.481	14.254	10659.08*
USD/ITL	2000	−0.004	0.467	−0.197	8.185	2260.57*
USD/ZAR	2000	0.001	0.877	1.010	17.404	17672.41*
USD/BRL	2000	−0.016	0.961	0.441	10.048	4215.97*

*Significant at the 5% level.

Table 1. Descriptive statistics for daily returns.

Series	ε_t^2	ε_t^3	ε_t^4
Stock indices			
NASDAQ100	1834.3 (0.000)	305.1 (0.000)	507.1 (0.000)
DAX30	2132.9 (0.000)	148.4 (0.000)	676.1 (0.000)
SSE	443.2 (0.000)	24.6 (0.216)	52.4 (0.000)
EZA	2597.2 (0.000)	305.8 (0.000)	647.8 (0.000)
EWC	3614.3 (0.000)	272.1 (0.000)	984.2 (0.000)
Exchange rates			
USD/GBP	1020.8 (0.000)	98.6 (0.000)	190.6 (0.000)
USD/AUD	2525.9 (0.000)	678.2 (0.000)	889.8 (0.000)
USD/ZAR	975.5 (0.000)	89.2 (0.000)	39.128 (0.006)
USD/ITL	536.2 (0.000)	94.477 (0.000)	77.6 (0.000)
USD/BRL	1555.3 (0.000)	406.1 (0.000)	1030.9 (0.000)

Note. For Ljung-Box statistics, the *p*-values are reported in parentheses.

Table 2. Ljung-Box statistics with order 20 of $\varepsilon_t^2, \varepsilon_t^3$ and ε_t^4 where ε_t is the error term for the mean equation for all daily returns of stock and exchange rate series.

statistics on the squared residuals ε_t^2, ε_t^3, and ε_t^4 are significant for the presence of time-varying volatility, skewness, and kurtosis for all daily returns of stock and exchange rate series.

2.2.1. Distributional assumptions

To complete the basic GARCH specification, an assumption about the conditional distribution of the error term ε_t is required. The expectation is that the excess kurtosis and skewness displayed by the residuals of conditional heteroscedastic models will be reduced, when a more appropriate distribution is used. The Johnson's SU distribution is resorted to in this study. This distribution has two shape parameters that allow a wide range of skewness and kurtosis levels of the type anticipated, and it is used in financial returns data [4, 18]. The Johnson's SU distribution was derived by Johnson [10] through transformation of a normal variable. Letting z ~ N(0,1) the standard normal distribution, the random variable y defined by the transformation:

$$z = \gamma + \delta \sinh^{-1}\left(\frac{y-\zeta}{\lambda}\right) \tag{1}$$

where $sinh^{-1}$ is the inverse hyperbolic sine function defines a Johnson's SU variable. The form of the density of the Johnson's SU distribution, which will be used for the estimation procedure, is that due to Yan [18]:

$$f_y(y) = \frac{\delta}{\lambda\sqrt{1+\left(\frac{y-\zeta}{\lambda}\right)^2}}\phi\left[\gamma + \delta \sinh^{-1}\left(\frac{y-\zeta}{\lambda}\right)\right] \tag{2}$$

where $y \in R$, ϕ is the density function of $N(0, 1)$, ξ and $\lambda > 0$ are location and scale parameters, respectively, while γ, $\delta > 0$ can be interpreted as skewness and kurtosis parameters, respectively. The parameters are not the direct moments of the distribution. The first four moments, the mean, variance, third central moment, and fourth central moment, respectively, of the distribution according to Yan [18] are as follows:

$$\mu = \zeta + \lambda\omega^{1/2}\sinh\Omega \tag{3}$$

$$\sigma^2 = \frac{\lambda^2}{2}(\omega - 1)(\omega\cosh 2\Omega + 1) \tag{4}$$

$$\mu_3 = -\frac{1}{4}\omega^2(\omega^2 - 1)^2\left[\omega^2(\omega^2 + 2)\sinh 3\Omega + 3\sinh\Omega\right] \tag{5}$$

$$\mu_4 = \frac{1}{8}(\omega^2 - 1)^2\left[\omega^4(\omega^8 + 2\omega^6 + 3\omega^4 - 3)\cosh 4\Omega + 4\omega^4(\omega^2 + 2)\cosh 2\Omega + 3(2\omega^2 + 1)\right] \tag{6}$$

The quantities Ω and ω in the moment formulas are $\Omega = \gamma/\delta$ and $\omega = \exp(\delta - 2)$. The skewness and kurtosis are jointly determined by the two shape parameters γ and δ. The standardized Johnson's SU innovations exist when $\xi = 0$ and $\lambda = 1$, but the mean and the variance are not 0 and 1, respectively. These can be done by setting the parameters in the following manner:

$$\zeta = -\omega^{1/2}\sinh\Omega\left[\sqrt{\frac{1}{2}(\omega - 1)(\omega\cosh 2\Omega + 1)}\right]^{-1} \tag{7}$$

$$\lambda = \left[\sqrt{\frac{1}{2}(\omega - 1)(\omega\cosh 2\Omega + 1)}\right]^{-1} \tag{8}$$

2.2.2. Maximum likelihood

Under the presence of heteroscedasticity (autoregressive conditional heteroscedasticity (ARCH) effects) in the residuals of the daily returns of stock and exchange rate series, the ordinary least square estimation (OLS) is not efficient, and the estimate of covariance matrix of the parameters will be biased due to invalid 't' statistics. Therefore, ARCH-type models cannot be estimated by simple techniques such as OLS. The method of maximum likelihood estimation is employed in ARCH models. For the formal exposition of the approach, each realization of the conditional variance h_t has the joint likelihood of realization:

$$L = \prod_{t=1}^{T}\left(\sqrt{\frac{1}{2\pi h_t}}\right)\exp\left(\frac{-\varepsilon_t^2}{2h_t}\right) \tag{9}$$

The log likelihood function is:

$$Log(L) = -\frac{T}{2}Ln(2\pi) - 0.5\sum_{t=1}^{T}h_t - 0.5\sum_{t=1}^{T}\left(\frac{\varepsilon_t^2}{h_t}\right) \tag{10}$$

The parameter values are selected so that the log likelihood function is maximized using a search algorithm by computers.

2.2.3. Model estimation with time-varying volatility, skewness, and kurtosis

As it was shown in Section 2.2, when the residuals were examined for heteroscedasticity, the Ljung Box test provided strong evidence of ARCH effects in the residuals series, which suggests proceeds with modeling the returns volatility using the GARCH methodology. The model to be estimated in this study is the standard GARCH(1, 1) model with constant shape parameters, and also, we impose dynamics on both shape parameters to obtain autoregressive conditional density (ARCD) models.[4] This allows for time-varying skewness and kurtosis assuming Johnson Su distribution for the error term in the two cases. Before presenting the estimation results obtained with both the stock return series and the exchange rate return series, the four nested models to be estimated are summarized as follows:

For stock return series:

Mean equation

$$r_t = \mu + \phi_1 r_{t-1} + \varepsilon_t \tag{11}$$

$\varepsilon_t = \sqrt{h_t} z_t,\ z_t = \sqrt{h_t} z_t \sim JSu\left(\xi_t, \lambda_t, \gamma_t, \delta_t\right)$

Variance equation (GARCH)

$$h_t = b_0 + b_1 \varepsilon_{t-1}^2 + b_2 h_{t-1} \tag{12}$$

Skewness equation

$$\gamma_t = c_0 + c_1 z_{t-1} + c_2 z_{t-1}^2 + c_3 \gamma_{t-1} \tag{13}$$

Kurtosis equation

$$\delta_t = d_0 + d_1 z_{t-1} + d_2 z_{t-1}^2 + d_3 \delta_{t-1} \tag{14}$$

For all stock return series, the study is going to use GARCH(1,1) model with a similar specification to that of Hansen [7] for shape parameters (γ_t, δ_t) but employs the standardized innovation z_{t-1} instead of nonstandardized ε_{t-1} as in Eqs. (13) and (14).

For exchange rate return series:

Mean equation

$$r_t = \theta_1 \varepsilon_{t-1} + \varepsilon_t \tag{15}$$

$\varepsilon_t = \sqrt{h_t} z_t,\ z_t = \sqrt{h_t} z_t \sim JSu\left(\xi_t, \lambda_t, \gamma_t, \delta_t\right)$

Variance equation (GARCH)

---

[4]ARCD is the approach, where dynamics imposed on shape parameters and skewness or kurtosis are derived from the time-varying shape parameters.

$$h_t = b_0 + b_1 \varepsilon_{t-1}^2 + b_2 h_{t-1} \tag{16}$$

Skewness equation

$$\gamma_t = c_0 + c_1 z_{t-1} I_{z_{t-1<y}} + c_2 z_{t-1} I_{z_{t-1 \geq y}} + c_3 \gamma_{t-1} \tag{17}$$

Kurtosis equation

$$\delta_t = d_0 + d_1 |z_{t-1}| I_{z_{t-1<y}} + d_2 |z_{t-1}| I_{z_{t-1 \geq y}} + d_3 \delta_{t-1} \tag{18}$$

For the exchange rate return series, a specification similar to that of [11] for shape parameters (γ_t, δ_t) is used with the exception that it utilizes the standardized innovation z_{t-1} instead of nonstandardized ε_{t-1} as in Eqs. (17) and (18). It also considers the absolute standardized shocks for the shape parameter in Eq. (18), Ghalanos [6]. So, first, we start by estimating the two standard models for the conditional variance: the AR(1)-GARCH(1,1) model (Eqs. (11) and (12)) for the stock return series and MA(1)-GARCH(1,1) model (Eqs. (15) and (16)) for the exchange rate return series. Second, the generalizations of both the standard GARCH and GARCH models with time-varying skewness and kurtosis (GARCHSK) as in Eqs. (11)–(14) for the stock return series and Eqs. (15)–(18) for the exchange rate return series are estimated.

The results for the stock return series are presented in **Tables 3** and **4** for both the standard GARCH and GARCHSK models, respectively. As expected, the results indicate high and significant presence of conditional variance, since the coefficient of lagged conditional variance (b_2) is high, positive, and significant. Volatility is found to be persistent, since the coefficient of lagged volatility (b_1) is positive and significant, indicating that high conditional variance is followed by high conditional variance. The sum of the two estimated coefficients ($b_1 + b_2$) in the estimation process is very close to one, implying that large changes in stock returns tend to be

Parameters		NASDAQ100	DAX30	SSE	EZA	EWC
Mean equation	μ	0.0536*	0.0940*	0.0207	0.1535*	0.0976*
	ϕ	−0.0578*	−0.0813*	0.0025	−0.0534*	−0.0461*
Variance equation	b_0	0.0082	0.0128*	0.0284*	0.0596*	0.0202*
	b_1	0.0499*	0.0646*	0.0756	0.1011*	0.0619*
	b_2	0.9468*	0.9311*	0.9225*	0.8894*	0.9285*
Log-likelihood		−3589.94	−3588.5	−3651.1	−4178.55	−3308.61
AIC		3.5969	3.5955	3.6580	4.1855	4.1445
ARCH-LM test for heteroscedasticity						
Statistic (T^*R^2)		6.596	7.775	0.5993	1.385	4.032
Prob. chi-square (5)		0.2525	0.1691	0.9880	0.9259	0.5447

*Significant at the 5% level.

Table 3. Maximum likelihood estimates of AR(1)-GARCH(1,1) model for stock return series.

Parameters		NASDAQ100	DAX30	SSE	EZA	EWC
Mean equation	μ	0.0155	0.0816*	0.0555	0.1312*	0.0851*
	ϕ	−0.0567*	−0.0947*	−0.0154	−0.0512*	−0.0540*
Variance equation	b_0	0.0104*	0.0167*	0.0506*	0.0620*	0.0250*
	b_1	0.0578*	0.0717*	0.1009*	0.0931*	0.0762*
	b_2	0.9436*	0.9239*	0.8997*	0.8998*	0.9183*
Skewness equation	c_0	−0.0038*	0.0035*	0.0015*	−0.0261*	−0.0256*
	c_1	0.00002	−0.0083*	−0.0054*	0.0838*	0.0163
	c_2	0.00355*	−0.0037*	−0.0017*	0.0004	0.0192*
	c_3	0.9939*	1.0000*	0.9898*	0.8661*	0.9165*
Kurtosis equation	d_0	0.0001	0.7193*	0.9625*	0.2245*	0.4362
	d_1	0.9869*	0.3126*	0.2684*	0.4848*	0.5166*
	d_2	0.0799	0.2929*	0.0591	0.0000	0.2638*
	d_3	0.8459*	0.0019	0.5469*	0.8143*	0.4358*
Log-likelihood		−3559.79	−3578.15	−3620.83	−3294.5	−3406.96
AIC		3.5728	3.5911	3.6338	4.1344	3.4200
ARCH-LM test for heteroscedasticity						
Statistic (T^*R^2)		6.942	6.604	1.678	0.7606	5.393
Prob. chi-square (5)		0.2250	0.2518	0.8917	0.9795	0.3698

*Significant at the 5% level.

Table 4. Maximum likelihood estimates of AR(1)-GARCH(1,1) model with time-varying skewness and kurtosis for stock return series.

followed by large changes, and small changes tend to be followed by small changes. This confirms that volatility clustering is observed in the stock returns series. For the skewness and kurtosis equations, it is found that for all stock return series, days with high conditional skewness and kurtosis are followed by days with high conditional skewness and kurtosis except DAX30 in kurtosis case, since the coefficients for lagged skewness (c_3) and for lagged kurtosis (d_3) are positive and significant. In summary, there is a significant presence of conditional skewness and kurtosis for all stock return series, since at least one of the coefficients associated with the standardized shocks or squared standardized shocks to (skewness and kurtosis) or to lagged (skewness and kurtosis) is found to be significant.

The results for the five exchange rates are presented in **Tables 5** and **6** for GARCH and GARCHSK models, respectively. As expected, the results are the same as in the case of stock return series, i.e., the results also indicate highest significant presence of conditional variance. Volatility is found to be persistent, and volatility clustering is also observed in exchange rate return series. A significant presence of conditional skewness and kurtosis for all exchange rate return series is confirmed, since at least one of the coefficients associated with the standardized

Parameters		USD/GBP	USD/AUD	USD/ITL	USD/ZAR	USD/BRL
Mean equation	θ	0.28470*	0.1886*	0.2495*	0.2619*	0.0945*
Variance equation	b_0	0.0009*	0.0015*	0.0006	0.0165*	0.0114
	b_1	0.0384*	0.0485*	0.0331*	0.0553*	0.1041
	b_2	0.9579*	0.9505*	0.9658*	0.9175*	0.8948*
Log-likelihood		−907.732	−1528.337	−922.161	−2257.187	−2159.827
AIC		0.9137	1.5343	0.9282	2.2632	2.1658
ARCH-LM test for heteroscedasticity						
Statistic (T^*R^2)		5.169	2.900	4.019	9.646	28.35
Prob. chi-square (5)		0.0754**	0.7155	0.1340**	0.0859	0.0016

*Significant at the 5% level.
**Significant at the 1% level.

Table 5. Maximum likelihood estimates of MA(1)-GARCH(1,1) model for exchange rate return series.

Parameters		USD/GBP	USD/AUD	USD/ITL	USD/ZAR	USD/BRL
Mean equation	θ	0.2978*	0.2111*	0.2626*	0.2590*	0.0978*
Variance equation	b_0	0.0009	0.0016	0.0006	0.0139*	0.0086*
	b_1	0.0502*	0.0597*	0.0425*	0.0760*	0.2626*
	b_2	0.9489*	0.9449*	0.9582*	0.9119*	0.8348*
Skewness equation	c_0	−0.0306	0.0368*	−0.0189	0.0168*	−0.0047
	c_1	0.0237	0.0610*	0.0195	0.0589*	−0.0051
	c_2	0.0808*	0.0036	0.0658*	0.0058	0.0150*
	c_3	0.0000	0.4814	0.0000	0.9018*	0.8807*
Kurtosis equation	d_0	0.2075	0.2939*	0.2128	0.4497	0.0405
	d_1	0.4029*	0.5678*	0.3459*	1.0000*	1.0000*
	d_2	0.0050	0.0000	0.0235	0.0000	0.0000
	d_3	0.8217*	0.7851*	0.8364*	0.5342*	0.9077*
Log-likelihood		−895.695	−1516.323	−910.919	−2227.667	−2135.46
AIC		0.9077	1.5283	0.9229	2.2397	2.1475
ARCH-LM test for heteroscedasticity						
Statistic (T^*R^2)		4.299	2.4075	3.308	8.659	9.116
Prob. chi-square (5)		0.1165	0.7904	0.1912**	0.1235	0.1045

*Significant at the 5% level.

Table 6. Maximum likelihood estimates of MA(1)-GARCH(1,1) model with time-varying skewness and kurtosis for exchange rate return series.

shocks (either negative or positive) to (skewness & kurtosis) or to lagged (skewness & kurtosis) are found to be significant.

Finally, it is worth noting that from the bottom of **Tables 3–6**, the value of Akaike information criterion (AIC) decreases monotonically when moving from the simpler model (standard GARCH) to the more complicated ones (GARCHSK) for all return series. Therefore, for all return series analyzed, the GARCHSK model specification seems to be the most appropriate one according to the AIC. Note that the ARCH-LM test statistics for all return series did not exhibit additional ARCH effect. This shows that the variance equations are well specified and adequate.

3. Comparison of models

One way to start comparing the models is to compute the likelihood ratio test. The LR test statistic has been used to compare the standard GARCH model (restricted model) and GARCHSK model (unrestricted model), where Johnson Su distribution is assumed for the standardized error z_t in both specifications. The results are contained in **Table 7**. The value of the *LR* statistic is quite large in all return series. This means that the GARCHSK model is showing superior performance than the standard GARCH model with constant shape parameters.

Series	LogL (GARCH)	LogL (GARCHSK)	LR
Stocks			
NASDAQ100	−3589.94	−3559.79	60.3*
DAX30	−3588.5	−3578.15	20.7*
SSE	−3651.1	−3620.83	60.54*
EZA	−3308.61	−3294.5	28.22*
EWC	−3415.2	−3406.96	16.48*
Exchange rates			
USD/GBP	−907.732	−895.695	24.07*
USD/AUD	−1528.337	−1516.323	24.03*
USD/ITL	−922.161	−910.919	22.48*
USD/ZAR	−2257.187	−2227.667	59.04*
USD/BRL	−2159.827	−2135.46	48.73*

*Significant at the 5% level.

Table 7. Likelihood ratio tests for all daily returns of stock and exchange rate series.

4. A new forecast scheme

In the literature, three alternative ways for generating the sequence of the forecasts, namely the recursive, rolling, and fixed schemes are suggested, see [13]. In this paper, the estimation sample of the models for all return series is based on $R = 2000$ observations, while the last $P = 1000$ observations are used for the out-of-sample forecast. Only the case of generating one-step ahead forecasts using the three alternative methods to generate a sequence of P one-step ahead forecasts is considered. For the estimation sample sizes R for all return series, the study will consider five different values for P for the three alternative schemes, namely $P = 200, 400, 600, 800, 1000$.

In this section, an attempt is made to introduce a new alternative scheme to generate the sequence of the forecasts by computing a weighted average of the last three alternative methods. The weights used are the reciprocals of the MSE of the methods. The rationale behind this is that a method with large mean square forecasting errors (MSE) (i.e., less reliability) should be given a smaller weight. The suggested name for the new method is "weighted average scheme." The four forecasting alternative schemes are applied using the estimated GARCHSK models for stock and exchange rate return series, which are given in the previous section and the results are shown in **Table 8**.

Table 8 presents the averages of the mean square forecasting errors over all levels of out-of-sample forecast ($P = 200, 400, 600, 800, 1000$) for the recursive, rolling, fixed, and weighted average schemes for all daily returns of stock and exchange rate series. The results show that the average forecasting mean squares errors for the four forecasting methods for all return series differ only either in the second decimal place or third decimal place. Although the weighted method shows clear superiority to the recursive and fixed methods, it failed to beat the rolling method which outperforms all other three methods in these data. We attribute the fair performance of weighted method compared to the rolling method possibly because of the

Forecasting alternative schemes				
Series	**Recursive**	**Rolling**	**Fixed**	**Weighted**
Stock				
NASDAQ100	1.521857	1.522096	1.522586	1.522166
DAX30	2.256312	2.238891	2.254930	2.249675
SSE	1.736101	1.736698	1.736048	1.736175
EZA	3.759198	3.752719	3.759654	3.756829
EWC	2.031167	2.027740	2.031093	2.029841
Currency				
USD/GBP	0.093255	0.092812	0.092784	0.092932
USD/AUD	0.255625	0.255306	0.255633	0.255505
USD/ITL	0.178520	0.178018	0.178496	0.178318
USD/ZAR	0.491262	0.489874	0.491256	0.490684
USD/BRL	0.377914	0.376564	0.377805	0.377420

Table 8. Averages of the mean square forecasting errors over all levels of out-of-sample forecast ($P = 200, 400, 600, 800, 1000$) for all forecasting alternative schemes for all daily returns of stock and exchange rate series.

small differences in the mean square errors of the un-weighted methods. We expect it to perform better in cases, where the three methods differ markedly with respect to their mean square errors.

5. Conclusions

This chapter proposes a GARCH-type model that allowing for time-varying volatility, skewness, and kurtosis where assuming a Johnson's SU distribution for the error term. Models estimated using daily returns of five stock indices and five exchange rate series. The results indicate significant presence of conditional volatility, skewness, and kurtosis. Moreover, it is found that specifications allowing for time-varying skewness and kurtosis outperform specifications with constant third and fourth moments. Also, a weighted average forecasting scheme is introduced to generate the sequence of the forecasts by computing a weighted average of the three alternative methods namely the recursive, rolling, and fixed schemes are suggested. The results showed that the weighted average scheme did not show clear superiority to the other three methods. Further work will consider linear and nonlinear combining methods and different forecasting horizons to forecast stock and return series.

Author details

Mohammed Elamin Hassan[1], Henry Mwambi[2] and Ali Babikir[2*]

*Address all correspondence to: ali.basher@gmail.com

1 Department of Economic and Applied Statistics, Sudan Academy for Banking and Financial Sciences, Khartoum, Sudan

2 School of Mathematics, Statistics and Computer Science, University of KwaZulu-Natal, Pietermaritzburg, South Africa

References

[1] Bollerslev T. Generalized autoregressive conditional heteroscedasticity. Journal of Econometrics. 1986;**31**:307-327

[2] Bond SA, Patel K. The conditional distribution of real estate returns: Are higher moments time varying. Journal of Real Estate Finance and Economics. 2003;**26**(2):319-339

[3] Brooks C, Burke SP, Heravi S, Persand G. Autoregressive conditional kurtosis. Journal of Financial Econometrics. 2005;**3**(3):399-421

[4] Cayton, Peter Julian A. and Mapa, Dennis S. Time-varying Conditional Johnson SU Density in Value-at-risk (VaR) Methodology. University of the Philippines Diliman, Philippine. MPRA Paper No. 36206; 2012. pp. 18-32

[5] Engle RF. Autoregressive conditional heteroscedasticity with estimates of the variance of U.K. inflation. Econometrica. 1982;**50**:987-1008

[6] Ghalanos A. Autoregressive Conditional Density Models, version 1.0-0. United Kingdom: R in Finance; 2013. pp. 1-14

[7] Hansen B. Autoregressive conditional density estimation. International Economic Review. 1994;**35**:705-730

[8] Hansen PR, Lunde A. A forecast comparison of volatility models: Does anything beat a GARCH(1,1)?. Journal of Applied Econometrics. 2005;**20**:873-889. DOI: 10.1002/jae.800

[9] Harvey CR, Siddique A. Autoregressive conditional skewness. Journal of Financial and Quantitative Analysis. 1999;**34**:465-487

[10] Johnson NL. Systems of frequency curves generated by methods of translation. Biometrika. 1949;**36**:149-176

[11] Jondeau E, Rockinger M. Conditional volatility, skewness, and kurtosis: Existence, persistence, and co-movements. Journal of Economic Dynamics and Control. 2003;**27**(10): 1699-1737

[12] León A, Rubio G, Serna G. Autoregressive conditional volatility, skewness and kurtosis. The Quarterly Review of Economics and Finance. 2005;**45**:599-618

[13] Pantelidis T, Pittis N. Forecasting Volatility with a GARCH(1, 1) Model: Some New Analytical and Monte Carlo Results. University of Kent, Canterbury, United Kingdom. Working Paper; 2005

[14] Peiró A. Skewness in financial returns. Journal of Banking and Finance. 1999;**23**:847-862

[15] Premaratne G and Bera AK. Modeling Asymmetry and Excess Kurtosis in Stock Return Data. Working Paper. Department of Economics, University of Illinois. United State; 2001

[16] Rockinger M, Jondeau E. Entropy densities with an application to autoregressive conditional skewness and kurtosis. Journal of Econometrics. 2002;**106**(1):119-142

[17] Tsay RS. Analysis of Financial Time Series. 3rd ed. New York, United States of America: John Wiley & Sons, Inc.; 2010

[18] Yan J. Asymmetry, Fat-tail, and Autoregressive Conditional Density in Financial Return Data with Systems of Frequency Curves. Working Paper in Department of Statistics and Actuarial Science. USA: University of Iowa; 2005

Chapter 5

Generation of Earth's Surface Three-Dimensional (3-D) Displacement Time-Series by Multiple-Platform SAR Data

Antonio Pepe

Additional information is available at the end of the chapter

http://dx.doi.org/10.5772/intechopen.71329

Abstract

In this chapter, the recent advancements of differential synthetic aperture radar interferometry (DInSAR) technique are presented, with the focus on the DInSAR-based approaches leading to the generation of three-dimensional time-series of Earth's surface deformation, based on the combination of multi-platform line-of-sight (LOS)-projected time-series of deformation. Use of pixel-offset (PO) measurements for the retrieval of North-South deformation components, which are difficult to be extracted from DInSAR data, only, is also discussed. A review of the principal techniques based on the exploitation of amplitude and phase signatures of sequences of SAR images will be first provided, by emphasizing the limitations and strength of each single approach. Then, the interest will be concentrated on the recently proposed multi-track InSAR combination algorithm, referred as minimum acceleration InSAR combination (MinA) approach. The algorithm assumes the availability of two (or more) sets of SAR images acquired from complementary tracks. SAR data are pre-processed through one of currently available multi-temporal DInSAR toolboxes, and the LOS-projected surface deformation time-series are computed. An under-determined system of linear equations is then solved, based on imposing that the 3-D displacement time-series have minimum acceleration (MA). The presented results demonstrate the validity of the MinA algorithm.

Keywords: ground displacement, SAR interferometry, pixel-offset, minimum acceleration, geodesy

1. Introduction

Over almost last two decades, the differential synthetic aperture radar interferometry (DInSAR) technique [1, 2] has evolved to become nowadays a common practice for the detection and monitoring of Earth's crust modifications over time, both in academic and operative frameworks. DInSAR is mainly used to detect the temporal evolution of surface deformation through the generation of long-lasting displacement time-series. Several multi-temporal advanced DInSAR algorithms have been proposed in the literature [3–9]. At the present days, the availability of large archives of SAR images collected by several radar instruments operating with different wavelengths, and with complementary side-looking angle geometries has posed the problem to effectively combine the information associated with the different SAR datasets. In particular, the combination of multiple-platform line-of-sight (LOS) displacement time series can improve the ability to retrieve the three-dimensional (East-West, Up-Down, and North-South) components of the on-going surface displacement phenomena. Thus, it allows overcoming the main limitation of DInSAR, which is able only to measure the radar LOS projection of the displacement. This research field is of particular interest; and in the recent years, a few solutions have been proposed [10–22] based on the effective combination of multiple-orbit/multiple-angle DInSAR-based measurements, as well as on merging of DInSAR data products with external measurements (e.g., derived from processing GPS data).

In this chapter, first, the basic rationale of the multi-temporal DInSAR techniques for the generation of Earth's surface displacements maps (see Section 2) is summarized; and then, the characteristics of the principal combination techniques for multi-track/multi-angle/multi-sensor SAR data recently proposed in the literature are discussed. In Section 3, the focus will be on the algorithm referred to as minimum acceleration combination technique (MinA) [23], which does not require the simultaneous process of very large sequence of differential SAR interferograms. The algorithm consists of a straightforward post-processing stage that involves the analysis of sequences of independently processed (potentially, also with different DInSAR toolboxes) multiple-platform LOS displacement time-series. Noteworthy, the adopted InSAR-combination scheme can be used in a wide context. Real SAR datasets are exploited to demonstrate the validity of the presented algorithm. Experimental results will be shown in Section 4. Conclusions and further perspectives will be provided in Section 5.

2. Retrieval of surface displacement components through DInSAR and pixel-offset-based techniques

In this section, the basic principles of differential SAR interferometry (DInSAR) for the detection of Earth's surface displacement are introduced. Moreover, the potential integration of DInSAR and pixel-offset-based measurement for the measurement of large deformation signals occurring in the case of large ruptures of Earth's crust is discussed.

2.1. Basics of InSAR technique

One of the major applications of the SAR technology is represented by the SAR interferometry (InSAR) technique [1, 2], which relies on the measurements of the phase difference between two complex-valued SAR images gathered from a satellite/airborne platform at different times and from different orbital positions, so as to measure the geomorphological characteristics of the ground (such as the topography height and the modifications of the surface over time, due to earthquakes, volcano eruptions, or other geophysical phenomena). Historically, InSAR has been used for the measurement of ground topography. To understand how InSAR works, let us consider the imaging geometry shown in **Figure 1**, and let us suppose the first SAR image (referred to as master image) is acquired from the orbital position labeled to as M, and the second image (i.e., the slave image) is taken from the orbital position labeled to as S, located at a distance b (usually referred to as baseline) from M. By applying simple geometrical rules, it is possible to uniquely identify the location of each ground targets on the image as well as to get an estimate of their heights (namely, z) relative to the reference plane. As evident by inspection of **Figure 1**, if a same target (namely, T) is observed form two orbital positions (master and slave), with two corresponding ranges its distances from the first (namely, r) and the second position (namely, $r + \delta r$) can be correctly measured and the target height can be unambiguously determined. This is obtained by finding out the solution of the following system of two equations (see **Figure 1**):

$$(r + \delta r)^2 = r^2 + b^2 - 2\, r\, b\, sin(\vartheta - \alpha) \tag{1}$$

$$z = H - r\, cos\vartheta \tag{2}$$

where δr and $\delta r + r$ represent the radar ranges from each antenna to the target point, ϑ represents the radar side-looking angle, α the angle of the baseline relative to the horizontal, and z is the scatterer height above the flat-earth reference. H is the height of the sensor above the reference surface and b is the distance between the antennas, which is referred to as baseline. The ability in successfully reconstructing the unknown topography (z) is strictly dependent on the capability to precisely measure the slant-range difference δr, which represents one of the known terms of the system of Eqs. (1) and (2).

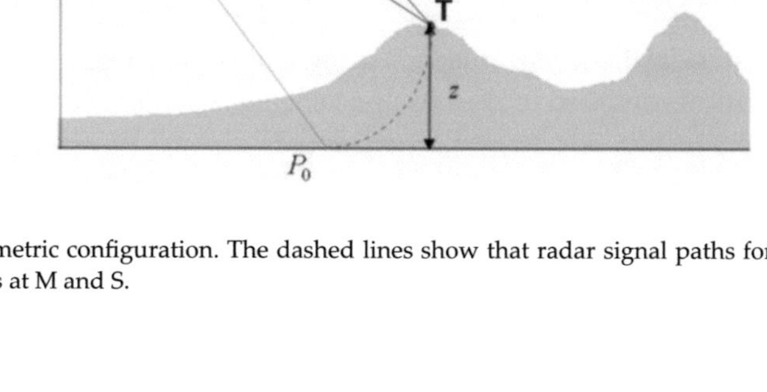

Figure 1. SAR interferometric configuration. The dashed lines show that radar signal paths for the first interferogram pair formed by antennas at M and S.

To understand how InSAR works, let us consider again the imaging geometry, let us assume the radar system has infinite bandwidth; under this condition the master and slave complex-valued SAR images (pixel-by-pixel) can be mathematically represented as follows:

$$\hat{\gamma}_1 = \gamma_1 \exp\left[-j\frac{4\pi}{\lambda}r\right] \quad (3)$$

$$\hat{\gamma}_2 = \gamma_2 \exp\left[-j\frac{4\pi}{\lambda}(r+\delta r)\right] \quad (4)$$

where γ_1 and γ_2 are the complex reflectivity functions of the master and slave scene, respectively, and λ denotes the operative radar wavelength. An interferogram is formed on a pixel-by-pixel basis by starting from two complex-valued co-registered SAR images, as outlined in the following. For each pixel, the phase difference between the two SAR images is computed, by multiplying the first image (master) by the complex conjugate of the second image (slave) and, then, by extracting the relevant phase.

From Eqs. (3) and (4), the interferometric phase is obtained, as follows:

$$\arg\left[\hat{\gamma}_1 \hat{\gamma}_2^*\right] = \arg\left[j\frac{4\pi}{\lambda}\delta r\right] + \arg[\gamma_1] - \arg[\gamma_2] \quad (5)$$

where the asterisk denotes the complex conjugate operation, and the symbol $\arg[\cdot]$ refers to the operator that extracts the phase of a complex number, which is restricted to the $[-\pi, \pi]$ interval. However, by assuming the scattering mechanism on the ground is the same ($\arg[\gamma_1] = \arg[\gamma_2]$) between the two passages of the sensor over the illuminated area (mutually coherent observations), the measured phase difference $\tilde{\psi}^k$ (where k identifies a specific interferometric pair of a multiple baseline configuration) depends upon on the range difference δr, only:

$$\tilde{\psi}^k = \arg\left[\exp\left(j\frac{4\pi}{\lambda}\delta r\right)\right] \quad (6)$$

The observed interferometic phase $\tilde{\psi}^k$ is 2π ambiguous, and the obtained image is called an interferogram. Since the ambiguity of the phase, which is measured modulo 2π, the information on range difference δr is retrieved from the interferogram by applying the phase unwrapping operation [24, 25], thus estimating the inherent absolute interferometric phase ψ^k, given by:

$$\psi^k = \frac{4\pi}{\lambda}\delta r \quad (7)$$

By considering the standard interferometric configuration depicted in **Figure 1** and a few mathematical calculations detailed in [26], it is possible to relate the computed interferometric phase difference to the (unknown) height topography as:

$$\psi^k \approx \psi_0^k + \frac{\partial \psi^k}{\partial z}\Delta z = -\frac{4\pi}{\lambda} b^k \sin\left(\vartheta_0^k - \alpha^k\right) - \frac{4\pi}{\lambda}\frac{b_\perp^k}{r \sin\vartheta_0^k} \quad (8)$$

where Δz is the surface height variation above the flat-earth reference plane, ϑ_0^k is the side-looking angle of each point in the image, assuming zero local height, $b_\perp^k = b^k \cos(\vartheta_0^k - \alpha^k)$ represents the projection of the baseline in the direction perpendicular to the line-of-sight from the radar to the target. The first term $\psi_0^k = \frac{4\pi}{\lambda} b^k \sin(\vartheta_0^k - \alpha^k)$ in Eq. (8) accounts for the phase contribution corresponding to the flat-Earth (z = 0), which is the term that is present in the absence of any height elevation on the ground. From Eq. (8), it is clear that the sensitivity of the InSAR measurement can be improved by increasing the baseline. However, the perpendicular baseline, cannot exceed the limiting value (critical baseline) for which the variation of the phase difference across one single ground range resolution element is 2π.

SAR interferometry nowadays is mostly used for the detection of surface changes occurring over time. In such a case, when a slight change of the surface across the two SAR acquisition times occurs in the imaged scene, an additive term arises in the interferometric phase, which is associated with the radar line-of-sight (LOS) component of the surface displacement, in addition to a phase term that depends on topography. By the inspection of the imaging geometry depicted in **Figure 2**, we get:

$$\Delta\psi^k = \frac{\partial\psi^k}{\partial z}\Delta z + \frac{\partial\psi^k}{\partial d_{Los}^k}\Delta d_{Los}^k = -\frac{4\pi}{\lambda}\frac{b_\perp^k}{r \sin\vartheta_0^k}\Delta z + \frac{4\pi}{\lambda}\Delta d_{Los}^k \quad (9)$$

where Δd_{Los}^k represents the projection of the surface displacement vector onto LOS (range) direction pertinent to the kth interferometric pair. Note that the presence of the flat earth phase contribution was neglected, for the sake of convenience.

In order to measure the interferometric phase term related to the surface displacement, it is thus essential to remove the interferometric phase contribution pertinent to the topography in Eq. (9). Specifically, a differential SAR interferogram is formed by synthesizing the topographic phase from an available digital elevation model (DEM) of the area (using the so

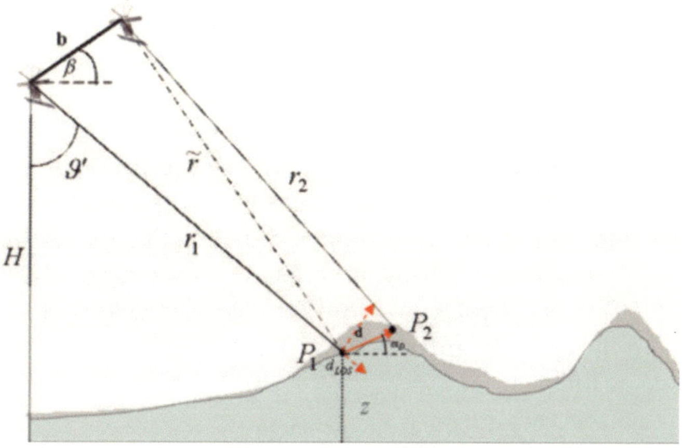

Figure 2. Differential SAR interferometry imaging geometry.

so-called back-geocoding process) and by subtracting, pixel-by-pixel, these synthetic fringes to the corresponding InSAR phase, thus leaving only the terms associated with the displacement. Accordingly, computed differential SAR interferograms can be expressed as:

$$\Delta\psi^k = \Delta\psi^k_{disp} + \Delta\psi^k_{topo} + \Delta\psi^k_{orb} + \Delta\psi^k_{prop} + \Delta\psi^k_{scat} \tag{10}$$

where $k \in \{1, .., M\}$ specifies the considered interferometric pair (master/slave);

$\Delta\psi^k_{disp} = \frac{4\pi}{\lambda}\Delta d^k_{Los}$ represents possible displacement of the scatterer between observations, where d_{LOS} is the projection of the relevant displacement vector on the line of sight;

$\Delta\psi^k_{topo} = \frac{4\pi}{\lambda}\frac{b^k_{\perp}}{r\sin\vartheta^k_0}\Delta\tilde{z}$ represents the residual-topography induced phase due to a non-perfect knowledge of the actual height profile (i.e., the DEM errors $\Delta\tilde{z}$);

$\Delta\psi^k_{orb}$ accounts for possible inaccurate orbital information;

$\Delta\psi^k_{prop}$ denotes the phase components due to the variation of propagation conditions (pertinent to the change in the atmospheric and ionospheric dielectric constant) between the two master/slave acquisitions;

$\Delta\psi^k_{scat}$ accounts for change in scattering behavior [13].

2.2. Combination of ascending/descending displacement maps

Availability of InSAR results computed from SAR data obtained from ascending and descending orbits allows also for the separation of the East-West (E-W) and the vertical components of the detected deformation. In particular, for all the pixels that are common to both radar geometries, the sum and the difference of LOS-projected deformations computed for the ascending and the descending orbits are calculated. In particular, the sum of the ascending/descending LOS-projected displacement measurements is related to the vertical component of the ground deformation, whereas the difference of the ascending/descending components gives an estimate for the E-W component of the deformation. Also, because modern spaceborne radar systems are mounted on-board satellites that fly nearly polar orbits, the North-South (N-S) component of the deformation cannot be reliably measured. To explain the rationale for the retrieval of the E-W and the vertical components of the deformation, the following assumptions are made: (i) ascending and descending radar LOS directions ($d^{(Asc)}_{LOS}$ and $d^{(Desc)}_{LOS}$, respectively) lay wholly in the east–z plane and (ii) the sensor side-looking angle is approximately the same along the ascending and descending orbits. Both these assumptions are acceptable. If we refer to the same homologous pixel imaged by the ascending and descending orbits, the E-W and Up-Down components of the measured surface deformation can be estimated from the ascending/descending LOS measurement (e.g., the LOS-projected rates of deformation) as follows:

$$d^{(East)}_{LOS} \approx \frac{d^{(Desc)}_{LOS} - d^{(Asc)}_{LOS}}{2\sin\vartheta} \tag{11}$$

$$d^{(Up)}_{LOS} \approx \frac{d^{(Desc)}_{LOS} + d^{(Asc)}_{LOS}}{2\cos\vartheta} \tag{12}$$

Geometric scheme to interpret the deformation component is portrayed in **Figure 3**. Finally, it is worth emphasizing that a fundamental advantage of InSAR technology, with respect to o GPS networks, resides in its dense sampling grid of the displacement field.

2.3. The advanced multi-temporal small baseline subset (SBAS) technique

In the following, the small baseline subset (SBAS) algorithm is presented. SBAS was developed in 2002 by a team of researchers from National Council Research (CNR) of Italy [19]. To introduce the rationale of the algorithm, let us consider a set of Q single-look-complex (SLC) SAR images acquired by a radar instrument over a certain area of interest. One of these images is selected and assumed as the reference (master) image, with respect to which all available SAR images are properly co-registered. The set is characterized by the corresponding acquisition times $\{t_1, \ldots, t_Q\}$ and the inherent perpendicular baselines vector $\{b_{\perp 1}, \ldots, b_{\perp Q}\}$ estimated with respect to the reference image. Application of the standard SBAS technique starts with the generation of a set of M of small baseline multi-look (differential) interferograms. On these interferograms, the retrieval of the original (unwrapped) phase signals from the modulo-2π measured (wrapped) phases is carried out. The expression of the kth interferometric phase is as follows:

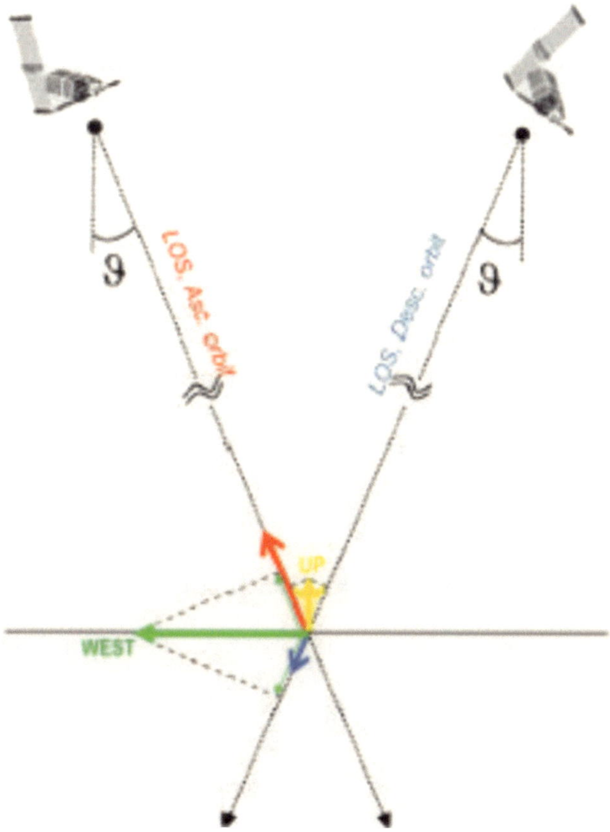

Figure 3. Combination scheme of ascending and descending displacement fields.

$$\Delta\psi^k = \frac{4\pi}{\lambda}\Delta d^k_{LOS} - \frac{4\pi}{\lambda}\frac{b^k_\perp}{r\sin\vartheta^k_0}\Delta\tilde{z} + \Delta\psi^k_{orb} + \Delta\psi^k_{prop} + \Delta\psi^k_{scat} \quad (13)$$

The system of Eq. (13) can be re-organized in a matrix form as:

$$\mathbf{A}\cdot\Psi = \Delta\Psi \quad (14)$$

wherein A is the incidence-like matrix directly related to the selected set of small baseline (SB) interferometric data-pairs. Let us now manipulate the system of Eq. (14) to replace the unknown phase vector Ψ with the mean phase velocities between adjacent time acquisitions (see [6]). Accordingly, the new unknowns become:

$$\mathbf{v} = \left[v_1 = \frac{\psi_2 - \psi_1}{t_2 - t_1}, \ldots, v_{Q-2} = \frac{\psi_{Q-1} - \psi_{Q-2}}{t_{Q-1} - t_{Q-2}}\right]^T \quad (15)$$

and the system (14) can be re-formulated as follows:

$$\mathbf{B}\cdot\mathbf{v} = \Delta\Psi \quad (16)$$

wherein **B** is the incidence matrix of the linear transformation in Eq. (15), whose detailed expression can be found in [6]. It is worth remarking that, depending upon the selection of small baseline interferometric data pairs, it is possible that SAR data could be separated into some independent subsets separated one another by large baselines. Mathematically, this leads the rank deficiency of matrix **B** and, accordingly, the system (16) can have infinite possible solutions. In order to figure it out a solution among the infinite ones, the singular value decomposition (SVD) method is applied. This allows us to evaluate the pseudo-inverse of the matrix **B**, which gives the minimum norm least-squares (LS) solution of the system (16). In this context, the minimum-norm constraint on the velocity vector **v** allows mitigating the presence of temporal discontinuities in the final result, so as to guarantee a physically sound solution. Finally, an additional integration step is necessary to compute the solution from the estimated vector **v**. After solving the system (16) an estimate of the spurious terms due to the presence of some residual topographic artifacts in the generated interferograms is usually performed [6]. Atmospheric phase screen (APS) is also estimated and filtered out [6]. The quality of retrieved LOS time-series is finally evaluated pixel-by-pixel by calculating the values of the temporal coherence factor, defined in [26].

2.4. Pixel-offset (PO) technique for the estimation of large rupture deformations

In areas where large and/or rapid deformation phenomena occur, the exploitation of the differential interferograms, thus the generation of displacement time series, can be however strongly limited by the presence of very high fringe rates, which in turn introduce additional difficulties in the phase unwrapping step and may lead to significant misregistration errors. A pictorial representation of how the interferometric phase degrades as the displacement amount increases is given in **Figure 4**. Nevertheless, the information on the occurred displacements might be preserved in the amplitude of the investigated data pair, considering the offset of the image's pixels in range and azimuth directions.

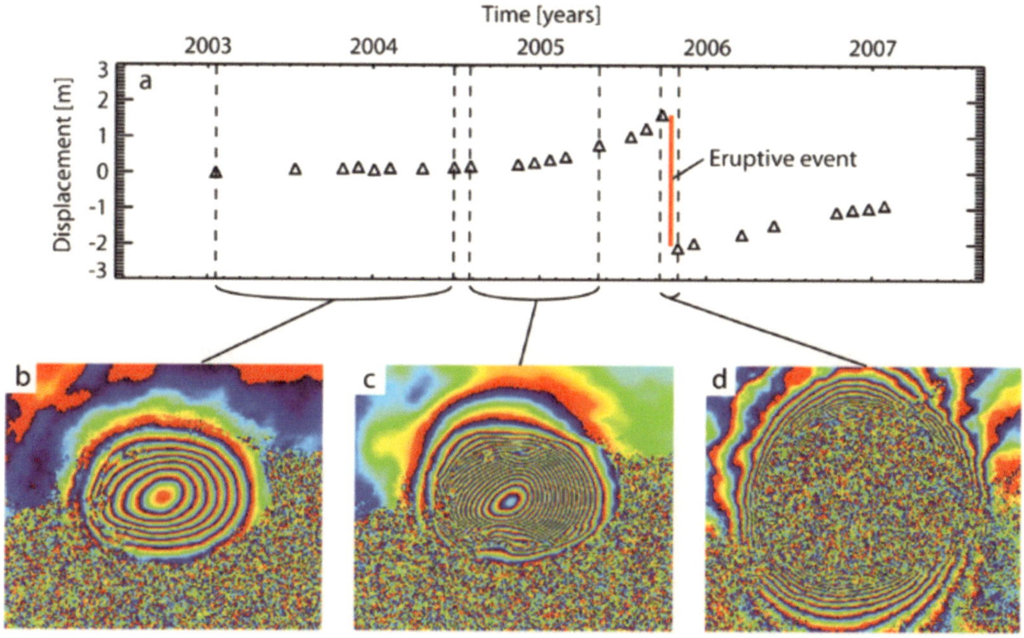

Figure 4. Pictorial representation of the effects due to different amounts of deformations. (a) Plot of the deformation time-series showing the temporal evolution of displacement in the Sierra Negra Caldera, as computed from a sequence of ENVISAT DInSAR interferograms. (b)–(d) Differential interferograms relevant to different deformation regimes and time epochs: when the deformation rate is low the information conveyed in the phase is fully preserved (b). As deformation rate increases the fringe spatial frequency increases (c), and in the occurrence of the large rupture of terrain the fringe rate is so high that the corresponding interferometric phase (d) is completely corrupted by decorrelation noise, thus making the use of phase not effective. This figure is a re-adaptation of **Figure 1** originally presented in [27].

Pixel-offset (PO) is a technique that attempts to find the same distinctive features within sub-scenes of two images relevant to the same target area. In remote sensing, this is usually performed by considering either the Fourier shift theorem [28], or normalized cross-correlation (NCC) algorithms [29]. In SAR applications, PO allows co-registering image pairs or, while already co-registered, identifying the residual shifts related to the motion of distinctive features with accuracies in the order of 1/20th of pixel.

In this scenario, the availability of a sequence of full resolution SAR data pairs, already co-registered, was assumed. For this purpose, the NCC algorithm, which is widely used for SAR images, is applied. This step, carried out on across-track and along-track directions, provides for each pixel an estimation of range and azimuth shifts, finally leading to two offset maps for each data pair. The performed NCC analysis might be evaluated through an estimator of the "goodness" of the retrieved offsets.

At this stage, in order to obtain the corresponding time series, the SBAS strategy is applied (see Section 2.3) by substituting the amplitude-driven information to the phase-driven displacement measurements. This operation was performed to the sequences of smoothed range and azimuth pixel-offset maps. Hence, the small baseline constraint in the data pair's selection, implicit in the SBAS strategy, is convenient in order to maximize the amount of the exploitable pixels. Notice that this algorithm, which is known in the literature to as pixel offset SBAS (POSBAS) [27], is particularly attractive in the case of large deformation, because it allows us to have an estimate of the North-South deformation components, with accuracy in the order of some centimeter, whereas (as said before) the information related to North-South displacement is almost absent in the conventional DInSAR interferometric phase, being the sensors' flight trajectories almost parallel to the North-South direction. The results of the performed experiments are shown in Section 4.

3. Minimum acceleration (MinA) algorithm

In this section, the minimum acceleration (MinA) combination algorithm [23] used for the extraction of displacement time-series of the Up-Down, East-West, and North-South components is detailed. To introduce the right mathematical framework, let us assume the availability of K independent sets of multiple-platform SAR data collected at ordered times $t^{(j)} = \left[t_0^{(j)}, t_1^{(j)}, \ldots, t_{Q_j-1}^{(j)}\right]^T \ \forall j = 1, \ldots, K$ over the same area on the ground, consisting of Q_j distinctive time epochs, respectively. The MinA algorithm [23] requires the preliminary generation from each single SAR data-track of the inherent LOS-projected deformation time-series. This task can be achieved by independently applying either the SBAS technique [6] or other alternative multi-temporal DInSAR approaches [4–9] to the available K SAR datasets. During this preliminary stage, the residual topography as well as the atmospheric phase screen (APS) artifacts corrupting differential SAR interferograms might be estimated and successfully filtered out from the generated LOS-projected displacement time-series [7–16]. The so-obtained LOS-projected time-series of deformation along with other ancillary information, such as the maps of temporal coherence (quantifying the goodness of obtained time-series) as well as the LOS mean deformation velocity maps are geocoded to a common spatial grid of points where to apply the subsequent combination stage. During this preliminary stage the location of high coherent targets is also identified. Henceforth, let $\mathbf{d}^{(j)} = \left[d_0^{(j)}, d_1^{(j)}, \ldots, d_{Q_j-1}^{(j)}\right]^T \ \forall j = 1, \ldots, K$ be the geocoded LOS-projected deformation time-series relevant to a generic pixel P that belongs to the group of high-coherent pixels common to all the available K SAR datasets.

LOS-projected time-series of deformation are expressed with respect to the instants $t_0^{(j)}, \forall j = 1, \ldots, K$, which are singularly taken as reference for each dataset, that is to say $d_0^{(j)} = 0, \forall j = 1, \ldots, K$. Let us now describe the algorithm works, and $Q = \sum_{j=1}^{K} Q_j$ be the total number of the available SAR images collected at the "whole" ordered times $T = \cup_{j=1}^{K} t^{(j)} = \left[T_0, T_1, \ldots, T_{Q-1}\right]^T$.

Let us start by observing that a generic LOS-projected deformation measurement, namely d_{LOS}, can be related to its inherent 3-D components, namely $[d_{E-W}, d_{U-D}, d_{N-S}]^T$, as [18, 22]:

$$d_{LOS} = d \cdot \hat{i}_{LOS} = \sin\vartheta \cos\varphi \, d_{East-West} - \cos\vartheta \, d_{Up-Down} + \sin\vartheta \sin\varphi \, d_{North-South} \quad (17)$$

where $\hat{\imath}_{LOS}$ is the LOS-direction versor. Note that θ and φ represent the radar side-looking and the satellite heading angles, respectively; the imaging geometries for ascending/descending data-tracks are shown in **Figure 5**. Extending to our case what originally proposed in [6] and subsequently adapted in [22], let us relate the available LOS deformations $d^{(j)}(P), \ j = 1, \ldots, K$

http://dx.doi.org/10.5772/intechopen.71329

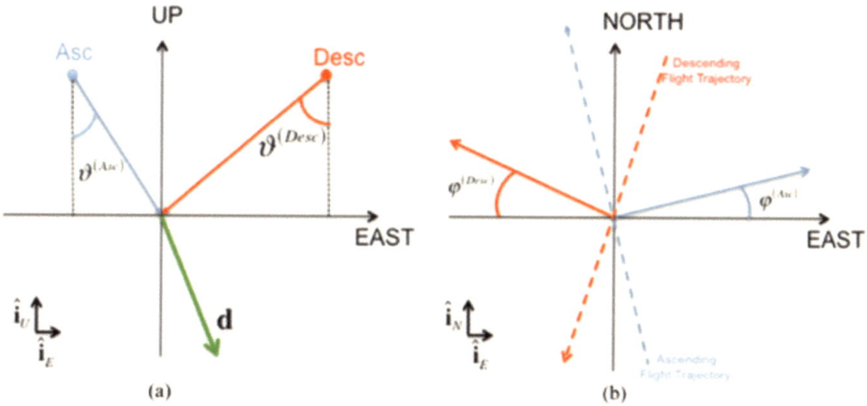

Figure 5. SAR data acquisition geometries for descending (a) and ascending (b) orbits, respectively.

(for each high coherent pixel) to their unknown 3-D components. This leads writing a system of Q-K independent linear equations with respect to the M = 3(Q-1) unknowns representing the East-West (E-W), Up-Down (U-D), and North-South (N-S) deformation velocities components between adjacent time-acquisitions, namely $V_E = [V_{E_1}, V_{E_2}, \dots, V_{E_{Q-1}}]^T$, $V_U = [V_{U_1}, V_{U_2}, \dots, V_{U_{Q-1}}]^T$ and $V_N = [V_{N_1}, V_{N_2}, \dots, V_{N_{Q-1}}]^T$. This system of linear equations can be expressed using matrix formalism as follows

$$\mathbf{B}\cdot\begin{bmatrix}\mathbf{V}_\mathbf{E}\\ \mathbf{V}_\mathbf{U}\\ \mathbf{V}_\mathbf{N}\end{bmatrix} = \begin{bmatrix}\Gamma^1\left(d^{(1)} - d_0^{(1)}\right)\\ \Gamma^2\left(d^{(2)} - d_0^{(2)}\right)\\ \cdots\\ \Gamma^K\left(d^{(K)} - d_0^{(K)}\right)\end{bmatrix} = \tilde{\mathbf{d}} \tag{18}$$

where Γ^j $j = 1, \dots, K$ are the values of temporal coherence associated to the K different datasets (representing a quality factor of the obtained LOS displacement time-series) and **B** is the incidence-like matrix of the linear transformation that converts LOS-projected measurements into their inherent 3-D components. It is defined by taking into account (1) as:

$$\mathbf{B} = \begin{bmatrix}\mathbf{B}^{(1)}\Gamma^{(1)}\sin\vartheta^{(1)}\cos\varphi^{(1)} & -\mathbf{B}^{(1)}\Gamma^{(1)}\cos\vartheta^{(1)} & \mathbf{B}^{(1)}\Gamma^{(1)}\sin\vartheta^{(1)}\sin\varphi^{(1)}\\ \mathbf{B}^{(2)}\Gamma^{(2)}\sin\vartheta^{(2)}\cos\varphi^{(2)} & -\mathbf{B}^{(2)}\Gamma^{(2)}\cos\vartheta^{(2)} & \mathbf{B}^{(2)}\Gamma^{(2)}\sin\vartheta^{(2)}\sin\varphi^{(2)}\\ \vdots & \vdots & \vdots\\ \mathbf{B}^{(K)}\Gamma^{(K)}\sin\vartheta^{(K)}\cos\varphi^{(K)} & -\mathbf{B}^{(K)}\Gamma^{(K)}\cos\vartheta^{(K)} & \mathbf{B}^{(K)}\Gamma^{(K)}\sin\vartheta^{(K)}\sin\varphi^{(K)}\end{bmatrix} \tag{19}$$

wherein $\mathbf{B}^{(j)}, j = 1, \dots, K$ is the jth incidence-like matrix of the linear transformation that relates displacement time-series with velocity deformation rates between consecutive time intervals for the jth SAR data set. Derivation of that incidence-like matrix is detailed in the paper [6]. Note that this matrix is the same as the one used in SBAS and discussed in the previous section.

The system (18) and (19) has fewer linear independent equations (Q-K) than unknowns (M), thus it is an under-determined system that does not admit a unique solution. The matrix **B** of the system has singular values that gradually decay to zero, thus rendering any solution much sensitive to noise level corrupting the vector $\tilde{\mathbf{d}}$. It represents a canonical example of a linear discrete ill-posed problem whose meaningful solution can be obtained by replacing the "original" linear system (18) and (19) by a nearby system that is less sensitive to perturbations of the right-hand side of the system, and considers the solution of this new system as a good approximation of the original one. This operation is known as regularization and can be performed using truncated singular value decomposition (TSVD) [30], Tikhonov regularization [31], maximum entropy principle [32]. TSVD practically consists in decomposing the matrix **B** with SVD and truncating (putting to zeros) the small singular values, in such a way that they do not dominate the solution leading to spurious oscillations. In turn, Tikhonov regularization consists in replacing the solution of the system (2) and (3) by the following minimization problem:

$$\min_{V \in \mathbb{R}} \left\{ \|\mathbf{B} \cdot \mathbf{V} - \tilde{\mathbf{d}}\|_2 + \alpha^2 \|\mathbf{V}\|_2 \right\} \tag{20}$$

for a suitable value of the regularization parameter α, which can effectively be found using (for instance) L-curve method [31]. The goal of L-curve is to search for a regularization parameter α for which the solution has an optimal balance between the minimization of residual norm $\|\mathbf{B} \cdot \mathbf{V} - \tilde{\mathbf{d}}\|_2$ and the "weight" of the minimum-norm velocity regularization $\|\mathbf{V}\|_2$.

A similar regularized problem was proposed within the MSBAS algorithm [22], even though in that case the relevant system of linear equations was derived from a sequence of unwrapped multiple-tracks differential SAR interferograms. In the case of MinA algorithm, the regularization problem is achieved differently, by adding to the original system (18) and (19) other equations imposing the condition that the (unknown) 3-D (E-W, U-D, N-S) displacement time-series are with minimum curvature, that is to say the velocity deformation differences (for all the 3-D components) between consecutive time intervals is minimal. Such conditions can formally be expressed by adding to Eq. (2) the following set of 3(Q-2) additional equations:

$$\begin{cases} V_{E_{i+1}} - V_{E_i} & i = 1, \ldots, Q-2 \\ V_{U_{i+1}} - V_{U_i} & i = 1, \ldots, Q-2 \\ V_{N_{i+1}} - V_{N_i} & i = 1, \ldots, Q-2 \end{cases} \tag{21}$$

Accordingly, the regularized system of linear equations becomes:

$$\begin{bmatrix} \mathbf{B} \\ \mathbf{C} \end{bmatrix} \cdot \begin{bmatrix} \mathbf{V}_E \\ \mathbf{V}_U \\ \mathbf{V}_N \end{bmatrix} = \begin{bmatrix} \tilde{\mathbf{d}} \\ \mathbf{0} \end{bmatrix} \tag{22}$$

where **C** is the incidence-like matrix related to the minimum-acceleration-regularization linear transformation. The solution of Eq. (6) is finally obtained in the LS sense by applying Truncated SVD to the matrix $\mathbf{\Omega} = \binom{\mathbf{B}}{\mathbf{C}}$. Once the problem in Eqs. (21) and (22) is solved, the

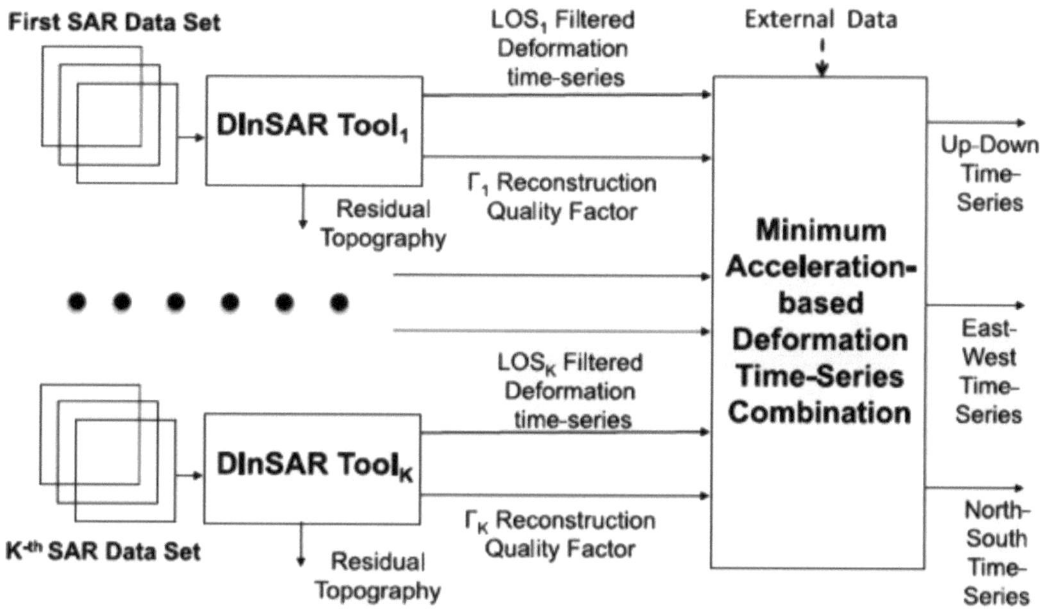

Figure 6. MinA diagram block. K independent sets of LOS measurements of the surface ground displacement, as obtained by processing data from K multi-angle/multi-sensor SAR systems also using independent DInSAR toolboxes, are combined (taking into account the associated quality reconstruction maps). Combination is based on the application of minimum-acceleration constraints on the achievable Up-Down, East-West, and North-South time-series of deformation. Use of external data is helpful for better constraining the solutions.

3-D velocity deformation components are independently time-integrated to recover the relevant 3-D displacement time-series.

As earlier said, a similar system of equations was also derived within the MSBAS algorithm [22] but, at variance with MinA, it relies on searching for a minimum-velocity-norm (MN) solution considering the Tikhonov regularization. Moreover, MSBAS requires the simultaneous inversion of several (a few hundreds or more) unwrapped interferograms for the retrieval of the 3-D components of deformation, and the achieved time-series were however still affected by possible topographic and atmospheric artifacts (although considering several hundreds of interferograms various sources of noise and related artifacts are averaged and only partly filtered out) that need to be subsequently filtered out in a post-processing phase. Accordingly, even though the adopted combination strategy shares some similarities with the MSBAS algorithm, MinA does not require simultaneous processing of multi-platform/multi-angle SAR datasets and can be applied with no restrictions at all on the method (permanent scatterers and/or small baseline-oriented) used for the retrieval of LOS DInSAR time-series, making its field of applicability extremely wide.

Noteworthy, the MinA algorithm can also be extended to include azimuth- and range-pixel-offset (AZPO and RGPO) time-series, as computed using the PO-SBAS method (or alternative solutions). This case is very suitable when large deformation phenomena have to be monitored, being the accuracy of these methods is on the order of 10 cm (or larger). In this case, the strategy here adopted can be extended using AZPO and RGPO time-series of deformation, instead of the LOS deformation measurements, and applying the minimum-acceleration (MA) regularization.

The diagram block of the MinA algorithm is shown in **Figure 6**.

4. Experimental results

This section shows some experimental results obtained by applying the PO-SBAS and the MinA techniques for the estimation of three-dimensional components of terrain displacements.

4.1. Sierra Negra PO-SBAS results

The experiments carried out in this case were related to the area of Sierra Negra caldera, which is the most active among shield volcanoes located on Isabela Island, Galapagos Archipelago. Following an Mw 5.4 earthquake, in October 2005 Sierra Negra caldera erupted, interrupting a period of quiescence that lasted almost 30 years. The investigation of several analyses of the Sierra Negra caldera geodetic signals revealed Sierra Negra is almost continuously in an uplift phase, which started in 1992, and accelerated so as to reach about 5 m of cumulative ground displacement before the 2005 eruption. On the other hand, the October 2005 catastrophic event induced a subsidence of the inner caldera of more than 5 m [33].

Due to the large deformation dynamics affecting Sierra Negra caldera, the retrieval of ground displacements using DInSAR is a challenging task. Indeed, the application of conventional SBAS-DInSAR time series analysis on the 2003–2007 Galapagos dataset provides only a partial picture of the deformation field. In particular, a set of 25 ENVISAT SAR images were processed (see [27] for further details). **Figure 7(a)** and **(b)** shows the retrieved mean ground velocity maps relevant to the 2003–2007 period. The behavior of the northern flanks of the volcano, being the displacements still in the order of centimeters, is clearly imaged by the SBAS-DInSAR analysis, and it is in agreement with previous studies. However, due to the lack of coherence caused by the large deformation dynamics, the interferometric phase analysis is not able to measure displacements around the crater and inner caldera due to the lack of coherence caused by the large deformation dynamics.

In order to image the spatial and temporal evolution of the deformation in these areas, the SAR amplitude information was exploited. Thus, the PO-SBAS approach was applied to the same data pairs considered for the generation of the SBAS-DInSAR time series. Following the PO-SBAS steps explained, the offsets for each data pair were calculated, and a common mask of "good" pixels was selected by considering only those having a high QI value that were present at least in 70% of the whole dataset. At this stage, the PO-SBAS time-series were generated for each of the selected pixels. The accuracies for the PO-SBAS measurements, relevant to the herein analyzed test-case, were obtained by calculating the standard deviation of the measurements in an area that is known to be stable. Estimated accuracy values are in

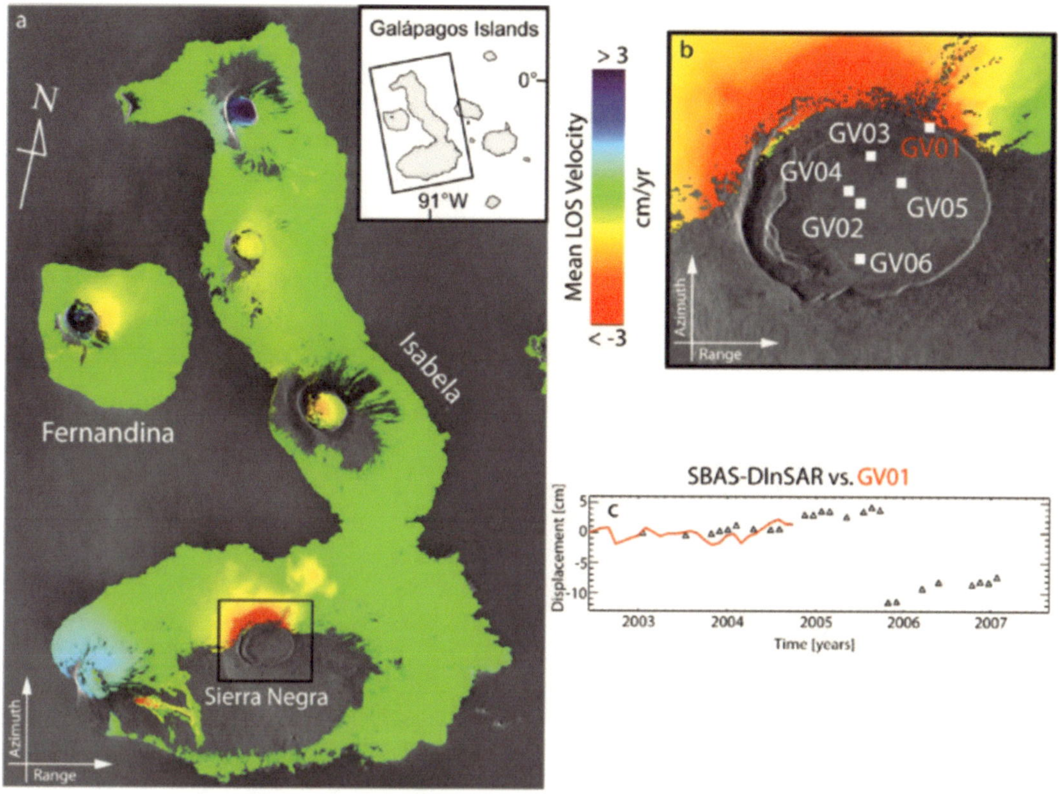

Figure 7. SBAS-DInSAR results. (a) Mean deformation velocity map of the Galapagos Islands retrieved by applying the SBAS technique and (b) zoom of the study area, (c) Comparison between PO-SBAS and GPS measurements corresponding to the GV01 station.

the order of 1/20th of pixel, in agreement with those expected. However, since the aim of this analysis is to emphasize the areas characterized by large deformations, the pixels whose dynamics are smaller than 1/10th of pixel were masked out. **Figure 8** shows the PO-SBAS time-series and the comparison with external GPS measurements available in the area.

4.2. Piton de La Fournaise MinA results

To further demonstrate the capabilities of the DInSAR-driven minimum-acceleration combination algorithm, it has been applied for studying the settlements of the area of Piton de La Fournaise (Reunion Islands), which is characterized by the presence of a large volcanic system that erupted on April 3, 2007 and lead to large fractures on the ground. Such volcanic system has extensively been studied [34], however new data can provide additional information on the state of volcanism of the island. The presented experiments are based on processing three independent sets of SAR images collected by the ENVISAT/ASAR (C-band) radar instrument along ascending (48 images) and descending passes (35 images) as well as by the ALOS-1/PALSAR (L-band) sensor (11 images), spanning the 2003–2010 time interval (see Table III in [23]). These three SAR datasets were independently processed by the

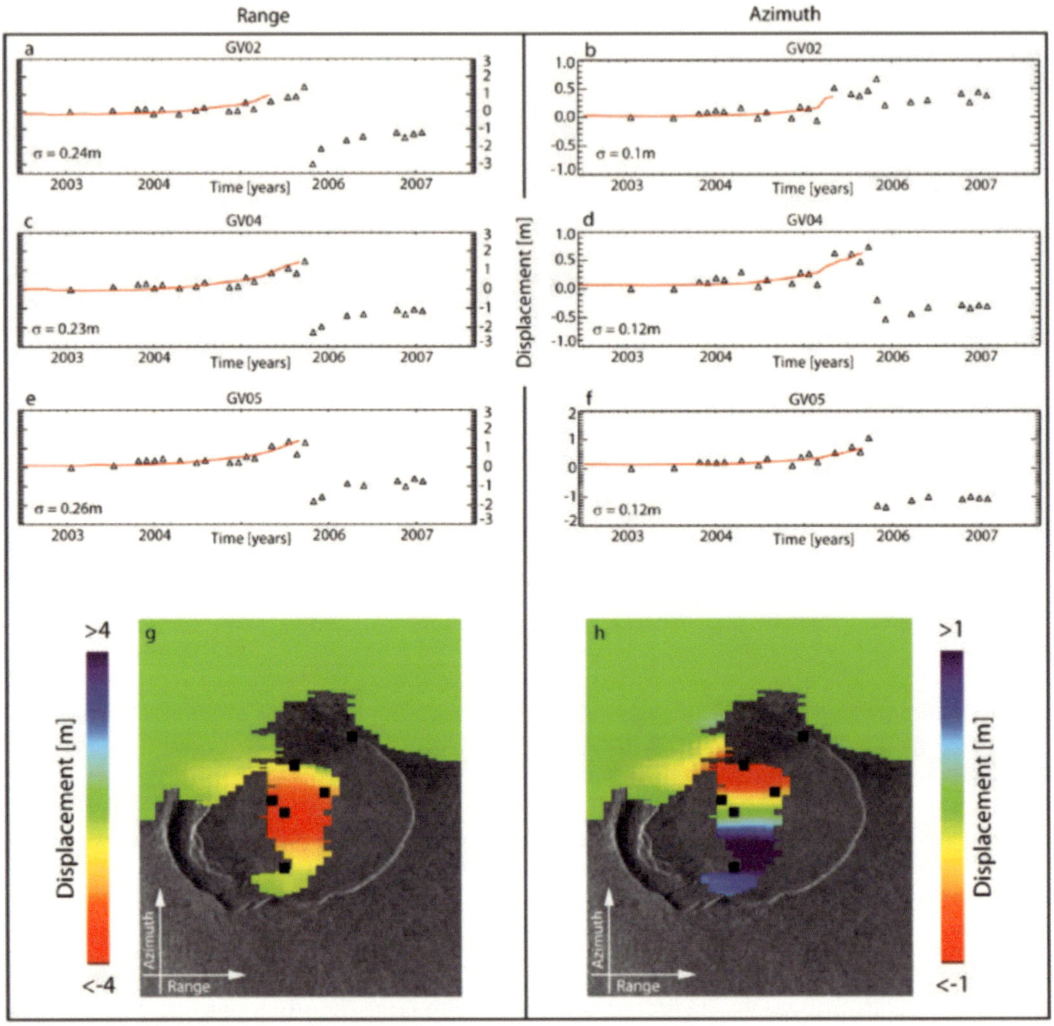

Figure 8. Examples of PO-SBAS time-series in azimuth (right) and range (left) directions, respectively. (a)-(f) Comparison between PO-SBAS and GPS measurements in the proximity of selected GPS stations. (g)-(h) AZO and RGO displacement mean velocity maps. The figure is adapted from [27].

SBAS-DInSAR processing chain, and corresponding LOS-projected displacement time-series (and mean deformation maps) were generated. The MinA combination method is applied (as a post-processing stage) only to those pixels that remain coherent in all three independent SBAS-DInSAR processing analyses, and this permitted discriminating from the LOS-projected deformations the time-series of the 3D deformation components.

Figure 9(a)–(c) shows the maps of retrieved E-W, U-D, and N-S mean deformation velocity maps, superimposed to a gray-scale SAR amplitude image of the zone common to all the three SAR data-tracks. Also, one point, labeled to as P in **Figure 9** and located in the summit

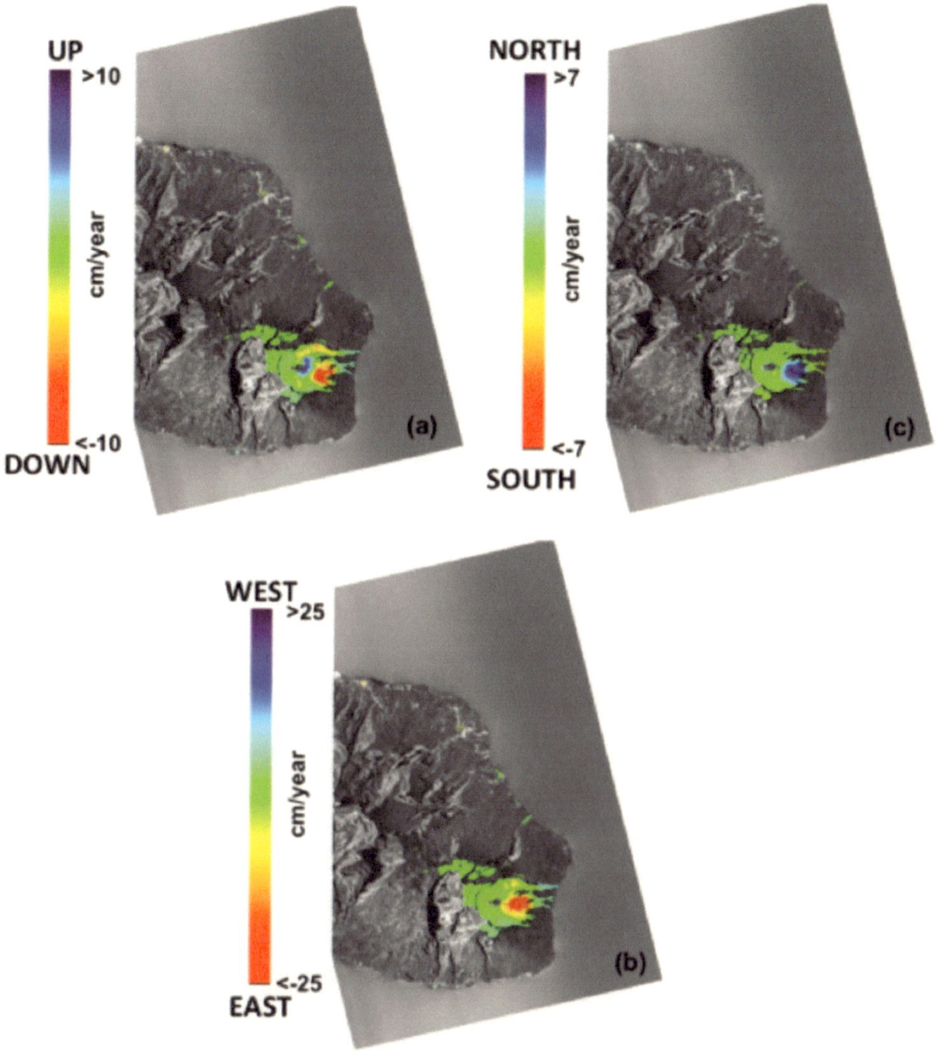

Figure 9. Geocoded maps of the Up-Down (a), east–west (b), and north–south (c) mean velocity deformation.

area of the crater, was selected. The inherent (combined) E-W and Up-Down deformation time-series relevant to this point are shown in the plots of **Figure 10**. They make it evident the large cumulative E-W displacement, moving mostly eastward, affects the upper part of the Eastern flank with velocity of about 10 cm/year. This trend is abruptly interrupted by a jump of about 40 cm in correspondence of the April 2, 2007 eruption, which induced a widespread flank movement starting at the time of dike injection to feed an initial eruption, a few days before the main eruptive event; also a significant U-D signal was active even with a more moderate deformation value (around 8 cm).

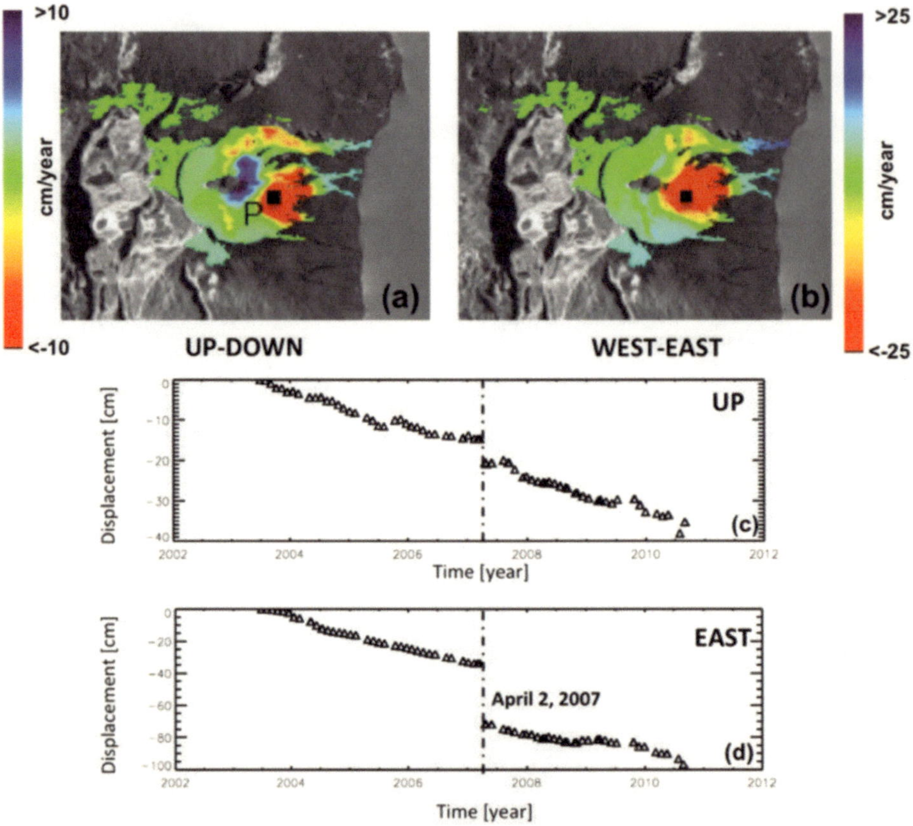

Figure 10. DInSAR results retrieved for the Piton de la Fournaise study area. Zoom view of the Up-Down (a) and East-West (b) mean deformation displacement maps. (c) and (d) are the MinA-driven time-series obtained by combining the LOS time-series for the Up (c) and East-West (d) components, respectively.

5. Conclusions

In this chapter, a review of some existing DInSAR methods for the retrieval of the 3-D (2-D) deformation time-series is first provided. In particular, we review some recently published methods and then we focus on the MinA method. With respect to previous works, this method has the advantage to be a post-processing algorithm, thus it does not require the simultaneous processing of hundreds of differential SAR interferograms. Information on the quality of LOS-projected deformation time-series (e.g., the temporal coherence maps) as well as the *a priori* identification of very coherent targets is very proficient for the discrimination of the 3-D deformation components. One strength of the algorithm is represented by the opportunity to complement LOS measurements with other external sources of information (such as GPS/leveling data). This technique has primarily been developed as an ultimate extension of the SBAS processing chain; however, it can be used, without any further modification, to work with other general-purpose DInSAR toolboxes. Several examples are provided, thus also clarifying how this method can be easily integrated in the currently available DInSAR toolboxes.

Acknowledgements

The author would like to thank Giuseppe Solaro, Fabiana Calò, Claudio Dema, Francesco Casu, and Riccardo Lanari, who was the co-authors of the MinA and POSBAS algorithms, which have been summarized in this Chapter. The author is also grateful to Simone Guarino, Fernando Parisi, and Maria Consiglia Rasulo for their technical support. ENVISAT data were provided by the European Space Agency, ALOS-1 data we provided by JAXA within the project entitled "Advanced Interferometric SAR Techniques for Earth Observation at L-band" of the four Research Agreement for the Advanced Land Observing Satellite-2. The DEM of the investigated zones were acquired through the SRTM archive.

Author details

Antonio Pepe

Address all correspondence to: pepe.a@irea.cnr.it

Institute for Electromagnetic Sensing of the Environment (IREA), National Research Council of Italy (CNR), Napoli, Italy

References

[1] Massonnet D, Feigl KL. Radar interferometry and its application to changes in the earth's surface. Reviews of Geophysics. 1998;**36**:441-500

[2] Massonnet D, Rossi M, Carmona C, Adragna F, Peltzer G, Feigl K, Rabaute T. The displacement field of the landers earthquake mapped by radar interferometry. Nature. 1993;**364**:138-142

[3] Ferretti A, Prati C, Rocca F. Permanent scatterers in SAR interferometry. IEEE Transactions on Geoscience and Remote Sensing. 2001;**39**(1):8-20

[4] Werner C, Wegm¨uller U, Strozzi T, Wiesmann A. Interferometric point target analysis for deformation mapping, In: Proceedings of the Geoscience and Remote Sensing Symposium; 21-25 July 2003; Toulouse, France; 2003;**7**:4362-4364

[5] Hooper A, Zebker H, Segall P, Kampes BM. A new method for measuring deformation on volcanoes and other natural terrains using InSAR persistent scatterers. Geophysical Research Letters. 2004;**31**(23):L23611. DOI: 10.1029/2004GL021737

[6] Berardino P, Fornaro G, Lanari R, Sansosti E. A new algorithm for surface deformation monitoring based on small baseline differential SAR interferograms. IEEE Transactions on Geoscience and Remote Sensing. 2002;**40**(11):2375-2383

[7] Usai S. A least squares database approach for SAR interferometric data. IEEE Transactions on Geoscience and Remote Sensing. 2003;**41**(4):753-760

[8] Mora O, Mallorqui JJ, Broquetas A. Linear and nonlinear terrain deformation maps from a reduced set of interferometric SAR images. IEEE Transactions on Geoscience and Remote Sensing. 2003;**41**(10):2243-2253

[9] Crosetto M, Crippa B, Biescas E. Early detection and in-depth analysis of deformation phenomena by radar interferometry. Engineering Geology. 2005;**79**(1/2):81-91

[10] Wright TJ, Parsons BE, Lu Z. Toward mapping surface deformation in three dimensions using InSAR. Geophysical Research Letters. 2004;**31**. DOI: L01607, 10.1029/2003GL018827

[11] Gray L. Using multiple RADARSAT InSAR pairs to estimate a full three-dimensional solution for glacial ice movement. Geophysical Research Letters. 2011;**38**(5):L05502

[12] Gudmundsson S, Sigmundsson F, Carstensen J. Three-dimensional surface motion maps estimated from combined interferometric synthetic aperture radar and GPS data. Journal of Geophysical Research. 2002;**107**(B10):2250-2264

[13] Spata A, Guglielmino F, Nunnari G, Puglisi G. SISTEM: A new approach to obtain three-dimensional displacement maps by integrating GPS and DInSAR data. Presented at the FringeWorkshop; November 30–December 4 2009; Frascati, Italy; 2009

[14] Fialko Y, Simons M, Agnew D. The complete (3-D) surface displacement field in the epicentral area of the 1999 M(w)7.1 Hector mine earthquake, California, from space geodetic observations. Geophysical Research Letters. 2001;**28**(16):3063-3066

[15] Fialko Y, Sandwell D, Simons M, Rosen P. Three-dimensional deformation caused by the Bam, Iran, earthquake and the origin of shallow slip deficit. Nature. 2005;**435**(7040):295-299. DOI: 10.1038/nature03425

[16] Jun H, Wei LZ, Jun ZJ, Chong RX, XiaoLi D. Inferring three-dimensional surface displacement field by combining SAR interferometric phase and amplitude information of ascending and descending orbits. Science China Earth Sciences. 2010;**53**(4):550-560. DOI: 10.1007/s11430-010-0023-1

[17] Shirzaei M. A seamless multitrack multitemporal InSAR algorithm. Geochemistry, Geophysics, Geosystems. 2015;**16**:1656-1669. DOI: 10.1002/2015GC005759

[18] Hu J, Ding X, Li Z, Zhu J, Sun Q, Zhang L. Kalman-filter based approach for multisensor, multitrack, and multitemporal InSAR. IEEE Transactions on Geoscience and Remote Sensing. 2013;**51**(7):4226-4239

[19] Manzo M et al. Surface deformation analysis in the Ischia Island (Italy) based on spaceborne radar interferometry. Journal of Volcanology and Geothermal Research. 2006;**151**:399-416

[20] Gourmelen N, Amelung F, Casu F, Manzo M, Lanari R. Mining related ground deformation in Crescent Valley, Nevada: Implications for sparse GPS networks. Geophysical Research Letters;**34**:L09309. DOI: 10.1029/2007GL029427

[21] Ozawa T, Ueda H. Advanced interferometric synthetic aperture radar (InSAR) time series analysis using interferograms of multiple-orbit tracks: A case study on Miyake-jima. Journal of Geophysical Research. 2011;**116**:B12407. DOI: 10.1029/2011JB008489

[22] Samsonov S, d'Oreye N. Multidimensional time-series analysis of ground deformation from multiple InSAR data sets applied to Virunga Volcanic Province. Geophysical Journal International. 2012;**191**:1095-1108

[23] Pepe A, Solaro G, Calò F, Dema C. A minimum acceleration approach for the retrieval of multiplatform InSAR deformation time-series. IEEE Journal of Selected Topics in Applied Earth Observations and Remote Sensing, August 2016;**9**(8)

[24] Gens R. Two-dimensional phase unwrapping for radar interferometry: Developments and new challenges. International Journal of Remote Sensing. 2003;**24**(4):703-710

[25] Chen CW, Zebker HA. Phase unwrapping for large SAR interferograms: Statistical segmentation and generalized network models. IEEE Transactions on Geoscience and Remote Sensing. 2002;**40**(8):1709-1719

[26] Pepe A, Lanari R. On the extension of the minimum cost flow algorithm for phase unwrapping of multi-temporal differential SAR interferograms. IEEE Transactions on Geoscience and Remote Sensing. 2006;**44**(9):2374-2383

[27] Casu F, Manconi A, Pepe A, Lanari R. Deformation time-series generation in areas characterized by large displacement dynamics: The SAR amplitude pixel-offset SBAS technique. IEEE Transactions on Geoscience and Remote Sensing. 2011;**49**(7):2752-2763

[28] Michel R, Avouac JP, Tabouri J. Measuring ground displacement from SAR amplitude images: Application to the Landers earthquake. Geophysical Research Letters. 1999; **26**(7):875-878

[29] Scambos T, Dutkiewicz M, Wilson J, Bindschadler R. Application of image cross-correlation to the measurement of glacier velocity using satellite image data. Remote Sensing of Environment. 1992;**42**:177-186

[30] Hansen PC. The truncated SVD as a method for regularization. BIT. 1987;**27**:354-553

[31] Rezghi M, Hosseini SM. A new variant of the L-curve for Tikhonov regularization. Journal of Computational and Applied Mathematics. 2009;**231**:914-924

[32] Skilling J, Gull SF. Algorithms and applications, in maximum-entropy and bayesian methods in inverse problems. In: Fundamental Theories of Physics. Vol. 14. Netherlands: Springer; ISBN: 978-94-017-2221-6

[33] Geist D, Harpp K, Naumann T, Poland M, Chadwick W, Hall M, Rader E. The 2005 eruption of Sierra Negra volcano, Galapagos. Bulletin of Volcanology. 2008;**70**(6):655-673

[34] Peltier A, Bianchi M, Kaminski E, Komorowski J-C, Rucci A, Staudacher T. PSInSAR as a new tool to monitor pre-eruptive volcano ground deformation: Validation using GPS measurements on piton de la Fournaise. Geophysical Research Letters. 2010;**37**. DOI: L12301, 10.1029/2010GL043846

Chapter 6

Time Series and Renewable Energy Forecasting

Mahmoud Ghofrani and Musaad Alolayan

Additional information is available at the end of the chapter

http://dx.doi.org/10.5772/intechopen.70845

Abstract

Renewable energy generation has been constantly increasing during recent years. Wind and solar have had the most significant growths among all renewable resources. Wind and solar resources are highly intermittent and dependent on meteorological parameters and climatic conditions. The power output of wind turbines is subject to various meteorological parameters, such as wind speed, wind direction, air temperature, relative humidity, etc., among which the wind speed is the most direct and influential factor in wind power generation. Solar photovoltaic (PV) power is a function of solar radiation. Wind speed and solar radiation time series data exhibit unique features which complicate their prediction. This makes wind and solar power forecasting challenging. Accurate wind and solar forecasting enhances the value of renewable energy by improving the reliability and economic feasibility of these resources. It also supports integrating solar and wind power into electric grids by reducing the integration and operation costs associated with these intermittent generation sources. This chapter provides an overview of the time series methods that can be used for more accurate wind and solar forecasting.

Keywords: forecasting, renewable energy, solar, time series, wind

1. Introduction

Power generation forecasting is the fundamental basis in managing existing and newly constructed power systems. Without having accurate predictions for the generated power, serious implications such as inappropriate operational practices and inadequate energy transactions are inevitable. High penetrations of intermittent renewable energy sources such as wind and solar significantly increase uncertainties of power systems which in turn, complicate the system operation and planning. Accurate forecasting of these intermittent energy sources provides a valuable tool to ease the complication and enable independent system operators (ISOSs) to more efficiently and reliably run power systems.

There are three major methods for wind and solar forecasting; classical statistical techniques, computational intelligent methods, and hybrid algorithms. Each category includes several methods.

Time series methods are one of the most commonly used statistical techniques for forecasting. Time series can be defined as "the evolution of a set of observations sampled at regular intervals along time. The specificity of time series models, compared to other statistic methods, is that it introduces 'time' as one of its explicative variables" [1]. Time series develop mathematical models that can forecast future observations on the basis of available data. Section below provides definitions and explanations for time series methods commonly in use for forecasting.

2. Time series methods

This section provides an overview of the most commonly used time series methods for solar and wind forecasting. A brief description is provided for each method along with its mathematical representation.

2.1. Autoregressive (AR)

The autoregressive (AR) model presents a process whose current value can be represented as a linear combination of the past values and a signal noise ω_t. The AR model of order m, AR(m), is described by [2]:

$$\tilde{x}_t = \sum_{i=1}^{m} \Phi_i\, x_{t-i} + \omega_t = \Phi_1\, x_{t-1} + \Phi_2\, x_{t-2} + \ldots + \Phi_m\, x_{t-m} + \omega_t \tag{1}$$

where x_t is the time series values, ω_t is the noise, $\Phi = (\Phi_1, \Phi_2, \ldots, \Phi_m)$ is the vector of model coefficients and m is a positive integer.

2.2. Moving average (MA)

Unlike the AR model that uses a weighted sum of past values ($\tilde{x}_{t-i}$) to provide a time-series representation, the moving average (MA) model combines n past noise values ($\omega_t, \omega_{t-1}, \omega_{t-2}, \omega_{t-n}$) to develop a time-series process. The MA model of order n, MA(n), is describes as, is describes as [3]:

$$\tilde{x}_t = \sum_{j=0}^{n} \theta_j\, \omega_{t-j} = \omega_t + \theta_1\, \omega_{t-1} + \theta_2\, \omega_{t-2} + \ldots + \theta_n\, \omega_{t-n} \tag{2}$$

where $\theta = (\theta_1, \theta_2, \ldots, \theta_n)$ is the vector of model coefficients and $\theta_0 = 1$.

2.3. Autoregressive moving average (ARMA)

The autoregressive moving average (ARMA) model is developed by combining AR and MA terms to provide a parsimonious parametrization for a process. The ARMA model of orders m and n, ARMA(m, n) is given by [3]:

$$\tilde{x}_t = \sum_{i=1}^{m} \Phi_i x_{t-i} + \sum_{j=0}^{n} \theta_j \omega_{t-j} \tag{3}$$

where Φ_i and θ_j are the autoregressive and moving average coefficients of the ARMA model.

2.4. Autoregressive moving average model with exogenous variables (ARMAX)

The auto regressive moving average model with exogenous variables (ARMAX) provides a multivariate time-series representation to enhance the accuracy of the univariate ARMA model by including relevant information in addition to the time-series under consideration. For example, climate information such as cloud cover, humidity, wind speed and direction can be included as exogenous variables in an ARMA model to develop an ARMAX for more accurate forecasting of solar radiation time series. The ARMAX model of orders m, n and p, ARMAX (m, n, p), is defined as [3]:

$$\tilde{x}_t = \sum_{i=1}^{m} \Phi_i x_{t-i} + \sum_{j=0}^{n} \theta_j \omega_{t-j} + \sum_{k=1}^{p} \lambda_k e_{t-k} \tag{4}$$

where Φ_i, θ_j and λ_k are the autoregressive, moving average and exogenous coefficients of the ARMAX model, and e_t is the exogenous input term.

2.5. Autoregressive integrated moving average (ARIMA)

The autoregressive integrated moving average (ARIMA) model is used for non-stationary time series. Despite representing differences in local trend or level, different sections of non-stationary processes exhibit certain levels of similarity. A stationary ARMA (m, n) process with the dth difference of the time-series develops an ARIMA (m, d, n) model. The ARIMA (m, d, n) model is represented by [4]:

$$\tilde{x}_t = \sum_{i=1}^{m} \Phi_i S^d x_{t-i} + \sum_{j=0}^{n} \theta_j \omega_{t-j} \tag{5}$$

where $S = 1 - q^{-1}$ and $\Phi_m(q)$ is a stationary and invertible AR(m) operator; x_t, ω_t, Φ_i and θ_j are the observed time series values, error, AR and MA parameters, respectively; d is the number of non-seasonal differences; m is the number of autoregressive terms, and n is the number of lagged forecast errors.

2.6. Autoregressive fractionally integrated moving average (ARFIMA)

The autoregressive fractionally integrated moving average (ARFIMA) model is used for long-memory forecasting. ARFIMA generalizes ARIMA by allowing the differencing to take fractional values. An ARFIMA model is given by [5]:

$$\left(1-\sum_{i=1}^{m}\Phi_i L^i\right)(1-L)^d\tilde{x}_t=\left(1+\sum_{j=1}^{n}\theta_j L^j\right)\omega_t \tag{6}$$

where powers of L indicate a corresponding number of shifts backward in the time series, and $(1-L)^d$ is the fractional differencing operator.

2.7. Autoregressive integrated moving average with exogenous variables (ARIMAX)

The autoregressive integrated moving average with exogenous variables (ARIMAX) includes the previous values of an exogenous time-series in the ARIMA to enhance its performance and accuracy. It is more applicable to time-series with sudden changes in trends. An ARIMA (m,d,n) process including the past p values of an exogenous variable e_t develops an ARIMAX process of order (m,d,n,p). The ARIMAX (m,d,n,p) model is represented by [3]:

$$\tilde{x}_t=\sum_{i=1}^{m}\Phi_i S^d x_{t-i}+\sum_{j=0}^{n}\theta_j\,\omega_{t-j}+\sum_{k=1}^{p}\lambda_k\,e_{t-k} \tag{7}$$

where ω_t is the white noise. Φ_i, θ_j and λ_k are the coefficients of the autoregressive, moving average and exogenous inputs, respectively.

2.8. Vector autoregressive (VAR)

The vector autoregressive (VAR) model characterizes linear dependences between two or more time-series. VAR model uses multiple variables to generalize the univariate autoregressive model (AR model). A k-dimensional VAR model of order L is given by [6].

$$\tilde{x}_t=v+\sum_{i=1}^{L}A_i\,x_{t-i}+\omega_t=v+A_1\,x_{t-1}+\ldots+A_L\,x_{t-L}+\omega_t \tag{8}$$

where x_t and v are $k\times 1$ vectors of variables and constants, respectively. L is the maximum lag in the VAR model, A_i is a $k\times k$ matrix of lag order parameters, and $\omega_t=(\omega_{1t},\ldots,\omega_{kt})$ is the vector of white noise [6, 7].

2.9. Autoregressive conditional heteroscedasticity (ARCH)—generalized ARCH (GARCH)

The autoregressive conditional heteroscedasticity (ARCH) is used for time series with specific variances for the error terms [7].

Estimated values are calculated using the following equations [8]:

$$x_t = \varepsilon_t \sigma_t \tag{9a}$$

$$\sigma_t = \sqrt{a_0 + \sum_{i=1}^{q} a_i x_{t-i}^2} \tag{9b}$$

where x_t is the observed time series values; ε_t is the error; σ_t is the conditional standard deviation; and a_0 is the constant added to the model.

The generalized ARCH (GARCH) model estimates the values by:

$$x_t = \varepsilon_t \sigma_t \tag{10a}$$

$$\sigma_t = \sqrt{a_0 + \sum_{i=1}^{p} a_i x_{t-i}^2 + \sum_{i=1}^{q} \beta_j \sigma_{t-i}^2} \tag{10b}$$

By setting $p = 0$, the GARCH model reduces to an ARCH process with parameter q.

3. Performance metrics

The performance of the forecast methods is measured by various metrics related to the forecast error. Higher values of errors correspond to less forecast accuracies. This section provides the definitions and equations for performance metrics which are commonly used to calculate the forecast error. Note that x represents the observed value, $\tilde{x}$ is the predicted value (forecast) and n is the total number of samples.

3.1. MSE

Mean square error (MSE) is calculated by:

$$\text{MSE} = \frac{1}{n} \sum_{i=1}^{n} (\tilde{x}_i - x_i)^2 \tag{11}$$

3.2. NMSE

Normalized mean square error (NMSE) is calculated by normalizing the MSE as:

$$\text{NMSE} = \frac{n \sum_{i=1}^{n} (\tilde{x}_i - x_i)^2}{\sum_{i=1}^{n} x_i \sum_{i=1}^{n} \tilde{x}_i} \tag{12}$$

3.3. RMSE

Root mean square error is given by calculating the square root of the MSE as:

$$\text{RMSE} = \sqrt{\frac{1}{n}\sum_{i=1}^{n}\left(\tilde{x}_i - x_i\right)^2} \quad (13)$$

3.4. NRMSE

Normalized root mean square error (NRMSE) is calculated by normalizing the RMSE as:

$$\text{NRMSE} = \frac{\sqrt{\frac{1}{n}\sum_{i=1}^{n}\left(\tilde{x}_i - x_i\right)^2}}{\frac{1}{n}\sum_{i=1}^{n} x_i} \quad (14)$$

3.5. MAE

Mean absolute error is calculated by:

$$\text{MAE} = \frac{1}{n}\sum_{i=1}^{n}\left|\tilde{x}_i - x_i\right| \quad (15)$$

3.6. NMAE

Normalized mean absolute error (NMAE) is calculated by normalizing the MAE as:

$$\text{NMAE} = \frac{1}{n}\sum_{i=1}^{n}\frac{\left|\tilde{x}_i - x_i\right|}{\max(x_i)} \quad (16)$$

3.7. MRE

Mean relative error (MRE) is calculated by:

$$\text{MRE} = \frac{1}{n}\sum_{i=1}^{n}\frac{\left|\tilde{x}_i - x_i\right|}{x_i} \quad (17)$$

3.8. MBE

Mean bias error (MBE) is calculated by:

$$\text{MBE} = \frac{1}{n}\sum_{i=1}^{n}\left(\tilde{x}_i - x_i\right) \quad (18)$$

3.9. MAPE

Mean absolute percentage error is calculated by:

$$\text{MAPE} = \frac{1}{n}\sum_{i=1}^{n}\left|\frac{\tilde{x}_i - x_i}{x_i}\right| \times 100\% \tag{19}$$

3.10. MASE

Mean absolute scaled error is calculated by:

$$\text{MASE} = \frac{\sum_{i=1}^{n}|\tilde{x}_i - x_i|}{\frac{n}{n-1}\sum_{i=2}^{n}|x_i - x_{i-1}|} \tag{20}$$

3.11. MSPE

Mean square percentage error is calculated by:

$$\text{MSPE} = \frac{1}{n}\sum_{i=1}^{n}\left(\frac{\tilde{x}_i - x_i}{x_i}\right)^2 \times 100\% \tag{21}$$

4. Time series methods for solar energy/wind power forecasting

Time series methods have been extensively used to forecast solar radiation/power and wind speed/power. Typically, solar and wind data exhibit features such as non-linearity and non-stationarity which cannot be captured by most of the time series methods. To address this limitation, these methods are used in combination with other computational intelligent or data processing methods to take advantage of their capabilities to better characterize wind and solar data for more accurate forecasting. These combinations are referred to as hybrid methods which are proven effective for renewables forecasting.

4.1. Time series methods for solar energy forecasting

This section provides a review of the articles that use time series methods individually or in hybrid algorithms for solar radiation/power forecasting. The literature review provides a summary of the solar-related variable that is predicted, the horizon for which the variable is predicted, the performance metrics in use to calculate the forecast error, the time series methods and data in use, and the research findings of each article. **Table 1** provides the summary.

4.2. Time series methods for wind power forecasting

This section provides a review of the articles that use time series methods individually or in hybrid algorithms for wind speed/power forecasting. The literature review provides a summary of the wind variable that is predicted, the horizon for which the variable is predicted, the performance metrics in use to calculate the forecast error, the time series methods and data in use, and the research findings of each article. **Table 2** provides the summary.

References	Forecast variable	Forecast horizon	Error metric	Time series method	Data	Finding
[9]	5, 15, 30, and 60 min averaged global horizontal irradiance (GHI)	5 min to several hours	MAPE	Regressions in logs, ARIMA, and hybrid (ARIMA and ANN)	4 years of hourly GHI data for three locations in USA	ARIMA can obtain better results if used in logs with time varying coefficients
[10]	Daily GHI	1 day	RMSE, NRMSE, MAE, and MBE	AR, ARMA	19 years of daily GHI from the metrological station of Ajaccio, France	AR and ANN models perform better than other prediction methods (ARMA, k-Nearest Neighbors, Markov Chains, etc.), if the time-series data is not pre-processed
[11]	Hourly GHI	1 h	MBE and RMSE	ARIMA	Meteorological data including GHI, diffuse horizontal irradiance (DHI), direct normal irradiance (DNI) and cloud cover from two weather stations in USA (Miami and Orlando)	Cloud cover information yields to more accurate forecasting
[12]	Half daily values of GHI	Up to 3 days	NRMSE	AR	Hourly GHI measurements from stations of the Spanish National Radiometric Network	Neural network models obtain better results for almost all stations except for Lerida station where the clearness index-based models outperform
[13]	Hourly solar irradiance	1 h	RMSE, and NRMSE	Naive, ARMA	144 months of hourly solar irradiance of the Paris suburb of Alfortville	ARMA model has competitive results as compared to similarity method (SIM), support vector machine (SVM) and neural network (NN)
[14]	Hourly solar radiation	1 h	RMSE, and NRMSE	Hybrid (ARMA and time delay neural network (TDNN))	10 months of solar radiation data from the observation station in Nanyang Technological University	The combination of the ARMA and TDNN provides more accurate results than each individual forecaster
[15]	Daily average of solar irradiance	1–15 h	MAPE	ARIMA	Solar irradiance data from a 4.0 kW PV panel in the city of Awali, Kingdom of Bahrain	ARIMA models are proved to effectively capture the auto-correlative structure of the solar irradiance
[16]	Daily solar irradiance	1 day	NA	ARIMA	Solar irradiance and surface air temperature	Various climate time series are dependent on

References	Forecast variable	Forecast horizon	Error metric	Time series method	Data	Finding
	and surface air temperature				data from 10 meteorological stations in Europe and 4 stations in Asia	long-range variability of solar irradiance
[17]	Hourly solar power from PV systems	1 h up to 36 h	RMSE	AR, AR with exogenous input (ARX), RX (regressive model with no endogenous variables)	1 year of solar power observations from 21 PV systems in Denmark	ARX model with both solar power observations and numerical weather predictions (NWPs) as the input outperforms the AR model for forecast horizons longer than 2 h ahead
[18]	Hourly GHI, DHI and DNI	1 h	RMSE, and MBE	AR	5 min GHI data from Jeddah, Saudi Arabia for a five-year interval	Using sunshine duration, relative humidity and air temperature as the inputs result in the most accurate forecast by the developed adaptive model
[19]	Monthly average solar radiation	1 month	RMSE	Linear regression (LR)	Daily GHI and meteorological data in Darwin, Australia from 2000 to 2011	LR obtains the best predictions compared to Angstrom-Prescott-Page (APP) and ANN models
[20]	Hourly PV power	1 and 2 h	MAE, MBE, RMSE, and NRMSE	ARIMA	Hourly average power of a 1 MW PV power plant located in Merced, California collected between November 2009 and August 2011	ANN-based forecasting models including the ANN and GA-optimized ANN obtain better predictions than Persistent, ARIMA and k-NN models
[21]	Hourly GHI	1 h	NRMSE	Hybrid (ARMA and ANN)	6 years of hourly solar radiation and meteorological data from five locations in the Mediterranean area in France	Combining ARMA and ANN enhances the forecast accuracy
[22]	Hourly solar irradiation	24 h	NRMSE	ARMA	2 years of meteorological data from Ajaccio, France	ANN outperforms the ARMA by 1.3 points reduction in the error estimate
[23]	Daily GHI	1 day	RMSE, NRMSE, MAE, and MBE	AR, ARIMA	30 min global solar radiation data in Corsica Island, France from January 1998 to December 2007	An ANN with exogenous and endogenous data outperforms univariate forecasters such as ARMA models
[24]	Solar irradiance	12 h		Hybrid (ARIMA-Back Propagation)	Hourly solar irradiance observations from	

References	Forecast variable	Forecast horizon	Error metric	Time series method	Data	Finding
			RMSE, and MASE		National Solar Radiation Data Base (NSRDB) site between 2008 and 2009	The hybrid ARIMA-BP does not outperform ARIMA
[25]	Solar power	1 min	MAE, MSE, and MAXE	Hybrid (Wavelet, ARMA, and Nonlinear Autoregressive model with exogenous variables (NARX))	1 min solar power data from the solar panel at UCLA for nearly 200,000 observations	Capability of the ARMA process to model the linear features of the data and the NARX advantage to compensate the error of Wavelet-ARMA enhances the forecast accuracy of the hybrid Wavelet-ARMA-NARX method
[26]	Solar generation	1–5 h	MAE, and MSE	ARMA	14 years of hourly solar radiation data from SolarAnywhere	ARMA outperforms the persistence model for short and medium term solar predictions
[27]	Hourly solar irradiance	1 h and 3 h	RMAE	Hybrid (non-linear regression and PR)	Solar radiation data from sensors, and National Digital Forecast Database, as well as the meteorological measurements from local airports in Los Angeles region	The hybrid method excels the benchmark methods including the regression, ARIMA and ANN by 40% and 33.33% for 1-h and 3-h ahead, respectively

Table 1. Summary of the articles with time series methods (individual or hybrid) for solar radiation/power forecasting.

References	Forecast variable	Forecast horizon	Error metric	Time series method	Data	Finding
[28]	Hourly average wind Speed	1 h	NA	ARMA	2 years of wind speed data from Quetta in Pakistan	ARMA is more appropriate for prediction intervals and probability forecasts
[29]	Wind power density	1–10 days	MAE, and RMSE	AR-GARCH, ARFI-GARCH	Daily midday wind speed measurements from 1995 to 2004, as well as weather ensemble predictions from 1997 to 2004 for five wind farms in UK	Weather ensemble-based forecasters are shown to perform better than time series models and atmospheric-based models
[30]	Mean hourly wind speed	1 h	RMSE	AR, and ARIMA	744 hours of wind speed measurements in Odigitria of the Greek island of Crete in March 1996	The neural logic-based models perform better than the time series methods

References	Forecast variable	Forecast horizon	Error metric	Time series method	Data	Finding
[15]	Daily average of wind speed	1–15 h	MAPE	ARIMA	Wind speed data from a 1.7 kW wind turbine in the city of Awali, Kingdom of Bahrain	ARIMA models are proved to effectively capture the auto-correlative structure of the wind speed
[31]	Wind speed	3 h	RMSE	AR	Wind speed data measured every 3-h in three Mediterranean sites in Corsica	AR is sufficient to simulate 3-h wind speeds
[32]	Wind speed	1, 2 and 3-step(s)	MAE, MAPE and MSE	Hybrid (Wavelet Packet-ARIMA-BFGS (Broyden-Fletcher-Goldfarb-Shanno))	Half-hourly wind speed measurements from 20 December 2011 to 5 January 2012 in Chinese Qinghai wind farm	The ARIMA models have better time performance than the ANN models in approximating wind speed time series while providing a little lower accuracy
[33]	Hourly mean wind speed and direction	1 h	MAE	ARMA, and VAR	Hourly average wind data from May 1 to October 21, 2002 in two wind sites in North Dakota, USA	ARMA forecasts the wind speed better than the component model whereas the opposite is observed for wind direction forecasting
[34]	Wind power	3 h	MAPE, and NMAE	ARIMA	Wind power data in Portugal	The ARIMA model is used as a benchmark to evaluate the performance of the proposed hybrid Wavelet-PSO-ANFIS forecasting method
[35]	Wind speed	1–24 h	MAE, and RMSE	AR, ARX, ARX-GARCH, Hybrid (ARX-TN (truncated normal), ARX-GARCH-TN)	3 years of hourly wind speed observations from a meteorological station in Denmark, as well as wind speed predictions based on a NWP model from the Danish Meteorological Institute	The time series models are used as benchmark methods to evaluate the performance of the developed stochastic differential equation for probabilistic wind speed forecasting
[36]	Wind speed/ power	1–24 h	MAE, MBE, RMSE, MASE NMBE, NMAE, and NRMSE	AR, ARMA, and ARIMA	Wind speed, wind direction, humidity, solar radiation, temperature, atmospheric pressure, and heat radiation data from two anemometric measuring towers in La Ventosa, Mexico	Results show that the developed method based on support vector regression is more accurate than the persistence and autoregressive models
[37]	Wind speed/ power	1 and 2 day(s)	Daily mean	fractional-ARIMA (*f*-ARIMA)	4 weeks of hourly average wind speed data from four wind	The proposed *f*-ARIMA is more accurate than the persistence method

References	Forecast variable	Forecast horizon	Error metric	Time series method	Data	Finding
			error (DME)		monitoring sites in North Dakota	
[38]	Average hourly wind speed	1 h	ME, MSE, and MAE	Hybrid (ARIMA-ANN)	1 month of wind speed measurements in three regions of Mexico	The combination of ARIMA and ANN predicts the wind speed with more accuracy than the individual ARIMA and ANN
[39]	Wind speed	1 day	MAPE	Hybrid (KF-ANN model based on ARIMA)	Daily wind speed observations from two meteorological stations in Mosul, Iraq and Johor, Malaysia	The ARIMA model provides inaccurate wind speed forecasts due to its limitation to capture the nonlinearity of the wind speed patterns
[40]	Wind speed	1, 2 and 3-step(s)	MAE, MSE, and MAPE	Hybrid (ARIMA-ANN and ARIMA-Kalman)	Hourly wind speed measurements from a station	Both hybrid methods can obtain accurate forecasts and are appropriate for non-stationary wind speed datasets
[41]	Wind speed	1 h	NA	ARMA-GARCH	7 years of hourly wind speed data from an observation site in Colorado, USA	The ARMA-GARCH model is proved efficient in capturing the trend change of wind speed mean and volatility over time
[42]	Hourly average wind speed	1 h up to 10 h	RMSE	ARMA	9 years of hourly wind speed data of five locations in Navarre, Spain	For longer term forecasting, the ARMA models with transformed and standardized data perform better than the persistence model
[43]	Wind speed	1 month	MSE, MAE, and MAPE	ARIMA	7 years of wind speed measurements from the South Coast of Oaxaca, Mexico	ARIAM models provide more sensitivity than the ANN methods to the adjustment and prediction of the wind speed
[44]	Win speed	1–6 min (s), and 1–6 hour (s)	MAE, and MAPE	Hybrid (Empirical mode decomposition (EMD)-Least squares support vector machines (LSSVM)-AR)	1 year of wind speed data measurements in Beloit, Kansas, USA	The proposed hybrid approach is proved more accurate than the existing forecasting approaches

References	Forecast variable	Forecast horizon	Error metric	Time series method	Data	Finding
[45]	Wind speed/ power generation	1 h	MAE, and RMSE	Hybrid (ARIMA-ANN/SVR)	2 years of hourly wind data from a 1.5 MW wind turbine in North Dakota, USA	The hybrid approaches are practical for both wind speed and power forecasting but not the best for all the forecasting time horizons
[46]	Wind speed	15 min	MAPE, MSPE, and MAE	Univariate and multivariable ARIMA	Wind speed data from the Wind Engineering Research Field Laboratory (WERFL) at five different heights at Texas Tech University	Multivariate models are more accurate than the univariate models and they are both less accurate than the recurrent neural network models

Table 2. Summary of the articles with time series methods (individual or hybrid) for wind speed/power forecasting.

5. Conclusion

This chapter provides a comprehensive literature review to demonstrate the application of time-series methods for renewable energy forecasting. In spite of recent developments in intelligent methods and their extensive applications for more accurate solar energy/wind power forecasting, our literature review concludes that time-series methods, individually or in combination with intelligent methods, are still viable options for short-term forecasting of intermittent renewable energy sources due to their less computational complexities.

Author details

Mahmoud Ghofrani* and Musaad Alolayan

*Address all correspondence to: mrani@uw.edu

Electrical Engineering, Engineering and Mathematics Division, School of STEM, University of Washington Bothell, Bothell, WA, USA

References

[1] Ding N, Besanger Y. Time series method for short-term load forecasting using smart metering in distribution systems. In: Proceeding of the IEEE Trondheim PowerTech; 2011. pp. 1-6

[2] AR, MA and ARMA models, Available: www.math.unm.edu/~ghuerta/tseries/week4_1.pdf

[3] Inman R, Pedro H, Coimbra C. Solar forecasting methods for renewable energy integration. Progress in Energy and Combustion Science. Jul. 2013;**39**:535-576

[4] Wang W, Niu Z. Time series analysis of NASDAQ composite based on seasonal ARIMA model. In: Proceeding of the International Conference on Management and Service Science; 2009. pp. 1-4

[5] Contrearas-Reyes J, Palma W. Statistical analysis of autoregressive fractionally integrated moving average models. Computational Statistics. 2013;**28**(5):2309-2331

[6] Hatemi A. Multivariate tests for autocorrelation in the stable and unstable VAR models. Economic Modelling. 2004;**21**(4):661-683

[7] Engle RF. Autoregressive conditional heteroscedasticity with estimates of the variance of United Kingdom inflation. Econometrica. 1982;**50**(4):987-1007

[8] Stepnicka M, Dvorak A, Pavliska V, Vavrickova L. Linguistic approach to time series analysis and forecasts. In: Proceeding of the IEEE International Conference on Fuzzy Systems; July 2010. pp. 1-9

[9] Reikard G. Predicting solar radiation at high resolutions: A comparison of time series forecasts. Solar Energy. 2009;**83**:342-349

[10] Paoli C, Voyant C, Muselli M, Nivet M-L. Forecasting of preprocessed daily solar radiation time series using neural networks. Solar Energy. 2010;**84**:2146-2160

[11] Dazhi Y, Jirutitijaroen P, Walsh WM. Hourly solar irradiance time series forecasting using cloud cover index. Solar Energy. 2012;**86**:3531-3543

[12] Martín L, Zarzalejo LF, Polo J, Navarro A, Marchante R, Cony M. Prediction of global solar irradiance based on time series analysis: Application to solar thermal power plants energy production planning. Solar Energy. 2010;**84**:1772-1781

[13] Touati T, Same A, Oukhellou L, Hourly solar irradiance forecasting based on machine learning models. In: Proceedings of the 2016 15th IEEE International Conference on Machine Learning and Applications; 2016. pp. 441–446

[14] Wu J, Chan CK. Prediction of hourly solar radiation using a novel hybrid model of ARMA and TDNN. Solar Energy. 2011;**85**:808-817

[15] Shams MB, Haji S, Salman A, Abdali H, Alsaffar A. Time series analysis of Bahrain's first hybrid renewable energy system. Energy. 2016;**103**:1-15

[16] Kärner O. ARIMA representation for daily solar irradiance and surface air temperature time series. Journal of Atmospheric and Solar—Terrestrial Physics. 2009;**71**:841-847

[17] Bacher P, Madsen H, Nielsen HA. Online short-term solar power forecasting. Solar Energy. 2009;**83**:1772-1783

[18] Mellit A, Eleuch H, Benghanem M, Elaoun C, Massi Pavan AP. An adaptive model for predicting of global, direct and diffuse hourly solar irradiance. Energy Conversion and Management. 2010;**51**:771-782

[19] Yap WK, Karri V. Comparative study in predicting the global solar radiation for Darwin, Australia. Journal of Solar Energy Engineering. 2012 August;**134**:1-6

[20] Pedro HTC, Coimbra CFM. Assessment of forecasting techniques for solar power production with no exogenous inputs. Solar Energy. 2012;**86**:2017-2028

[21] Voyant C, Muselli M, Paoli C, Nivet M-L. Numerical weather prediction (NWP) and hybrid ARMA/ANN model to predict global radiation. Energy. 2012;**39**:341-355

[22] Voyant C, Randimbivololona P, Nivet ML, Paolic C, Muselli M. Twenty four hours ahead global irradiation forecasting using multi-layer perceptron. Metrological Application. 2014;**21**:644-655

[23] Voyant C, Muselli M, Paoli C, Nivet M-L. Optimization of an artificial neural network dedicated to the multivariate forecasting of daily global radiation. Energy. 2011;**36**: 348-359

[24] Ren Y, Suganthan PN, Srikanth N. Ensemble methods for wind and solar power forecasting—A state-of-the-art review. Renewable and Sustainable Energy Reviews. 2015;**50**:82-91

[25] Nazaripouya H, Wang B, Wang Y, Chu P, Pota HR, Gadh R. Univariate time series prediction of solar power using a hybrid wavelet-ARMA-NARX prediction method. In: Proceedings of the IEEE Transmission and Distribution Conference and Exposition (T&D); 2016

[26] Huang R, Huang T, Gadh R. Solar generation prediction using the ARMA model in a laboratory-level micro-grid. In: Proceedings of the IEEE SmartGridComm 2012 Symposium–Support for Storage, Renewable Sources, and MicroGrid; 2012. pp. 528–533

[27] Hall J, Hall J. Forecasting solar radiation for the Los Angeles Basin – phase II report. In: Proceedings of the American Solar Energy Society annual SOLAR 2011 Conference; 2011

[28] Kamal L, Jafri YZ. Time series models to simulate and forecast hourly average wind speed in Quetta, Pakistan. Solar Energy. 1997;**61**:23-32

[29] Taylor JW, McSharry PE. Wind power density forecasting using ensemble predictions and time series models. Proceedings of the IEEE Transactions on Energy Conversion. 2009;**24**(3):775-782

[30] Sfetsos A. A comparison of various forecasting techniques applied to mean hourly wind speed time series. Renewable Energy. 2000;**21**:23-35

[31] Poggi P, Muselli M, Notton G, Cristofari C, Louche A. Forecasting and simulating wind speed in Corsica by using an autoregressive model. Energy Conversion and Management. 2003;**44**:3177-3196

[32] Liu H, Tian H, Pan D, Li Y. Forecasting models for wind speed using wavelet, wavelet packet, time series and artificial neural networks. Applied Energy. 2013;**107**:191-208

[33] Erdem E, Shi J. ARMA based approaches for forecasting the tuple of wind speed and direction. Applied Energy. 2011;**88**:1405-1414

[34] Catalão JPS, Pousinho HMI, Mendes VMF. Hybrid wavelet-PSO-ANFIS approach for short-term wind power forecasting in Portugal. IEEE Transactions on Sustainable Energy. 2011;**2**(1):50-59

[35] Iversen EB, Morales JM, Moller JK, Madsen H. Short-term probabilistic forecasting of wind speed using stochastic differential equations. International Journal of Forecasting. 2016;**32**: 981-990

[36] Bonfil GS, Reyes-Ballesteros A, Gershenson C. Wind speed forecasting for wind farms: A method based on support vector regression. Renewable Energy. 2016;**85**:790-809

[37] Kavasseri RG, Seetharaman K. Day-ahead wind speed forecasting using f-ARIMA models. Renewable Energy. 2009;**34**:1388-1393

[38] Cadenas E, Rivera W. Wind speed forecasting in three different regions of Mexico, using a hybrid ARIMA-ANN model. Renewable Energy. 2010;**35**:2732-2738

[39] Shukur OB, Lee MH. Daily wind speed forecasting through hybrid KF-ANN model based on ARIMA. Renewable Energy. 2015;**76**:637-647

[40] Liu H, Tian H, Li Y. Comparison of two new ARIMA-ANN and ARIMA-Kalman hybrid methods for wind speed prediction. Applied Energy. 2012;**98**:415-424

[41] Liu H, Erdem E, Shi J. Comprehensive evaluation of ARMA–GARCH (−M) approaches for modelling the mean and volatility of wind speed. Applied Energy. 2011;**88**:724-732

[42] Torres JL, Garcia A, De Blas M, De Francisco A. Forecast of hourly average wind speed with ARMA models in Navarre (Spain). Solar Energy. 2005;**79**:65-77

[43] Cadenas E, Rivera W. Wind speed forecasting in the South Coast of Oaxaca, Mexico. Renewable Energy. 2007;**32**:2116-2128

[44] Tatinati S, Veluvolu KC. A hybrid approach for short-term forecasting of wind speed. The Scientific World Journal. 2013:1-8

[45] Shi J, Guo J, Zheng S. Evaluation of hybrid forecasting approaches for wind speed and power generation time series. Renewable and Sustainable Energy Reviews. 2012;**16**: 3471-3480

[46] Cao Q, Ewing BT, Thompson MA. Forecasting wind speed with recurrent neural networks. European Journal of Operational Research. 2012;**221**:148-154

Chapter 7

Modeling Nonlinear Vector Time Series Data

Jiancheng Jiang and Sha Yu

Additional information is available at the end of the chapter

http://dx.doi.org/10.5772/intechopen.70825

Abstract

In this chapter, we review nonlinear models for vector time series data and develop new nonparametric estimation and inference for them. Vector time series data exist widely in practice. In financial markets, multiple time series are usually correlated. When analyzing several interdependent time series, in general one should consider them as a single vector time series fitted by multivariate models, which provides a useful tool for modeling interdependencies among multiple time series and for simultaneously analyzing feedback and Granger causality effects. Since nonlinear features are widely observed in time series, we consider nonlinear methodology for modeling nonlinear vector time series data, which allows flexibility in the model structure and avoids the curse of dimensionality.

Keywords: cointegration, VAR, multivariate threshold autoregressive model, nonparametric smoothing, generalized likelihood ratio

1. Introduction

Multiple time series are of considerable interest in an array of domains, such as finance, economics, engineering and so on. The data are collected in time order and consist of several related variables of interest, for instance, the data of stock price indexes and the status data of important instruments such as shuttles. It is of much practical significance to model this kind of data well. Moreover, a lot of commonly seen multiple time series are correlated, which makes it reasonable to regard them as a single vector and to fit them using multivariate models. Multivariate models perform well in exploring the interdependencies among multiple time series and capturing the dynamic structure.

Plenty of contributions have been made in the field of parametric models for multivariate time series. For instance, Sims proposed vector autoregressive (VAR) models in 1980 [1], Engle and Kroner considered multivariate generalized autoregressive conditional heteroscedastic (GARCH) models in 1995 [2], and Tsay developed the multivariate threshold models in 1998 [3]. Compared to parametric models, nonparametric models require less assumption about the model structure and are more flexible. Combined with the fact that nonlinearity widely exists in time series, it is ideal to model the multiple time series using nonparametric models. However, not much of achievements have been made about this. This is partly due to the complexity of nonparametric smoothing as well as the curse of dimensionality. With these objectives in mind, Jiang proposed the multivariate functional-coefficient model in 2014 [4], which provides a useful tool for modeling vector time series data.

In this chapter, we first review some vector time series models, next extend them to include an error-correction term by incorporating cointegration among integrated variables, then develop a single index model for choosing the smoothing variable and a variable selection method for the multivariate functional-coefficient models, and finally study multivariate time-varying coefficient models and related hypothesis testing problems.

The remainder of this chapter is organized as follows. In Section 2 we review vector autoregressive (VAR) models. In Section 3, we consider multivariate functional-coefficient regression models and their extensions, where a model selection rule is also proposed. In Section 4 we introduce multivariate time-varying coefficient models and propose a generalized likelihood ratio test. In Section 5 we make a conclusion and discuss some interesting research topics to be completed.

2. Review of VAR models

The vector autoregressive model is a generalization of the univariate autoregressive model for forecasting a vector of time series. This model was pioneered by Sims in Ref. [1] and it has acquired a prominent role in analyzing macroeconomic time series. Prior to 1980, large-scale statistical dynamic simultaneous equations model (DSEMs) was widely used in empirical macroeconomics, which often contained dozens or even hundreds of equations. As the economic environment has grown more complicated, the traditional simultaneous models have grown. Sims believed that since these models do not dichotomize variables into "endogenous" and "exogenous," the exclusion restrictions used to identify the simultaneous equations models make little sense. Thus, he advocated the vector autoregressive model (VAR) to model the interrelationships among a set of macroeconomic variables. In the structure of VAR models, each variable is a linear function of past lags of itself and past lags of the other variables. Sims demonstrated that VARs provide a flexible and tractable framework for analyzing economic time series. While hardly relying on economic theorems, VAR models have proven efficient in capturing the dynamics of multivariate systems as well as forecasting [1]. Specifically, a vector autoregressive model of order p [VAR(p)] has the following general form:

$$y_t = c + A_1 y_{t-1} + \ldots A_p y_{t-p} + e_t \tag{1}$$

where $y_t = (y_{1t}, \ldots, y_{Kt})'$ is a set of K time series variables, c is a $K \times 1$ vector of constant, A_i's are $K \times K$ coefficient matrices, and e_t are error terms. Usually, e_t are assumed to be zero-mean independent white noise with time-invariant and positive-definite covariance matrix Σ. For example, a VAR (1) model with two time series components can be written as:

$$\begin{pmatrix} y_{1t} \\ y_{2t} \end{pmatrix} = \begin{pmatrix} c_1 \\ c_2 \end{pmatrix} + \begin{pmatrix} A_{11} & A_{12} \\ A_{21} & A_{22} \end{pmatrix} \begin{pmatrix} y_{1,t-1} \\ y_{2,t-1} \end{pmatrix} + \begin{pmatrix} e_{1,t} \\ e_{2,t} \end{pmatrix}$$

or the equation set

$$\begin{aligned} y_{1t} &= c_1 + A_{11}y_{1,t-1} + A_{12}y_{2,t-1} + e_{1,t} \\ y_{2t} &= c_2 + A_{21}y_{1,t-1} + A_{22}y_{2,t-1} + e_{2,t} \end{aligned}$$

Using lag-operator L, Eq. (1) can be written as the following form:

$$y_t = c + \left(A_1L + A_2L^2 + \ldots + A_pL^p\right)y_t + e_t \tag{2}$$

Let $A(z) = I - A_1z - A_2z^2 - \ldots A_pz^p$, where z is a complex number. Then the VAR process is stable if

$$\det(A(z)) \neq 0 \,\text{for}\, |z| \leq 1. \tag{3}$$

In other words, the determinant of the matrix polynomial has no roots in and on the complex unit circle. If the stability conditions are satisfied and the process can be extended to the infinite past, then the VAR process is stationary.

For model (1), since the right-hand side consists of only predetermined variables and the error terms are assumed to be independent white noise with time-invariant covariance, each equation can be estimated by ordinary least squares (OLS). Zellner proved that the OLS estimator coincides with the generalized LS (GLS) estimator [5].

The celebrated model (1) is easy to fit, and its autoregressive structure allows one to study the feedback effects and the Granger causality. However, model (1) employs only the lagged values of y_t for forecast and ignores other potentially important variables' effect. In addition, as time evolved, the coefficients remain constant, which may contrast the real situations where the dynamic structure of the relationship among different time series involves with time.

3. Multivariate functional-coefficient regression models and extensions

We briefly reviewed VAR models in the previous section. This parametric method has been significantly developed and widely applied to econometric dynamics as well as other domains. An alternative to modeling vector time series is the nonparametric method, which requires much fewer assumptions on the model structure and may shed light on the later parametric fitting. To illustrate the basic idea of this approach, let us begin with the multivariate threshold autoregressive model [3].

3.1. Multivariate threshold autoregressive model

The multivariate threshold autoregressive model is a generalization of the univariate threshold autoregressive model [6]. The idea is to partition one-dimensional variable into s regimes and impose an AR model with exogenous variables in each regime. Consider a $k-$ dimensional time series $y_t=(y_{1t}, \ldots, y_{kt})'$ and a v-dimensional exogenous variable $x_t=(x_{1t}, \ldots, x_{vt})'$, for $t=1,\ldots,n$. Let $-\infty=r_0<r_1<\cdots<r_s=\infty$. The multivariate threshold model with threshold variable z_t and delay d has the following form:

$$y_t = c_j + \sum_{i=1}^{n} \phi_i^{(j)} y_{t-i} + \sum_{i=1}^{q} \beta_i^{(j)} x_{t-i} + \varepsilon_i^{(j)} \text{ if } r_{j-1} < z_{t-d} \le r_j (j = 1, \ldots, s), \tag{4}$$

where p and q are nonnegative integers and $\varepsilon_t^{(j)} = \Sigma_j^{\frac{1}{2}} a_t$, with $\Sigma_j^{\frac{1}{2}}$ being a positive-definite matrix and $\{a_t\}$ a sequence of serially uncorrelated random vectors with mean zero and covariance matrix I_k. The threshold variable z_t is assumed to be stationary and has a continuous distribution.

Model (4) is piecewise linear in the threshold space of z_{t-d}, but it is nonlinear when $s>1$ [3]. This model has proven to be useful in practice. Nevertheless, the assumption embedded in this model weakens the practicability, that is, the coefficients are assumed to be constants in the threshold space of z_{t-d} in model (4). This assumption is questionable since the economic conditions tend to change slowly over time and the coefficient functions may vary smoothly. Motivated by this, Jiang proposed the multivariate functional-coefficient model, in which the coefficients are functions of threshold variable z_{t-d} instead of constants [4].

3.2. Multivariate functional-coefficient models

The multivariate functional-coefficient model has the following form:

$$y_t = c(z_{t-d}) + \sum_{i=1}^{p} \phi_i(z_{t-d}) y_{t-i} + \sum_{i=1}^{q} \beta_i(z_{t-d}) x_{t-i} + \varepsilon_t, \tag{5}$$

where $c(\cdot)$ is a $k \times 1$ functional vector, $\phi_i(\cdot)$ are $k \times k$ functional matrices, and $\beta_i(\cdot)$ are $k \times v$ functional matrices. The innovation satisfies $\varepsilon_t = \sigma_t^* a_t$, where σ_t^* is a positive-definite matrix and $\{a_t\}$ as in Eq. (4). Assume that σ_t^* is measurable with respect to the σ-field generated by the historical information $\mathcal{F}_{t-1}=\{(w_j, z_{j-d}): j\le t\}$, where $w_j=(x_{j-1}, \ldots, x_{j-q}, y_{j-1}, \ldots, y_{j-p})$. For model (5), we are interested in estimating the regression part. Once it is estimated, one may consider making simultaneous inference about parameters and using the residuals to study the structure of the volatility matrix. This model is a generalization of vector autoregressive models [1], threshold models [3] and functional-coefficient models [7–10]. Even for one-dimensional settings with k = 1, model (5) includes important predictive regression models in econometrics, such as the linear predictive models with nonstationary predictors [11–13] and functional-coefficient models for nonstationary time series data [14]. Model (5) can also be used to investigate the Granger Causality [15–17] and the feedback effect in engineering and finance [18, 19].

For model (5), a weighted local least squares estimation method was provided in [4]. Let $X_t = vec(1, y_{t-1}, \ldots, y_{t-p}, x_{t-1}, \ldots, x_{t-p})$ and $\Phi(z) = (c(z), \phi_1(z), \cdots, \phi_p(z), \beta_1(z), \ldots, \beta_q(z))$. Then model (5) becomes

$$y_t = \Phi(z_{t-d})X_t + \varepsilon_t, \tag{6}$$

where $\Phi(\cdot)$ is a $k \times m$ matrix-valued function and X_t is an $m \times 1$ vector with $m = 1 + pk + qv$. For any z_{t-d} in the neighborhood of z, by the Taylor expansion, we have

$$\Phi(z_{t-d}) \approx \Phi(z) + \Phi'(z)(z_{t-d} - z) \equiv A + B(z_{t-d} - z).$$

Let S and V be 2×2 matrices whose $(i, j)th$ elements are $\mu_{i+j-2} = \int u^{i+j-2}K(u)du$ and $\nu_{i+j-2} = \int u^{i+j-2}K^2(u)du$, respectively, and let $s = (\mu_2, \mu_3)'$. Given any invertible working variance matrix σ_t^2 of σ_t^{*2}, the estimator $(\tilde{A}, \tilde{B})$ is achieved by minimizing

$$\sum_{t=s'+1}^{n} \|\sigma_t^{-1}[y_t - AX_t - BX_t(z_{t-d} - z)]\|^2 K_{h_n}(z_{t-d} - z),$$

where $\|\cdot\|$ denotes the Euclidean norm, $s' = \max(p, d, q)$, and $K_{h_n}(x) = h_n^{-1}K(x/h_n)$ for kernel function $K(\cdot)$ with bandwidth h_n controlling the amount of smoothing. Let $K_{h_n}^{(i)}(z_{t-d} - z) = h_n^{-i}(z_{t-d} - z)K_{h_n}(z_{-d} - z)$ and $\tilde{S}_{ni} = \sum_{t=s'+1}^{n} (X_t X_t^T) \otimes \sigma_t^{-2} K_{h_n}^{(i)}(z_{t-d} - z)$ for $i = 0, 1, 2$. Then the weighted estimators $(\tilde{A}, \tilde{B})$ admit the closed form:

$$\begin{pmatrix} vec(\tilde{A}) \\ vec(h_n\tilde{B}) \end{pmatrix} = \begin{pmatrix} \tilde{S}_{n0} & \tilde{S}_{n1} \\ \tilde{S}_{n1} & \tilde{S}_{n2} \end{pmatrix}^{-1} \begin{pmatrix} \sum_{t=s'+1}^{n} (X_t \otimes \sigma_t^{-2}) y_t K_{h_n}(z_{t-d} - z) \\ \sum_{t=s'+1}^{n} (X_t \otimes \sigma_t^{-2}) y_t K_{h_n}^{(1)}(z_{t-d} - z) \end{pmatrix}.$$

Under certain conditions, the weighted estimators are asymptotically normal (see [4]).

Recall that, in model (5), σ_t^* is a positive-definite matrix measurable with respect to the sigma-algebra generated by historical information. If there is a parametric structure of σ_t^*, for example, the generalized autoregressive conditional heteroscedastic (GARCH) errors [4], then it helps to improve the efficiency of the weighted estimation. Example 3 in [4] exemplifies this point. Our intuition is that, if a parametric structure of σ_t^* is correctly specified, then the weighted estimation mimics the oracle estimation in the sense that σ_t^* is known. This intuition can be verified theoretically since σ_t^* can be estimated at rate of $\sqrt{n}$ which is faster than what we can do for the regression function in model (5).

3.3. Extension of multivariate functional-coefficient models

Due to the fact that many economic factors are not stationary, classic regression analysis requiring the stationarity condition suffers from a great limitation. Cointegration analysis has become a formidable toolkit in analyzing non-stationary economic time series. The concept of cointegration goes back to Granger [20] and initiated a literal research boom. Engle & Granger proposed the well-known Engel-Granger test to examine whether there is a cointegrating relationship among a set of first-order integrated variables [21].

Motivated by Granger and Engel & Granger, Jiang proposed an error-correction version of model (5) by incorporating the cointegrating relationship of first-order integrated variables [4]. This allows us to cope with the nonstationarity of vector time series and to improve the accuracy of forecasting.

Let s_t denote a $k \times 1$ vector of first-order integrated variables and let $y_t = s_t - s_{t-1}$. Assume that there is a co-integrating relationship for s_t; that is, there exists a unique $k \times r(0<r<k)$ deterministic matrix θ of rank r and a stationary process u_t such that $\theta^T s_t = u_t$. Then an error-correction form of model (5) is

$$y_t = c(z_{t-d}) + \gamma(z_{t-d})u_{t-1} + \sum_{i=1}^{p} \phi_i(z_{t-d})y_{t-i} + \sum_{i=1}^{q} \beta_i(z_{t-d})x_{t-i} + \varepsilon_t, \tag{7}$$

where $\gamma(z_{t-d})$ is a $k \times r$ coefficient matrix. This model simplifies to the Granger representation theorem if the coefficient functions are constant and there are no exogenous variables [4].

Due to the widespread presence of cointegrating variables in finance and economics, model (7) should improve the practicability of model (5). However, model (7) requires specification of variable z_t. This can be relaxed by using the idea of single index models. Recall that model (5) can be represented in succinct form (6). The similar operations can be applied to model (7). Now set $z_t = \gamma^T X_t$ and let data decide the value of γ. Then model (7) can be extended as

$$y_t = \Phi(\gamma^T X_{t-d})X_t + \varepsilon_t, \tag{8}$$

where γ is a directional vector such that its first nonzero entry is positive. Model (8) is more flexible than model (7), it is key to estimate γ. We introduce the profile lease squares method to estimate model (8). The estimation procedure consists of several steps:

Step 1. Given an initial value of γ, one obtains the weighted estimator $\widehat{\Phi}(\cdot;\gamma)$ of coefficient function in the same way as for model (6).

Step 2. Find the value $\widehat{\gamma}$ to minimize

$$\sum_{t=s'+1}^{n} \|y_t - \widehat{\Phi}(\gamma^T X_{t-d};\gamma)X_t\|^2. \tag{9}$$

Step 3. Update the value of γ by $\widehat{\gamma}$, and repeat Step 1 and Step 2 many times until convergence. The coefficient function $\Phi(\cdot)$ is estimated by $\widehat{\Phi}(\cdot;\widehat{\gamma})$.

It can be shown that $\widehat{\Phi}(\cdot;\widehat{\gamma})$ shares the same asymptotic normality as the Oracle weighted estimator in the sense that it knows the true value of γ, since $\widehat{\gamma}$ is $\sqrt{n}$-consistent.

3.4. Variable selection of multivariate functional-coefficient models

In this section, we consider variable selection of model (6). Increasing the lags p and q will necessarily reduce the sum of squared errors. However, doing so will increase the burden of coefficient estimation and may also lead to overfitting. Hence, for the multivariate functional-coefficient model, order selection is of much importance.

Two widely used model selection criteria are Akaike Information Criterion (AIC) and Bayesian Information Criterion (BIC). However, these stepwise methods yield heavy burden on computation and furthermore bring difficulty in establishing asymptotics for the estimation of selected models. The problems become more severe for high-dimensional data. Various regularization methods have been proposed to deal with these problems. Among them, a popular approach, called LASSO, proposed by Tibshirani, performs variable selection and parameter estimation simultaneously. See Ref. [22]. For univariate varying-coefficient regression models with i.i.d. data, Wang and Xia [23] developed a shrinkage estimation method by combining the idea of group LASSO [24] and kernel smoothing. In the following we develop a shrinkage estimation method for multivariate functional-coefficient model (6):

$$y_t = \Phi(z_{t-d})X_t + \varepsilon_t,$$

where the functional-coefficient matrix $\Phi(z) = (c(z), \phi_1(z), \ldots, \phi_p(z), \beta_1(z), \ldots, \beta_q(z))$. Since each column of $\Phi(\cdot)$ corresponds to the effect of a component of X_t, for variable selection of X_t we should penalize each column of $\Phi(\cdot)$ as a whole. This leads to minimizing

$$Q_\lambda(\Phi) = \sum_{i=s'+1}^{n} \sum_{t=s'+1}^{n} \|y_t - \Phi(z_{i-d})X_t\|^2 K\left(h^{-1}(z_{t-d} - z_{i-d})\right) + \sum_{j=1}^{p+q+1} \lambda_j \|\Phi_j\|, \tag{10}$$

where $\Phi_j = (\Phi_j(z_{s'+1-d}), \ldots, \Phi_j(z_{n-d}))$ with $\Phi_j(\cdot)$ being the jth column of $\Phi(\cdot)$, λ_j's are tuning parameters, and for any matrix A we use $\|A\|$ to denote the Hilbert-Schmidt norm of matrix. It is interesting to establish model selection consistency and the oracle property of the shrinkage estimation.

4. Multivariate time-varying coefficient models

Parallel to functional-coefficient model (5), it is natural to consider its alternative with time-varying coefficients [25]:

$$y_t = c(t/T) + \sum_{i=1}^{p} \phi_i(t/T) y_{t-i} + \sum_{i=1}^{q} \beta_i(t/T) x_{t-i} + \varepsilon_t, t = 1, \ldots, T, \tag{11}$$

where y_t is a $k \times 1$ vector, x_t is a $v \times 1$ vector, $c(s)$ a $k \times 1$ vector, $\varphi_i(\cdot)$ are $k \times k$ smooth matrices and $\beta_i(\cdot)$ are $k \times v$ smooth matrices. The innovation satisfies the same conditions as model (5). It is known that as time involves the economic conditions change slowly and smoothly. Model (11) reflects this smoothing change by allowing the coefficients being smoothing functions of time.

Let

$$\Phi(t/T) = \left(c(t/T), \phi_1(t/T), \ldots, \phi_p(t/T), \beta_1(t/T), \ldots, \beta_q(t/T)\right).$$

Using similar arguments to model (6), we can rewrite model (11) as

$$y_t = \Phi(t/T)X_t + \varepsilon_t, t = 1, \ldots, T, \tag{12}$$

where $\Phi(\cdot)$ is a $k \times m$ matrix and X_t is the same as in model (6). By the Taylor expansion, for any t in the neighborhood of $t_0 \in (0, T)$, we have

$$\Phi(t/T) \approx \Phi(t_0/T) + \Phi'(t_0/T)((t - t_0)/T) \equiv P + Q((t - t_0)/T).$$

Running the local linear smoother for model (12), we minimize

$$\sum_{t=s+1}^{T} \|y_t - PX_t - QX_t((t - t_0)/T)\|^2 K_h(t - t_0) \tag{13}$$

over P and Q, where $s = \max(p, q)$ and $K_h(x) = h^{-1}K(x/hT)$. Then it is straightforward to obtain an explicit form of the minimizer, $\left(\widehat{P}, \widehat{Q}\right)$, for the above optimization problem,

$$\begin{pmatrix} vec\left(\widehat{P}\right) \\ vec\left(h\widehat{Q}\right) \end{pmatrix} = \begin{pmatrix} S_{T0} & S_{T1} \\ S_{T1} & S_{T2} \end{pmatrix}^{-1} \begin{pmatrix} \sum_{t=s+1}^{T} (X_t \otimes I_k) y_t K_h(t - t_0) \\ \sum_{t=s+1}^{T} (X_t \otimes I_k) y_t K_h^{(1)}(t - t_0) \end{pmatrix}, \tag{14}$$

where $S_{Ti} = \sum_{t=s+1}^{T} (X_t X_t') \otimes I_k K_h^{(i)}(t - t_0)$ and $K_h^{(i)}(t - t_0) = (Th)^{-i}(t - t_0)^i K_h(t - t_0)$, for $i = 0, 1, 2$.

Define $M = E[(X_t X_t^T) \otimes I_k]$ and $N = E[(X_t X_t^T) \otimes (\sigma_t^*)^2]$. Let $\mu_i = \int u^i K(u)du$, $v_i = \int u^i K^2(u)du$,

$$U = \begin{pmatrix} \mu_0 & \mu_1 \\ \mu_1 & \mu_2 \end{pmatrix}, V = \begin{pmatrix} v_0 & v_1 \\ v_1 & v_2 \end{pmatrix}$$

Using similar arguments to [4], we can show that this estimator is asymptotically normal with mean zero and variance Σ, where $\Sigma = (U^{-1}VU^{-1}) \otimes (M^{-1}NM^{-1})$.

4.1. Generalized likelihood ratio tests

The multivariate time-varying coefficient regression model is flexible and powerful to estimate the dynamic changes of coefficients. After fitting a given dataset, some important questions arise, for example, whether the coefficient functions are actually constant or of some particular forms? This leads to statistical hypothesis testing. To answer these questions, we develop generalized likelihood ratio statistics to test corresponding hypothesis testing problems about the coefficient functions [26].

For the multivariate time-varying coefficient model (12), assume $\Sigma_0^{-1/2}\varepsilon_t$ has mean zero and covariance matrix I_k with Σ_0 being a symmetric positive-definite constant matrix.

Consider the following hypothesis testing problem

$$H_0 : \Phi(t/T) \in \Theta_0(t/T) \leftrightarrow H_a : \Phi(t/T) \notin \Theta_0(t/T), \tag{15}$$

where $\Theta_0(t/T)$ is some known constant matrix Φ_0 or a set of functionalmatrices. Let $\widehat{\Phi}(t/T)$ denote the nonparametric estimator of Φ, and let $\widehat{\Phi}_0(t/T)$ denote the true or estimated value of coefficients under the null hypothesis. Following Fan et al. [26] and Fan and Jiang [27], we define a generalized likelihood ratio statistic for testing problem (15):

$$\lambda_T = \frac{T}{2}\log\left(\frac{RSS_0 - RSS_a}{RSS_a}\right), \tag{16}$$

where $RSS_0 = \sum_{t=1}^{T}\left(y_t - \widehat{\Phi}_0(t/T)X_t\right)^T \Sigma^{-1}\left(y_t - \widehat{\Phi}_0(t/T)X_t\right)^T$, and $RSS_a = \sum_{t=1}^{T}\left(y_t - \widehat{\Phi}(t/T)\right.$ $\left.X_t\right)^T\Sigma^{-1}\left(y_t - \widehat{\Phi}(t/T)X_t\right)$ with Σ being a known constant covariance matrix from a working model. It is meaningful to study the asymptotic distributions of the test statistic under the null and alternatives.

In the following example, we consider the case when $\Theta_0(.)$ is a known constant. For any $u = t/T \in (0, 1)$, if we rewrite matrix $\Phi(u)$ as a vector, $\Delta(u) \equiv vec(\Phi_1(u), \ldots, \Phi_m(u))$, and denote $\Delta_0(u) \equiv vec(\Phi_{01}^*(u), \ldots, \Phi_{0M}^*(u))$, then the power of the test is evaluated against alternatives:

$$H_a : \Delta(u) = \Delta_0(u) + \frac{1}{\sqrt{Th}}G(u), \tag{17}$$

where $G(u) = (g_1(u), \ldots, g_m(u))^T$ is a vector of functions.

Example 1. To investigate the performance of the proposed generalized likelihood ratio test, 600 replications for each of sample sizes $T = 200$, $T = 400$ and $T = 800$ from the multivariate time-varying coefficient model were generated:

$$y_t = \Phi(t/T)X_t + \varepsilon_t, t = 1, \ldots, T$$

where $k = 2$, $v = p = q = 1$, $\Delta = vec(0.5, 0.0074, 0.08, 0.65, 0.25, 0.75)^T$. We set the initial values $x_1 = 0$ and $y_1 = (0.15, 0.2)$. Accordingly, $X_t = vec(y_{1,t-1}, y_{2,t-1}, x_{t-1})$ for $t = 2, \ldots, T$. Three distributions of the error term are considered: bivariate normal, bivariate log-normal, and bivariate $t(5)$, each with variance matrix $\Sigma = \begin{pmatrix} 1 & 0.5 \\ 0.5 & 1 \end{pmatrix}$. According to alternative (17), the power of the test is evaluated for a sequence of alternatives index by θ:

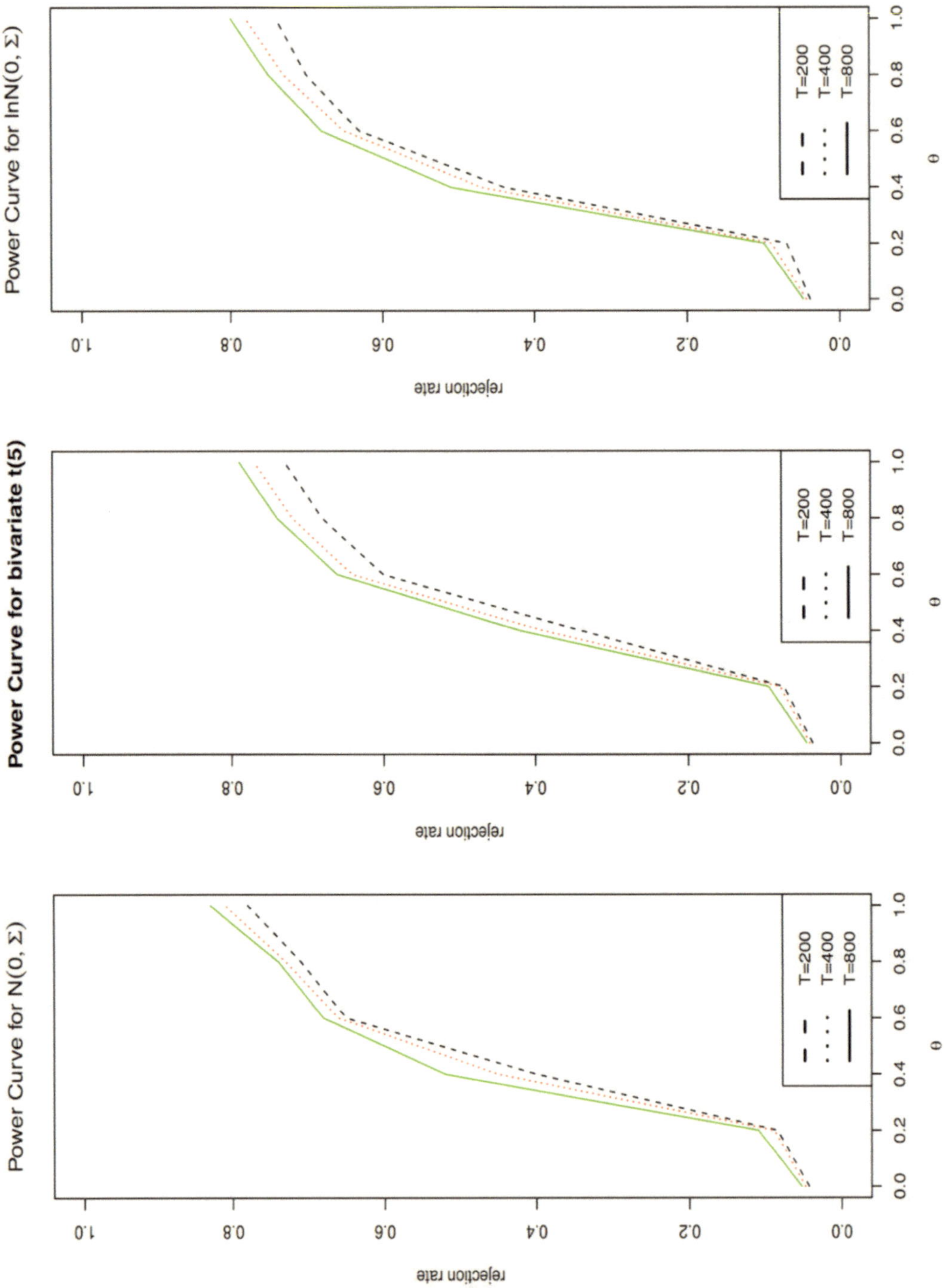

Figure 1. The power curves for Example 1. Significance level is 5%.

$$H_\theta : \Delta_\theta = (0.5, 0.0075, 0.08, 0.65, 0.25, 0.75)^T + \frac{\theta}{\sqrt{Th}} G(t/T), \tag{18}$$

where $G(t/T) = ((\sin(\sqrt{2}\pi/T), -0.09\cos(\pi t/T), 0.16\sin(\sqrt{3}\pi/T), 0.8\sin(\sqrt{2}\pi/T), 0.3\sin(t/T), \cos(\sqrt{1.5}\pi t/T))^T$ and $\theta = 0, 0.2, 0.4, 0.6, 0.8, 1$. The power function is estimated by the relative rejection frequency of H_0 in the above replicates.

The significance level is set to be 5%, and the critical values in simulations are calculated similarly by using the conditional bootstrap method in Ref. [26] for each given θ value. Detail of this method is as follows:

Step 1. Compute the estimators of the coefficient $\widehat{\Phi}(t/T)$ under both the null and the alternative by setting the optimal bandwidth as the estimated value $\widehat{h}_{opt}$.

Step 2. Compute the test statistic $\lambda_T(H_0)$ and the residuals $\{e_t\}$ from the alternative model.

Step 3. For each given X_t, draw a bootstrap residual e_t^* from the centered empirical distribution of e_t and compute $y_t^* = \widehat{\Phi}(t/T)X_t + e_t^*$. This forms a conditional bootstrap sample $\{X_t, y_t^*\}_{t=1}^T$.

Step 4. Compute the test statistic $\lambda_T^*(H_0)$ using the bootstrap sample constructed in Step 3.

Step 5. Repeat Step 3 and Step 4 to get a sample of the test statistic $\lambda_T^*(H_0)$. The critical values at significance level α are calculated by the $100(1-\alpha)$th percentile of the sample.

Figure 1 displays the power curves in difference scenarios. We can tell from **Figure 1** that the patterns of power curves look like half of an inverted normal density. All the curves rise monotonically from a height equal to the significance level of 5% until eventually it reaches its maximum height of around 90%. It is evident from **Figure 1** that the test is powerful for all three different distributions of error terms. Moreover, the test becomes more powerful as sample size increases. These indicate that the proposed test keeps the size and is powerful for distinguishing the difference between the null and the alternative.

5. Conclusions

In this chapter, we have reviewed some parametric and nonparametric methods for modeling nonlinear vector time series data, which include the VAR model, the multivariate threshold autoregressive model, and the multivariate functional-coefficient regression model. These models have great significance in econometrical and statistical theory and application. Based on the weighted local least square estimation, we have proposed a variable selection method for the functional-coefficient model. This model selection procedure is applicable to the proposed multivariate single index models and multivariate time-varying coefficient models. We have also extended the generalized likelihood ratio test to the time-varying coefficient model and demonstrated its performance through simulation. The proposed methodology is very useful for modeling nonlinear dynamic structures inherited in financial data. However, there are many problems remain unsolved for our procedure, such as the limiting theory about the proposed methodology. Future work includes, but not limited to, extending our models to nonstationary settings and exploring their performance in different applications.

Acknowledgements

This research was supported in part by NSFC grant 71361010 and by funds provided by the University of North Carolina at Charlotte.

Author details

Jiancheng Jiang* and Sha Yu

*Address all correspondence to: jjiang1@uncc.edu

University of North Carolina at Charlotte, Charlotte, NC, USA

References

[1] Sims CA. Macroeconomics and reality. Econometrica. 1980;**48**(1):1-48. DOI: 10.2307/1912017

[2] Engle RF, Kroner KF. Multivariate simultaneous generalized ARCH. Econometric Theory. 1995;**11**(1):122-150. DOI: 10.1017/S0266466600009063

[3] Tsay RS. Testing and modeling multivariate threshold models. Journal of the American Statistical Association. 1998;**93**(443):1188-1202. DOI: 10.1080/01621459

[4] Jiang J. Multivariate functional-coefficient regression models for nonlinear vector time series data. Biometrika. 2014;**101**(3):689-702. DOI: 10.1093/biomet/asu011

[5] Zellner A. An efficient method of estimating seemingly unrelated regressions and tests for aggregation bias. Journal of the American Statistical Association. 1962;**57**(298):348-368. DOI: 10.2307/2281644

[6] Tong H. On a threshold model. In: Chen C, editor. Pattern Recognition and Signal Processing. Netherlands: Sijthoff & Noordhoff; 1978. p. 575-586. DOI: 10.1007/978-94-009-9941-1_24

[7] Chen R, Tsay RS. Functional-coefficient autoregressive models. Journal of the American Statistical Association. 1993;**88**(421):298-308. DOI: 10.2307/2290725

[8] Hastie T, Tibshirani R. Varying-coefficient models. Journal of the Royal Statistical Society. Series B (Methodological). 1993;**55**(4):757-796

[9] Cai Z, Fan J, Yao Q. Functional-coefficient regression models for nonlinear time series. Journal of the American Statistical Association. 2000;**95**(451):941-956. DOI: 10.2307/2669476

[10] Huang JZ, Shen H. Functional coefficient regression models for non-linear time series: A polynomial spline approach. Scandinavian Journal of Statistics. 2004;**31**(4):515-534. DOI: 10.1111/j.1467-9469.2004.00404.x

[11] Campbell JY, Yogo M. Efficient tests of stock return predictability. Journal of Financial Economics. 2006;**81**:27-60

[12] Paye BS, Timmermann A. Instability of return prediction models. Journal of Empirical Finance. 2006;**13**:274-315

[13] Cai Z, Wang Y. Testing predictive regression models with nonstationary regressors. Journal of Econometrics. 2014;**178**:4-14

[14] Cai Z, Li Q, Park JY. Functional-coefficient models for nonstationary time series data. Journal of Econometrics. 2009;**148**:101-113

[15] Sims CA. Money, income, and causality. American Economic Review. 1972;**62**:540-552

[16] Psaradakis Z, Ravn MO, Sola M. Markov switching causality and the money-output relationship. Journal of Applied Econometrics. 2005;**20**:665-683

[17] Berger H, Österholm P. Does money still matter for U.S. output? Economics Letters. 2009;**102**:143-146

[18] Subrahmanyam A, Titman S. Feedback from stock prices to cash flows. Journal of Finance. 2001;**56**:2389-2413

[19] Åström KJ, Murray RM. Feedback Systems: An Introduction for Scientists and Engineers. Princeton University Press: Princeton, NJ; 2010

[20] Granger CWJ. Some properties of time series data and their use in econometric model specification. Journal of Econometrics. 1981;**16**(1):121-130. DOI: 10.1016/0304-4076(81)90079-8

[21] Engle RF, Granger CWJ. Co-integration and error correction: Representation, estimation, and testing. Econometrica. 1987;**55**(2):251-276. DOI: 10.2307/1913236

[22] Tibshirani, R. Regression Shrinkage and Selection via the Lasso. Journal of the Royal Statistical Society. Series B (Methodological). 1996;**58**(1):267-288. DOI: 10.1111/j.1467-9868.2011.00771.x

[23] Wang H, Xia Y. Shrinkage estimation of the varying coefficient model. Journal of the American Statistical Association. 2009;**104**(486):747-757. DOI: 10.1198/jasa.2009.0138

[24] Yuan M., Lin Y. Model Selection and Estimation in Regression With Grouped Variables. Journal of the Royal Statistical Society Series B (Statistical Methodology). 2006;**68**(1):49-67. DOI: 10.1111/j.1467-9868.2005.00532.x

[25] Liu Y. Generalized quasi-likelihood ratio statistics for multivariate time-varying coefficient regression models [dissertation]. Charlotte: University of North Carolina at Charlotte; 2013. 47 p

[26] Fan J, Zhang C, Zhang J. Generalized likelihood ratio statistics and Wilks phenomenon. The Annals of Statistics. 2001;**29**(1):153-193. DOI: 10.1214/aos/996986505

[27] Fan J, Jiang J. Nonparametric inference for additive models. Journal of the American Statistical Association. 2005;**100**:890-907

Chapter 8

Symbolic Time Series Analysis and Its Application in Social Sciences

Wiston Adrián Risso

Additional information is available at the end of the chapter

http://dx.doi.org/10.5772/intechopen.70826

Abstract

The present chapter intents to present the symbolic time series analysis (STSA) reviewing the recent developments in sciences. Even if there are very few works applied to social sciences, STSA has a potential to be developed. In particular, due to the limitations about historical data, fields such as Economics and Finance need to develop statistical tests to prove their hypotheses. An independence test and a causality test based on STSA are reviewed. They seem to be more powerful, detecting different kinds of nonlinearities compared with the classical tests, usually applied in social sciences. However, there is much work to do with STSA, and social sciences are a fertile field for the development of new powerful tools.

Keywords: STSA, information theory, entropy, independence, causality

1. Introduction

Time series has a long history in social sciences, especially in economics and finance. As it is well known, much of economics and finances are concerned with modeling dynamics, and systematization of data over time was a subject that appeared early. In particular, two empirical topics become important when working with time series in social sciences: inferences and forecasting. The cumulated historical data permitted to applied statistical methods in order to find evidence of causation between social variables, finding some support to social theories. Considering the nonexperimental nature of the social sciences, this also encourages the development of statistical techniques. In fact, while in physics, it is relatively easy to get hundreds of thousands of data for a given time series, in economics there are often only 50 or 100 data for a time series, and maybe we can obtain thousands of data in financial series. For this reason, much of the statistical effort, in particular econometric effort was focused on developing powerful statistical tests, considering the availability of small samples. This is an important different approach between econometrics and for example, statistical mechanics in theoretical physics.

We can identify two main groups in time series econometrics: univariate time series analysis concerning with techniques for the analysis of dependence in adjacent observations. It has increased importance since 1970 based on the main ideas underlying in [1]; multivariate time series analysis based on the vector autoregressive (VAR) models, made popular by [2]. In the first group, we find all the autoregressive integrated moving average (ARIMA) models and the related generalized autoregressive conditional heteroscedasticity (GARCH) models developed by [3]. The second group is a generalization of the AR models and we can find two important developments based on this: cointegration proposed by [4] focusing on finding a statistical relationship between variables; and noncausality test developed by [5], which takes the concept of predetermination try to test if a variable causes another. Much of the development in time series econometrics is found in books such as [6–18].

In summary, dependence and causation are two important topics in time series econometrics and time series analysis. These topics are related with the importance of inference and forecasting in social sciences. Econometrics has been focused in developing powerful test considering the available small samples. Most of these developments are based on linear models even if there are some developments considering nonlinearities; see for instance [19, 20].

Time series analysis in econometrics is mostly based on observations belonging to the set of the real numbers. Some variables can be categorical such as dummy variables. However, in this chapter, we will talk about a different approach that is known as symbolic time series analysis (STSA). It has been originally applied to physics and engineering as a statistical methodology to detect the very dynamic of highly noise time series. The application to social sciences such as economics or finance is very recent and there are some novel developments.

As mentioned before, the application of STSA in social sciences requires a different approach due to data limitation. In this sense, the design of powerful test considering the availability of data is crucial. As abovementioned, dependence and causation are two important topics. In this sense, we review an independence test and a first approach on testing noncausality, both based on STSA. The information theory was adopted as an approach to analyze the symbolic time series and the approximation of Shannon Entropy as an important measure, applied to test design.

The chapter is organized as follows. Section 2 presents the symbolic time series approach and its relation with the symbolic dynamics. In Section 3, we review some of the literature of STSA applied to the sciences. In Section 4, the information theory approach and Shannon Entropy measure is explained. Section 5 presents a review of the independence symbolic test. Section 6 focuses on causality test based on STSA. Section 7 discusses the difference between the proposed symbolic noncausality test and the traditional and well-known Granger noncausality test. Finally, in Section 8, we draw some conclusions and present some future lines of research.

2. Symbolic time series analysis

The concept of symbolization has its roots in dynamical systems theory, particularly in the study of nonlinear systems, which can exhibit bifurcation and chaos. In [21], it is asserted that symbolic dynamics is a method for studying nonlinear discrete-time systems by taking a previously codified trajectory using strings of symbols from a finite set, also called an alphabet. According to [22], symbolic dynamics and symbolic analysis are connected but are different concepts. In fact, the former is the practice of modeling a dynamical system by a discrete space. However, the latter is an empirical approach to characterize highly noisy data by considering a partition, discretizing the data, and obtaining a string representing the very dynamic of the process.

As asserted by [23], symbolization involves transformation of raw time series measurements into a series of discretized symbols that are processed to extract information about the generating process. In this way, we can search for nonrandom patterns and dependence by transforming a given time series $\{x_1, x_2,\ldots, x_T\}$ into a symbolic string $\{s_1, s_2, \ldots, s_T\}$.

The STSA approach is easy to apply but the definition of the right partition is the most difficult thing to do. Generally, it applied an equiprobable partition implying to take the empirical distribution of a given time series $\{x_1, x_2,\ldots, x_T\}$ and establishing two or more equally probable regions. For instance, for a Gaussian time series, we can define two equally probable regions considering as partition the mean equal to zero. After that, we can assign the symbol $s_i = 0$ for negative values and $s_i = 1$ for positive ones. In this way, we transform a continuously random series into a discrete string similar to the outcomes from flipping a coin.

3. STSA in applied sciences

In [23], the applications of STSA techniques to the different fields of science are reviewed. According to the authors, the different applications suggest that symbolization can increase the efficiency of finding and quantifying information from the systems. Mechanical systems were one of the first applications where symbolic analysis was successfully used to characterize complex dynamics. In [24–26], symbolic methods to the analysis of experimental combustion data from internal combustion engines are applied. Their objective was to study the onset of combustion instabilities as the fueling mixture was leaned. STSA has also been applied in Astrophysics and Geophysics. For instance, [27] analyzes weak-reflected radar signals from the planet Venus to measure the rotational period. In [28], a binary symbolization to analyze solar flare events is utilized. Biology and Medicine is another field where STSA has been applied. There have been many recent applications of symbolic analysis for biological systems, most notably for laboratory measurements of neural systems and clinical diagnosis of neural pathologies. STSA has been applied in neurosciences. In [29, 30], symbolization data is applied to equal-sized interval to partition EEG signals to identify seizure precursors in electroencephalograms. [31] proposed a new damage localization method based on STSA to detect and localize a gradually evolving deterioration in the system. They assert that this method could be demanded for implementation in real-time observation application such as structural health monitoring. In [32], the STSA is used in human gait dynamics. The results of this study can have implication modeling physiological control mechanism and for quantifying human gait dynamics in physiological and stressed conditions. In [33], the heart-rate dynamics is studied by using partitions aligned on the data mean and ± 1 and ± 2 sample standard deviations, for a symbol-set size of 6. In [34], the prevalence of irreversibility in human heartbeat is analyzed applying STSA.

Application of symbolization to fluid flow measurements has spanned a wide range of data types from global measurements of flow and pressure drop, to formation and coalescence of bubbles and drops, to spatiotemporal measurements of turbulence. In [35], an approach for transforming images of complex flow fields (as well as other textured fields) into a symbolic representation is developed. In [36], STSA is applied to the networks of genes, which is important underlying the normal development and function of organisms. Information about the structure of the genome of humans and other organisms is increasing exponentially. In [37], equiprobable symbols are used for analyzing measurements from free liquid jets in order to readily discriminate between random and nonrandom behavior. In [38], STSA is applied to the detection of incipient fault in commercial aircraft gas turbine engines. In [39], combustion instability in a swirl-stabilized combustor is investigated using STSA. Chemistry-related applications of symbolic techniques have been developed for chemical systems involving spontaneous oscillations or propagating reaction fronts. In [40], a type of symbolization for improving the performance of Fourier-transform ion-cyclotron mass spectrometry is applied. Artificial Intelligence, Control, and Communication are fields where symbolization has been incorporated. In [41], a phase-space partitioning to model communication is used. An example application of symbolization to communication is found in [42], utilizing small perturbations to encode messages in oscillations of the Belousov-Zhabotinsky (BZ) reaction. In robotics, a symbolic time series–based statistical learning method to construct the generative models of the gaits (i.e., the modes of walking) for a robot, see [43], has been developed. Efficacy of the proposed algorithm is demonstrated by laboratory experimentation to model and then infer the hidden dynamics of different gaits for the T-hex walking robot. In [44], an algorithm to intuitively cluster groups of agent trails from networks based on STSA is proposed. The authors assert that temporal trails generated by agents traveling to various locations at different time epochs are becoming more prevalent in large social networks. The algorithm was applied to real world network trails obtained from merchant marine ships GPS locations. It is able to intuitively detect and extract the underlying patterns in the trails and form clusters of similar trails.

The methods of data symbolization have also been applied for data mining, classification, and rule discovery. In [45], rule discovery techniques to real-valued time series via a process of symbolization are applied. Finally, we find some applications of STSA in Social Science. In [46–48], STSA and minimal spanning tree (MST) are applied to construct cluster of financial asset with application to portfolio theory. Utilizing a similar methodology, in [49], the dynamics of exchange market is studied, and in [50], the international hotel industry in Spain is analyzed. In [51, 52], STSA and entropy are applied to measure informational efficiency in financial markets.

4. Information theory and Shannon entropy

The term entropy was first used by Rudolf Clausius in [53] related to the second law of thermodynamics. Subsequently, the communication theory [54] used the Shannon entropy as a measure of uncertainty where the maximum entropy corresponds to the maximum degree of uncertainty. In this sense, a random process will take the maximum entropy value. In fact, English language is not a random process; some patterns such as "THE" are more probable than sequences such as "DXC". Note, that in a random process, the two sequences should have the same probability. This principle is very relevant because if a symbolic string is random, the entropy should be the maximum.

The entropy measure (H) must meet the following conditions:

1. $H(P)$ should be a function of the probability distribution of the n events expressed as the vector $P = (p_1, p_2, \ldots, p_n)$.
2. (*Continuity*), $H(P)$ should be a continuous function of vector P.
3. (*Symmetry*), the measure should be unchanged if the outcomes p_i are re-ordered.
4. (*Expansible*), Event of probability zero should not contribute to the entropy, $H(p_1, p_2, \ldots, p_n, 0) = H(p_1, p_2, \ldots, p_n)$.
5. (*Minimum*), the measure should take value 0 when there is not uncertainty.
6. (*Maximum*), the measure should be maximal if all the outcomes are equally likely. It means $p_1 = p_2 = \ldots = p_n = 1/n$.
7. For equiprobable events, the entropy increases with the number of outcomes. $H(p_1 = 1/(n+1), \ldots, p_{n+1} = 1/(n+1)) > H(p_1 = 1/n, \ldots, p_n = 1/n)$.

In [54], the Shannon entropy function is proposed:

$$H_n(P) = -\sum p_i log_2(p_i) \tag{1}$$

The entropy is frequently measured in bits by using log base 2 satisfying all the properties already mentioned. Note that the maximum property is confirmed solving the following Lagrangian expression (2).

$$-\sum p_i log_2(p_i) - \lambda\left(\sum p_i = 1\right) \tag{2}$$

The Shannon entropy is concaved with a global maximum when all the probabilities are equal. In addition, when $p_i = 0$, the convention that $0.log0 = 0$ is used. Thus, adding zero, probability terms do not change the entropy value.

In order to clarify the concept of Shannon, consider two possible events and their respective probabilities p and $q = 1-p$. The Shannon entropy will be defined by Eq. (3).

$$H = -(p.\log(p) + q.\log(q)) \tag{3}$$

Figure 1 shows graphically the function shape, note that the maximum is obtained when the probability is 0.5 for each event. This case corresponds to a random event; on the other hand, note that a certain event (when probability of one event is 1) will produce entropy equal to 0.

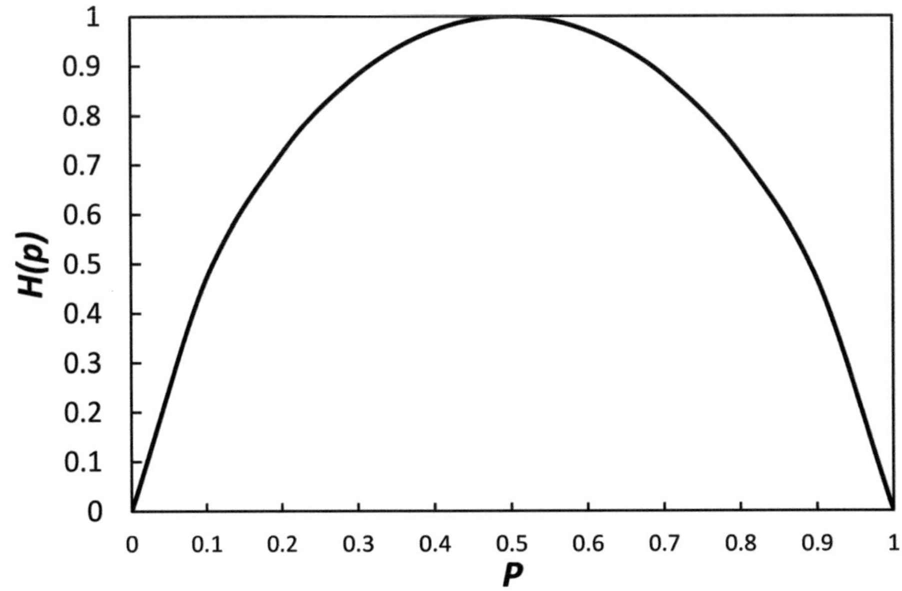

Figure 1. Shape of the Shannon entropy function. Note that maximum happens when the process is random (p = 0.5).

In general, [55] showed that any measure satisfying all the properties must take the following form:

$$-c\sum p_i log_2(p_i) \tag{4}$$

In order to normalize the Shannon entropy, c usually takes the value $1/log_2(n)$ allowing to compare events of different sizes.

5. Symbolic independence test

STSA seems to present a good performance when detecting independence in time series. A variety of dynamical processes are present in economics. Linearity, nonlinearity, deterministic chaos, and stochastic models have been applied when modeling a complex reality. In [56], a runs test is designed, asserting that the problem of testing randomness arises frequently in quality control of manufactured products. It is remarked that detecting dependence in time series is an essential task for econometricians and applied economist. In [57], the well-known BDS test is introduced, considered as a powerful test to detect nonlinearity. In [58], a simple and powerful test based on STSA is proposed and the results are compared with the BDS and runs test. On one hand, it is found that BDS is not able to detect processes such as the chaotic Anosov and the stochastic processes nonlinear sign model (NLSIGN), nonlinear autoregressive model (NLAR), and nonlinear moving average model (NLMA). On the other hand, runs test cannot detect the chaotic Anosov, the logistic process, the bilinear, the NLAR, and the NLMA stochastic processes. The experiments show that the test based on STSA has no problem detecting all these dynamics. It is concluded that proposed test is simple, easy to compute, and is powerful with respect to the other two tests. In particular, for small samples, it is the only one able to detect models such as chaotic Anosov and nonlinear moving average (NLMA). Besides, the test is applied to financial time series to detect nonlinearity on the residuals after applying a GARCH model. In this case, the BDS rejected the independence few times whereas the SRS test still detects nonlinearity in the residuals. It seems that BDS considers that the GARCH(1,1) model is a good model most of the time. However, the symbolic test suggests that GARCH(1,1) would not be a good model considering all the nonlinear components.

Here, we review briefly the test and repeat some experiments comparing the results with the well-known BDS and runs tests. At first, let us consider a finite time series generated by an independent or random process-sized T^* $\{x_t\}_{t=1,2,\ldots,T^*}$. Define a partition in the series in "a" equiprobable regions obtaining the symbolized time series $\{s_t\}_{t=1,2,\ldots,T^*}$, where each symbol s_t takes a symbolic value from the alphabet $A = \{A_1,A_2,\ldots,A_a\}$. Since, we want to derive a general statistic for different alphabet sizes a and different subsequences lengths w, we have to make two considerations: (1) from now, we will call n to the quantity of possible events. That is $n = a^w$, where for the simplest case ($w = 1$) implies $n = a$, then the quantity of events is equal to the symbol-set size; (2) in practice, we have a finite sample size T^*, there is no problem for $w = 1$, but when we compute subsequences or time-windows w of consecutive symbols we loss observations. For example, when we compute the frequency for two consecutive symbols, we have a total sample size T^*-1. In general, we can define the sample size $T = T^* + w-1$, again for the trivial case $w = 1$, $T^* = T$

Note that defining S_i for $i = 1,2,\ldots,n$ as the sum of the total i events in the time series, we can derive the multidimensional variable $S = \{S_i/T\}$ being distributed as a multinomial with $E(S_i/T) = (1/n)$, $Var(S_i/T) = (1/n)(n\text{-}1)/nT$ and $Cov(S_i/T,S_j/T) = -(1/n)(1/nT)\ \forall i \neq j$. As we will see, frequencies of the events should be important in the statistic and the vector of the n frequencies S_i/T could be approximated by a multivariate normal distribution $N(1/n,\sigma^2\Sigma)$ where σ^2 is $(1/nT)$ and Σ is a idempotent matrix as in (5)

$$\sum\nolimits_{nxn} \equiv \begin{bmatrix} (n-1)/n & -1/n & \ldots & -1/n \\ -1/n & (n-1)/n & \ldots & -1/n \\ \vdots & \vdots & \ddots & \vdots \\ -1/n & -1/n & \ldots & (n-1)/n \end{bmatrix} \tag{5}$$

For convenience, we can define the normalized vector variable $\{\varepsilon_i\} = \{(S_i/T)\text{-}(1/n)\}_{i=1,2,\ldots,n}$ having a multivariate normal distribution $N(\varnothing,\sigma^2\Sigma)$, being $\varnothing$, the null vector. Then, the statistic can be defined as a quadratic form in random normal variables (6).

$$\left\{\frac{\sum_{i=1}^{i=n}\varepsilon_i^2}{\sigma^2}\right\} \tag{6}$$

In [58] is applied the distribution of quadratic forms in normal variables presented in [59]. $X = (\varepsilon_1/\sigma,\varepsilon_2/\sigma,\ldots,\varepsilon_n/\sigma)$ is distributed multivariate normal $N(\varnothing,\Sigma)$. The theorem indicates that

$tr(A\Sigma) = n-1$, and thus $X'AX$ distributes Chi-square with $(n-1)$ degrees of freedom. In this case, A is the identity matrix I, and Σ is symmetric, singular, and idempotent. Remembering that $\sigma^2 = (1/nT)$, then we obtain that the distribution of the symbolic randomness statistic (SRS) as in (7).

$$SRS \equiv Tn\left\{\sum_{i=1}^{i=n}\left(\frac{S_i}{T}-\frac{1}{n}\right)^2\right\} \textit{ assymptotically distributes } \chi^2_{n-1} \quad (7)$$

Note that in practice computing the statistic is very simple. We just have to consider the symbols (a) and subsequences or length (w) and compute the frequencies for each event ($n = a^w$) in the time series.

The algorithm to compute the test is as follows:

Step 1: Considering time series $\{x_t\}_{t=1,2,\ldots,T^*}$, compute the empirical distribution, and define equiprobable regions according to the quantity of symbols or the alphabet size.

Step 2: According to the partition, translate $\{x_t\}_{t=1,2,\ldots,T^*}$ into $\{s_t\}_{t=1,2,\ldots,T^*}$, the symbolic time series when $w = 1$.

Step 3: Compute different symbolic time series for different lengths w, remember that the obtained series in step 2 corresponds to $w = 1$.

Step 4: For each w, compute the frequency of the n different events S_i/T for $i = 1,2,\ldots,n$.

Step 5: For each w, compute the $SRS(a,w) = Tn\{\Sigma(S_i/T - 1/n)^2\}$ as shown in Eq. (7).

Step 6: Compare the $SRS(a,w)$ with the Chi-2 with n-1 degree of freedom at 0.05 of significance, under the independence null hypothesis. When $SRS(a,w)$ is larger than the critical value we reject the null hypothesis.

In [58], it is found that the statistic introduced in (7) is related to the Shannon entropy (H). We can derive the approximation expressed in Eq. (8).

$$SRS \approx (1 - H).T.\ln(n) \quad (8)$$

Note the generalization implied in STSA permits to study different dynamical process. For instance, consider a string of the first 3000 letters from the book *"A Christmas Carol"*, s_1 = {*marleywasdeadtobeginwith…scroogecar*} and a random string of 3000 letters from an alphabet of 26, s_2 = {*iskynbmhjp…vbbihjfkk*}. Imagine testing this kind of process with BDS or runs test. However, note that would be easy to test this dynamics with the symbolic test. In this case, we can define an alphabet of 26 letters and the string. On the one hand, applying the *SRS* (26,1) and *SRS*(26,2) for the s_1, we obtain the following values 2102.40 and 12331.26, respectively. On the other hand, SRS(26,1) and SRS(26,2) for the string s_2 are 25.79 and 690.26, respectively. Considering that a Chi-2 with 25 degree of freedom at 95% is 37.65 and a Chi-2 with 675 degree of freedom (26^2–1) at 95% is 736.55. Since, the statistics for s_1 are large than the critical value, we can conclude that the process is not random. However, since the statistics for s_2 are less than critical values, we cannot reject the hypothesis of independence.

In [58] is shown that the test is conservative, rejecting the null hypothesis less time than expected. However, it is powerful in detecting nonrandom and nonlinear processes. Considering the four sample sizes, selecting two symbols and length 4 presents decent results in most of the cases. Selecting three symbols seems to be a relative good option for size of 200 or larger and three symbols for a sample size of 500 or larger. The best result is given for a sample of 2000 applying three symbols and length 4. **Table 1** presents the experiments using 1000 Monte Carlo simulations on Normal, Logistic, NLMA, Anosov, and NLSIGN processes reproducing the experiments in [58].

Note that the symbolic test is more conservative than BDS and Runs test when rejecting independence in a normal random process. However, the symbolic test is powerful in detecting nonlinearities in the studied processes. For a sample of 50, Logistic model is detected 100% by the symbolic test, but BDS detects 68%, and Runs test rejects independence 23.90% of the time. Logistic model is still hard to be detected by the run test when sample increases to 2000. Note that NLMA model is detected by the symbolic test when sample is 500 or larger, but it is not detected by BDS and Runs test. It is interesting to note that the chaotic process of Anosov is detected by the symbolic test for a sample larger than 500 but both BDS and Runs tests reject independence less than 6% of the cases. NLSIGN is hard to be detected, for a sample of 2000 the symbolic test detects more than 90% of the cases and Runs test detects 84% of the cases. However, BDS cannot detect the NLSIGN process. In [58] similar results are obtained, the proposed SRS is the only one that is able to detect chaotic Anosov and nonlinear process NLMA when T = 2000.

Sample size	Test	Normal (%)	Logistic (%)	NLMA (%)	Anosov (%)	NLSIGN (%)
$T = 50$	SRS(2,3)	1.20	41.00	1.30	2.90	0.20
	SRS(3,2)	0.70	100.00	0.40	0.80	0.50
	BDS	9.70	68.10	7.60	18.10	12.00
	RUN test	2.90	23.90	1.30	3.90	2.20
$T = 500$	SRS(2,3)	2.10	19.30	13.50	2.30	9.90
	SRS(3,2)	0.40	100.00	1.70	0.80	1.10
	SRS(4,3)	3.20	100.00	97.50	93.80	17.40
	BDS	3.60	66.40	7.20	5.30	4.40
	RUN test	3.80	14.70	16.30	5.50	24.10
$T = 2000$	SRS(2,3)	1.90	14.40	62.90	2.50	64.80
	SRS(3,2)	0.30	100.00	25.30	1.00	3.80
	SRS(4,3)	2.50	100.00	100.00	100.00	92.30
	SRS(5,3)	1.70	100.00	100.00	100.00	92.20
	BDS	2.80	80.40	14.60	3.60	4.00
	RUN test	4.40	12.20	50.00	5.70	84.30

Table 1. Simulated size of the SRS, Runs and BDS statistics.

6. Symbolic noncausality test

The present section reviews the symbolic noncausality test (SNC) and discusses the differences with the classical Granger noncausality test. As in the case of independence test, the main idea here is to derive the asymptotic distribution for the statistic when there is no causality between the series. A full explanation of the test is shown in [60].

Let us consider that X and Y are two independent random time series sized T + 1 and the symbolized time series can be expressed as $Sx = \{sx_1, sx_2, .., sx_{T+1}\}$ and $Sy = \{sy_1, sy_2, \ldots, sy_{T+1}\}$. To test causality, we have to define two new series, grouping Sx and Sy in the following way:

(1) $Sxy = \{(sx_1, sy_2), (sx_2, sy_3), \ldots, (sx_{t-1}, sy_t), \ldots, (sx_T, sx_{T+1})\}$

(2) $Syx = \{(sx_1, sy_2), (sx_2, sy_3), \ldots, (sx_{t-1}, sy_t), \ldots, (sx_T, sx_{T+1})\}$

If the alphabet is composed by three symbols, the combination (sx_{t-1}, sy_t) takes a value from the set of nine possible events {(1,1), (1,2), (1,3), (2,1), (2,2),(2,3),(3,1),(3,2),(3,3)}. Note that each event should be independent with probability 1/9 (Sx and Sy are random). Only if at least one event were deviated from 1/9, would there be evidence of noncausality.

An alphabet of $a = 3$ symbols determines $n = 3^2 = 9$ possible events in the set of pairs $\{(x_{t-1}, y_t)\}$ or $\{(y_{t-1}, x_t)\}$. Considering "a" symbols and the events $n = a^2$, the vector of the n frequencies Exy_i/T and Eyx_i/T could be approximated by a multivariate normal distribution $N(1/n, \sigma^2\Omega)$ where σ^2 is $(1/nT)$ and Ω is a idempotent matrix as in (9).

$$\Omega_{nxn} \equiv \begin{bmatrix} (n-1)/n & -1/n & \ldots & -1/n \\ -1/n & (n-1)/n & \ldots & -1/n \\ \vdots & \vdots & \ddots & \vdots \\ -1/n & -1/n & \ldots & (n-1)/n \end{bmatrix} \tag{9}$$

Following a similar approach as in Section 5, the statistics for the both hypothesis can be defined as in (10) and (11).

$$\left\{ \frac{\sum_{i=1}^{i=n} \varepsilon xy_i^2}{\sigma^2} \right\} \tag{10}$$

$$\left\{ \frac{\sum_{i=1}^{i=n} \varepsilon yx_i^2}{\sigma^2} \right\} \tag{11}$$

The term in brackets in (10), (11) are quadratic forms in random normal variables. Applying the theorem presented in [59], in the present case where vector $X = (\varepsilon_1/\sigma, \varepsilon_2/\sigma, \ldots, \varepsilon_n/\sigma)$ is distributed multivariate normal $N(\emptyset, \Omega)$. As mentioned in Section 5, $tr(A\Omega) = n\text{-}1$, thus $X'AX$ distributes Chi-square with $(n-1)$ degrees of freedom. In this case, A is the identity matrix I and Ω is symmetric, singular, and idempotent.

Note that we derive the test assuming that X and Y are random processes. However, we can apply the test for stationary time series and optionally apply an autoregressive process if we want to remove linear dependence and testing the noncausality between the residuals of the two series.

$$x_t = \alpha_0 + \alpha_1 x_{t-1} + ux_t \tag{12}$$

$$y_t = \beta_0 + \beta_1 y_{t-1} + uy_t \tag{13}$$

Finally, the statistics of noncausality SNC(X → Y) and SNC(Y → X) are defined as in (14) and (15).

$$SNC(X \to Y) \equiv nT\left\{\sum_{i=1}^{i=n}\left(\frac{Exy_i}{T} - \frac{1}{n}\right)^2\right\} assymptotically\ distributes\ \chi^2_{n-1} \tag{14}$$

$$SNC(Y \to X) \equiv nT\left\{\sum_{i=1}^{i=n}\left(\frac{Eyx_i}{T} - \frac{1}{n}\right)^2\right\} assymptotically\ distributes\ \chi^2_{n-1} \tag{15}$$

Note that in practice, computing the statistic is very simple. In summary, the test works as follows:

Step 1: Consider time series $\{x_t\}_{t=1,2,\ldots,T+2}$ and $\{y_t\}_{t=1,2,\ldots,T+2}$ we can optionally apply an AR (1) to both series as in (12) and (13) in order to eliminate autocorrelation and define the new residuals time series $\{ux_t\}_{t=1,2,\ldots,T+1}$ and $\{uy_t\}_{t=1,2,\ldots,T+1}$. Note that 1 observation is lost after applying AR(1).

Step 2: In $\{ux_t\}_{t=1,2,\ldots,T+1}$ and $\{uy_t\}_{t=1,2,\ldots,T+1}$ apply a partition in "a" equiprobable regions and translate the series into $\{sx_t\}_{t=1,2,\ldots,T+1}$ and $\{sy_t\}_{t=1,2,\ldots,T+1}$.

Step 3: According to the two hypothesis, $X \to Y$ and $Y \to X$ define the two sets $Sxy = \{(sx_1, sy_2), (sx_2,sy_3),\ldots,(sx_{t-1},sy_t),\ldots,(sx_T,sx_{T+1})\}$ and $Syx = \{(sx_1,sy_2), (sx_2,sy_3),\ldots,(sx_{t-1},sy_t),\ldots,(sx_T, sx_{T+1})\}$.

Step 4: For Sxy and Syx, compute the frequency of the $n = a^2$ different events Exy_i/T and Eyx_i/T considering $i = 1,2,\ldots, a^2$.

Step 5: Taking into account Eqs. (14) and (15) compute the $SNC(X \to Y) = nT\{\Sigma[(Exy_i/T)-(1/n)]^2\}$ and $SNC(Y \to X) = nT\{\Sigma[(Eyx_i/T) - (1/n)]^2\}$.

Step 6: Finally, two null hypotheses must be contrasted: X does not cause Y, and Y does not cause X. In the first case $SNC(X \to Y)$ should be compared with a Chi-2 with n-1 degree of freedom at 0.05 of significance, if $SNC(X \to Y)$ is larger than the critical value the null hypothesis is rejected. The same should be done with $SNC(Y \to X)$.

7. Symbolic noncausality and Granger noncausality

The concept of causality into the experimental practice is due to Clive Granger. The classical approach of Granger causality is based on temporal properties. Although the principle was formulated for wide classes of systems, the autoregressive modeling framework proposed by Granger was basically a linear model, and as mentioned in [61] the choice was made due to practical reasons. Granger noncausality test is among the most applied tool testing causality. Three limitations should be noted: (1) the classical test has a good performance when the process is linear. This is because it is based on the vector autoregressive model (VAR); (2) there are extension of the classical test to consider nonlinear causality but they are related with a particular nonlinear model; (3) some authors assert that empirical time series are generally contaminated with noise producing what is known as spurious causality or not allowing to detect the causality.

SCN test presented in [60] is a nonparametric noncausality test based on the symbolic time series analysis. The idea is to develop a complementary test to the Granger noncausality, showing strengths in the points where the Granger test is weak. In this sense, the proposed SNC test performs well detecting nonlinear processes, in particular the chaotic processes. In addition, the mentioned problem related with spurious causality should be alleviated. In fact, according to some experiments nonlinear models such as NLAR model, Lorenz map, and models with exponential terms are not detected by Granger test but the SNC identifies these processes. The test is based on information theory considering an approximation of the entropy as the measure of uncertainty of a random variable. Information theory is considered to be a subset of communication theory. However, in [62] is consider that it is much more. It has fundamental contributions to make in statistical physics, computer science, and statistical inference, and in probability and statistics. It is important to highlight and is an important idea relating symbolic analysis, information theory, and the concept of noise. Information theory considers that communication between A and B is a physical process in an imperfect ambient contaminated by noise. Another important concept is the discrete channel, defined as a system consisting of an input alphabet X and output alphabet Y and a probability transition matrix $p(y\,|\,x)$ that expresses the probability of observing the output symbol y given that we send the symbol x.

To compare the performance between the classical Granger noncausality and the proposed SNC test, the following stochastic and deterministic models were simulated:

1. AR(1). We consider two independent series generated by autoregressive (AR) processes: $X_t = 0.2 + 0.45X_{t-1} + \varepsilon_{1t}$ and $Y_t = 0.8 + 0.5Y_{t-1} + \varepsilon_{2t}$. Where ε_{1t} and ε_{2t} are i.i.d. and normally distributed (0,1).

2. Nonlinear with exponential component. $X_t = 1.4 – 0.5X_{t-1}e^{Y_{t-1}} + \varepsilon_{1t}$ and $Y_t = 0.4 + 0.23Y_{t-1} + \varepsilon_{2t}$; where ε_{1t} and ε_{2t} are i.i.d. normal(0,1).

3. NLAR (Autoregressive Nonlinear). $X_t = 0.2|X_{t-1}|/(2 + |X_{t-1}|) + \varepsilon_{1t}$ and $Y_t = 0.7|Y_{t-1}|/(1 + |X_{t-1}|) + \varepsilon_{2t}$; where ε_{1t} and ε_{2t} are i.i.d. normal(0,1).

4. Lorenz: $X_t = 1.96X_{t-1} – 0.8X_{t-1}Y_{t-1}$; $Y_t = 0.2Y_{t-1} + 0.8X^2_{t-1}$; with initial conditions X_1, Y_1 generated randomly. This is a discrete version of the Lorenz process as in [63].

Table 2 shows the results of the power experiments applying the SNC and the Granger noncausality test to 10,000 Monte Carlo simulations for the four models and for different sample sizes ($T = 50, 100, 500, 1000$, and 5000).

Sample size	Model	Symbolic noncausality		Granger noncausality	
		$X \to Y$	$Y \to X$	$X \to Y$	$Y \to X$
$T = 50$	**AR(1)** (None)	0.40	0.45	5.66	5.25
$T = 100$		0.42	0.37	5.28	5.09
$T = 500$		0.41	0.27	5.47	5.14
$T = 1000$		0.39	0.42	5.18	5.14
$T = 5000$		0.34	0.46	5.30	5.09
$T = 50$	**NLAR** (X → Y)	0.01	0.01	0.05	0.05
$T = 100$		0.73	0.34	4.82	4.74
$T = 500$		5.96	0.31	4.94	5.16
$T = 1000$		17.87	0.29	5.01	5.05
$T = 5000$		98.02	0.39	6.51	5.00
$T = 50$	**Nonlinear exponential** (Y → X)	0.51	3.76	2.89	16.89
$T = 100$		0.28	11.85	2.78	13.36
$T = 500$		0.43	89.50	2.53	11.48
$T = 1000$		0.40	99.22	2.73	11.29
$T = 5000$		1.42	100.00	2.67	11.19
$T = 50$	**Lorenz** (X → Y, Y → X)	96.61	31.90	30.77	13.86
$T = 100$		99.99	90.49	28.52	12.64
$T = 500$		100.00	100.00	23.60	11.74
$T = 1000$		100.00	100.00	24.42	11.69
$T = 5000$		100.00	100.00	23.87	11.52

Table 2. Simulated power of the SNC and the Granger non causality statistic.

Following [60], a 60% acceptance or rejection of the null hypothesis is considered as a threshold. SNC and Granger noncausality correctly identifies noncausality in AR(1) process. **Table 2** suggests that SNC is more conservative in the rejection of causality with percentages less than 5%. The nonlinear model with an exponential component implies causality from Y to X. Note that SNC detects the causality when the sample size is 500 or larger. However, Granger test does not detect causality in any case. As asserted by [58] the NLAR process is very difficult to detect. Note that SCN is the only one detecting the causality when $T = 5000$. The Lorenz discrete map is also chaotic, and it is detected by SNC starting from $T = 100$. However, note that Granger test never detects the causality. In particular, is highlighted that Granger test is not able to detect the model with an exponential component, the NLAR model and the chaotic Lorenz map.

Finally, we compare both tests with real data from US. In particular, we consider two well-known relationships in economics: the Phillips curve [64] about the relation between unemployment and inflation rates, the Okun's law [65] establishing a relation between unemployment and economic rate. We take annual data for the US unemployment rate, inflation rate, and economic growth for the period 1948–2016 representing a total of 69 observations. **Table 3** shows the results of the Granger noncausality test and the symbolic test considering a partition of two symbols.

The results are similar for both tests. On one hand, Granger and symbolic tests detect causality from inflation to unemployment in the Phillips curve. On the other hand, the two tests detect causality running from economic growth to unemployment in the Okun's law. The economic theory suggests that inflation increases unemployment while economic growth reduces it. Note that STSA allows thinking about causality in a more general way, whereas Granger noncausality needs to think of continuous measured variables, this should not be a problem for STSA. Let us consider the following example; we now can test the hypothesis of causality from economic growth (G) and inflation (P) to unemployment (U). The main problem is that we have to test causality from a two-dimensional variable to a one dimensional. Symbolization permits to transform the two-dimensional problem in one dimensional and then to apply the symbolic test as explained. We can follow a similar approach as in [66] where STSA is applied

Null hypothesis	Granger	SNC(2 symbols)
Phillips curve		
Unemployment does not cause inflation	0.04	1.53
Inflation does not cause unemployment	16.90*	9.41*
Okun's law		
Unemployment does not cause economic growth	3.37	2.94
Economic growth does not cause unemployment	61.01*	9.65*

* Indicates rejection of the null hypothesis at the 5% level significance.

Table 3. SNC and the Granger non causality for the Phillips Curve and Okun's Law in US.

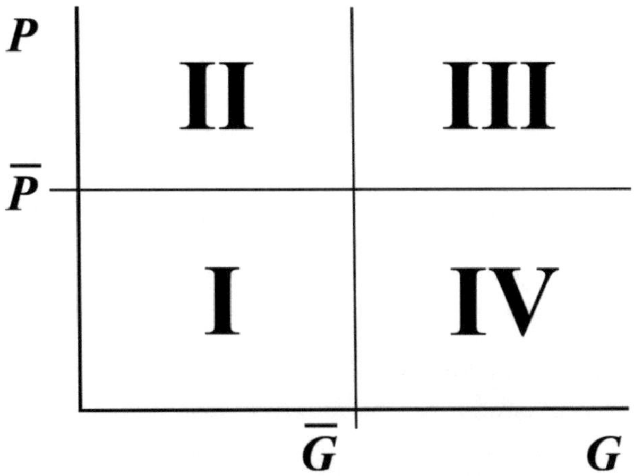

Figure 2. Two-dimensional variable (economic growth and inflation) is transformed into a four symbol variable.

to dynamic regimes. **Figure 2** shows the transformation of the variable (G, P) in a symbolic variable with an alphabet of four symbols (I: low economic growth and low inflation, II: low economic growth and high inflation, III: high economic growth and high inflation, IV: high economic growth and low inflation) considering as partition the mean of each variable. Note that now the application of symbolic causality is easy, the hypothesis that the economic regime (G, P) does not cause unemployment is rejected since the SNC is 31.76 and Chi-2 with 15 degree of freedom (4^2–1) at 95% is 25.00. The opposite hypothesis is not rejected because the SNC is 24.71. It is not possible to test this type of causality with the traditional Granger noncausality test.

8. Conclusion

STSA is a powerful tool being applied to many scientific fields. There are recent applications in robotic, biology, medicine, communication, and engineering. However, applications in social sciences are very recent. The main difficult is the few historical data produced by the social processes. Social sciences are used to applied statistical tests for proving their hypothesis. However, there is much work to do in developing statistical tests based on STSA to be applied in social sciences. There are some very recent efforts applied to economics and finance using STSA. In particular, we present a symbolic independence test, which seems to be powerful in detecting nonlinearities compared with well-known BDS and runs test. The symbolic test is better detecting models such as the chaotic Anosov and Logistic or some stochastic models such as NLMA or NLSIGN. A second symbolic test about causality detects complex processes such as NLAR, nonlinear exponential, or the Lorenz chaotic process when the traditional Granger noncausality cannot. The symbolic causality also enables causality to be tested in a more general perspective. The application of test from a two-dimensional economic variable to a one-dimensional economic variable is a clear example of the potential of STSA in economics and social sciences in general.

One future research line could be to develop a powerful nonlinear test for multidimensional variables. As it was explained, STSA permits to transform a multidimensional time series in a one-dimensional time series simplifying the analysis. This could have important applications in relationships involving vector functions. A more general line of research is to find methodologies to define the optimal partition. As mentioned before, equiprobable partition is generally applied but to find the right partition is still a theoretical and practical weakness in STSA.

Author details

Wiston Adrián Risso

Address all correspondence to: arisso@iecon.ccee.edu.uy

Institute of Economics (IECON), University of the Republic, Montevideo, Uruguay

References

[1] Box G, Jenkins G. Time Series Analysis: Forecasting and Control. San Francisco: Holden-Day ed; 1970

[2] Sims C. Macroeconomics and reality. Econometrica: Journal of the Econometric Society. 1980;**48**(1):1-48

[3] Engle R. Autoregressive conditional heteroscedasticity with estimates of the variance of United Kingdom inflation. Econometrica: Journal of the Econometric Society. 1982;**50**(4): 987-1007

[4] Engle R, Granger C. Co-integration and error correction: Representation, estimation, and testing. Econometrica: Journal of the Econometric Society. 1987;**55**(2):251-276

[5] Granger C. Investigating causal relations by econometrics models and cross-spectral methods. Econometrica. 1969;**37**(3):424-438

[6] Box G, Jenkins G, Reinsel G, Ljung G. Time Series Analysis: Forecasting and Control. 5th ed. John Wiley & Sons: New Jersey, US; 2015

[7] Granger C, Newbold P. Forecasting Economic Time Series. Academic Press: New York, US; 2014

[8] Hamilton J. Time Series Analysis. Princeton: Princeton University; 1994

[9] Harris R, Sollis R. Applied Time Series Modelling and Forecasting. Wiley: Chichester, UK; 2003

[10] Franses P. Time Series Models for Business and Economic Forecasting. Cambridge University Press: Cambridge, UK; 1998

[11] Chatfield C. Time-Series Forecasting. CRC Press: Florida, US; 2000

[12] Lütkepohl H. New Introduction to Multiple Time Series Analysis. Springer Science & Business Media: Berlin, Germany; 2005

[13] Clements M, Hendry D. Forecasting Economic Time Series. Cambridge University Press: Cambridge, UK; 1998

[14] Harris R. Using Cointegration Analysis in Econometric Modelling (Vol. 82). London: Prentice Hall; 1995

[15] Banerjee A, Dolado JJ, Galbraith JW, Hendry D. Co-integration, Error Correction, and The Econometric Analysis of Non-Stationary Data. OUP Catalogue: Oxford, UK; 1993

[16] Juselius K. The Cointegrated VAR Model: Methodology and Applications. Oxford University Press: Oxford, UK; 2006

[17] Johansen S. Likelihood-Based Inference in Cointegrated Vector Autoregressive Models. Oxford University Press: Oxford, UK; 1995

[18] Tsay R. Analysis of Financial Time Series (Vol. 543). John Wiley & Sons: New York, US; 2005

[19] Terasvirta T, Tjostheim D, Granger CW. Modelling Nonlinear Economic Time Series. OUP Catalogue: Oxford, UK; 2010

[20] Kantz H, Schreiber T. Nonlinear Time Series Analysis (Vol. 7). Cambridge University Press: Cambridge, UK; 2004

[21] Williams S. Symbolic dynamics and its applications. Proceeding of Symposia in Applied Mathematics. 2004;**60**:150

[22] Piccardi C. On the control of chaotic systems via symbolic time series analysis. Chaos. 2004;**14**(4):1026-1034

[23] Daw C, Finney C, Tracy E. A review of symbolic analysis of experimental data. Review of Scientific Instruments. 2003;**74**(2):915-930

[24] Daw CS, Kennel MB, Finney CEA, Connolly F. Observing and modeling nonlinear dynamics in an internal combustion engine. Physical Review E. 1998;**57**(3):2811

[25] Daw C, Green J, Wagner R, Finney C, Connolly F. Synchronization of combustion variations in a multicylinder spark ignition engine. Proceedings of the Combustion Institute. 2000;**28**(1):1249-1255

[26] Daw C, Finney C, Kennel M. Symbolic approach for measuring temporal "irreversibility". Physical Review E. 2000;**62**(2):1912

[27] Goldstein R. A technique for the measurement of the power spectra of very weak signals. IRE Transactions on Space Electronics and Telemetry. 1962;**2**:170-173

[28] Schwarz U, Benz A, Kurths J, Witt A. Analysis of solar spike events by means of symbolic dynamics methods. Astronomy and Astrophysics. 1993;**277**:215

[29] Hively L, Gailey P, Protopopescu V. Detecting dynamical change in nonlinear time series. Physics Letters A. 1999;**258**(2):103-114

[30] Hively L, Protopopescu V, Gailey P. Timely detection of dynamical change in scalp EEG signals. Chaos: An Interdisciplinary Journal of Nonlinear Science. 2000;**10**(4):864-875

[31] Makki M, Samali B, Li J. Damage localization based on symbolic time series analysis. Structural Control and Health Monitoring. 2015;**22**(2):374-393

[32] Qumar A, Aziz W, Saeed S, Ahmed I, Hussain L. Comparative study of multiscale entropy analysis and symbolic time series analysis when applied to human gait dynamics. In: 2013 International Conference on Open Source Systems and Technologies (ICOSST). IEEE: Lahore, Pakistan; December, 2013; 2013.

[33] Kim J, Park J, Seo J, Lee W, Kim H, Noh J, Yum M. Decreased entropy of symbolic heart rate dynamics during daily activity as a predictor of positive head-up tilt test in patients with alleged neurocardiogenic syncope. Physics in Medicine and Biology. 2003;**45**(11):3403

[34] Cammarota C, Rogora E. Time reversal, symbolic series and irreversibility of human heartbeat. Chaos, Solitons & Fractals. 2007;**32**(5):1649-1654

[35] Rao A, Jain R. Computerized flow field analysis: Oriented texture fields. IEEE Transactions on Pattern Analysis and Machine Intelligence. 1992;**14**(7):693-709

[36] Edwards R, Siegelmann H, Aziza K, Glass L. Symbolic dynamics and computation in model gene networks. Chaos: An Interdisciplinary Journal of Nonlinear Science. 2001;**11**(1): 160-169

[37] Godelle J, Letellier C. Symbolic sequence statistical analysis for free liquid jets. Physical Review E. 2000;**62**(6):7973

[38] Sarkar S, Mukherjee K, Sarkar S, Ray A. Symbolic transient time-series analysis for fault detection in aircraft gas turbine engines. In: American Control Conference (ACC); June 2002; 2002. pp. 5132–5137.

[39] Ramanan V, Chakravarthy SR, Sarkar S, Ray A Investigation of combustion instability in a swirl-stabilized combustor using symbolic time series analysis. In: American Society of Mechanical Engineers, editor. ASME 2014 Gas Turbine India Conference; December 2014; 2014. p. V001T03A012-V001T03A012.

[40] Hsu A, Marshall A, Ricca T. Clipped representations of fourier-transform ion-cyclotron resonance mass spectra. Analytica Chimica Acta. 1985;**178**:27-41

[41] Baptista M, Rosa E, Grebogi C. Communication through chaotic modeling of languages. Physical Review E. 2000;**61**(4):3590

[42] Dolnik M, Bollt E. Communication with chemical chaos in the presence of noise. Chaos: An Interdisciplinary Journal of Nonlinear Science. 1998;**8**(3):702-710

[43] Seto Y, Takahashi N, Jha D, Virani N, Ray A Data-driven robot gait modeling via symbolic time series analysis. In: American Control Conference (ACC); July 2016; 2016. p. 3904–3909.

[44] Gullapalli A, Carley K. Extracting ordinal temporal trail clusters in networks using symbolic time-series analysis. Social Network Analysis and Mining. 2013;**3**(4):1179-1194

[45] Das G, Lin KI, Mannila H, Renganathan G, Smyth P. Rule discovery from time series. KKD. 1998;**98**(1):16-22

[46] Brida J, Risso W. Dynamics and structure of the main italian companies. International Journal of Modern Physics C. 2007;**18**(11):1783-1793

[47] Brida J, Risso W. Multidimensional minimal spanning tree: The dow jones case. Physica A: Statistical Mechanics and its Applications. 2008;**387**(21):5205-5210

[48] Brida J, Risso W. Dynamic and structure of the Italian Stock Market based on returns and volume trading. Economics Bulletin. 2009;**29**(3):2417-2423

[49] Brida J, Gomez D, Risso W. Symbolic hierarchical analysis in currency markets. An application to contagion in currency crises. Expert Systems with Applications. 2009;**36**(4): 7721-7728

[50] Brida J, Esteban L, Risso W, Such S. The international hotel industry in Spain: Its hierarchical structure. Tourism Management. 2010;**31**(1):57-73

[51] Risso W. The informational efficiency and the financial crashes. Research in International Business and Finance. 2008;**22**(3):396-408

[52] Risso W. The informational efficiency: The emerging markets versus the developed markets. Applied Economics Letters. 2009;**16**(5):485-487

[53] Clausius R. The nature of the motion we call heat. In: Brush SG, editor. Kinetic Theory. (Selected Readings in Physics). Vol. Vol. 2. Pergamon Press: Oxford, UK; 1965. p. 111-134

[54] Shannon C. A mathematical theory of communication. Bell System Technical Journal. 1948;**27**:379-423

[55] Khinchin A. Mathematical Foundations of Information Theory. Courier Dover Publications: New York, US; 1957

[56] Wald A, Wolfowitz J. An exact test for randomness in the non-parametric case based on serial correlation. The Annals of Mathematical Statistics. 1943;**14**(4):378-388

[57] Brock W, Dechert W, LeBaron B, Scheinkman J. A test for independence based on the correlation dimension. Econometric Reviews. 1996;**15**:197-235

[58] Risso W. An independence test based on symbolic time series. International Journal of Statistical Mechanics. 2014;**2014**:809383

[59] Mathai A, Provost S. Quadratic Forms in Random Variables: Theory and Applications. Marcel Dekker, Inc.; 1992

[60] Risso W. A first approach on testing non-causality with symbolic time series. Economic Computation and Economic Cybernetics Studies and Research. 2015;**49**(3):123-142

[61] Hlaváčková-Schindler K, Paluš M, Vejmelka M, Bhattacharya J. Causality detection based on information-theoretic approaches in time series analysis. Physics Reports. 2007;**441**(1): 1-46

[62] Cover T, Thomas J. Elements of Information Theory, Wiley. 2nd ed2006

[63] Stork, M., Hrusak, J., Mayer, D.. Discrete-time chaotic systems impulsive synchronization and data transmission. In: Proc. 13th WSEAS Int. Conf. System; 2009.

[64] Phillips A. The relationship between unemployment and the rate of change of money wages in the United Kingdom 1861–1957. Economica. 1958;**25**(100):283-299. DOI: 10.1111/j.1468-0335.1958.tb00003.x

[65] Okun A. Potential GNP, its measurement and significance. Proceedings of the Business and Economics Statistics Section of the American Statistical Association. 1962:98-104

[66] Brida J, Punzo L. Symbolic time series analysis and dynamic regimes. Structural Change and Economic Dynamics. 2003;**14**(2):159-183

Chapter 9

State-Space Models for Binomial Time Series with Excess Zeros

Fan Tang and Joseph E. Cavanaugh

Additional information is available at the end of the chapter

http://dx.doi.org/10.5772/intechopen.71336

Abstract

Count time series with excess zeros are frequently encountered in practice. In characterizing a time series of counts with excess zeros, two types of models are commonplace: models that assume a Poisson mixture distribution, and models that assume a binomial mixture distribution. Extensive work has been published dealing with modeling frameworks based on Poisson-type approaches, yet little has concentrated on binomial-type methods. To handle such data, we propose two general classes of time series models: a class of observation-driven ZIB (ODZIB) models, and a class of parameter-driven ZIB (PDZIB) models. The ODZIB model is formulated in the partial likelihood framework, which facilitates model fitting using standard statistical software for ZIB regression models. The PDZIB model is conveniently formulated in the state-space framework. For parameter estimation, we devise a Monte Carlo Expectation Maximization (MCEM) algorithm, with particle filtering and particle smoothing methods employed to approximate the intractable conditional expectations in the E-step of the algorithm. We investigate the efficacy of the proposed methodology in a simulation study, which compares the performance of the proposed ZIB models to their counterpart zero-inflated Poisson (ZIP) models in characterizing zero-inflated count time series. We also present a practical application pertaining to disease coding.

Keywords: autocorrelation, count time series, observation-driven models, parameter-driven-models, particle methods, zero-inflation

1. Introduction

Count time series with excess zeros are commonly encountered in a variety of research fields. In principle, both zero-inflation and autocorrelation may be present in such series. Failing to adequately accommodate temporal dynamics and a high frequency of zeros can lead to incorrect inferential conclusions. Developing a general modeling framework that accounts for these characteristics poses a daunting challenge.

In characterizing data comprised of counts with excess zeroes, two types of models are commonplace: a model that assumes a Poisson mixture distribution, and a model that assumes a binomial mixture distribution. A considerable literature exists for regression models based on the zero-inflated Poisson (ZIP) distribution to deal with count data that are independently distributed [1]. Many researchers have extended the classical ZIP model to analyze repeated measures data by incorporating independent random effects, as these can account for within-subject correlation and between-subject heterogeneity [2, 3]. To deal with count time series with excess zeros, some researchers have proposed parameter-driven ZIP models that accommodate the temporal dynamics by incorporating correlated random effects, which can be represented by a latent autoregressive process [4, 5]. However, for data arising from a binomial mixture distribution, a survey of the literature for analogous frameworks reflects an absence of work dealing with binomial time series with excess zeros. To handle such data, we propose two general classes of models: a class of observation-driven ZIB (ODZIB) models, and a class of parameter-driven ZIB (PDZIB) models. The inspiration for the two proposed modeling frameworks arises from the work of Hall [6], Yau et al. [4], and Yang et al. [5, 7].

Depending on how the temporal correlation is conceptualized, count time series models can be classified as either observation-driven or parameter-driven [8]. For the former, serial correlation is characterized by specifying that the conditional mean of the current response depends explicitly on its past values [9–14]. For the latter, such correlation is characterized through an unobservable underlying process [15–19]. In this chapter, we employ the partial likelihood framework to formulate the ODZIB model, as this largely simplifies parameter estimation with negligible loss of information. The ODZIB model can be viewed as an extension of the observation-driven binomial model [20]. Such a model is often fit using standard statistical software available for classical ZIB regression models. For the PDZIB model, we employ a state-space approach, as this framework allows for the investigation of the underlying latent processes that govern the temporal correlation and zero inflation. Due to the non-Gaussian distribution of the count response, and the nonlinear nature of modeling its conditional mean, traditional state-space methods using the Kalman filter and the Kalman smoother are not available for parameter estimation. We thereby adopt a Monte Carlo Expectation Maximization (MCEM) algorithm based on the particle filter [21] and the particle smoother [22].

The remainder of the chapter is organized as follows. In Section 2, we briefly introduce a class of observation-driven models for a zero-inflated count time series that arises from a binomial mixture. Section 3 proposes a class of parameter-driven models in the state-space framework, and presents the MCEM algorithm devised to fit such models. A comprehensive simulation study is provided in Section 4. In Section 5, we illustrate the proposed methodology through a practical application. Section 6 concludes with a brief discussion.

2. Observation-driven ZIB models

2.1. ZIB models

A popular approach for modeling independent zero-inflated binomial data is the ZIB model proposed by Hall [6]. This model assumes that data are generated from a mixture distribution, comprised of a binomial distribution and a degenerate distribution at zero. For response variable Y, let y_i denote the observation for subject i, $i = 1, 2, \ldots, n$. The probability mass function for the ZIB model is defined as follows:

$$f(y_i|\pi_i, \omega_i) = \begin{cases} \omega_i + (1-\omega_i)(1-\pi_i)^{n_i}, & \text{if } y_i = 0, \\ (1-\omega_i)\binom{n_i}{y_i}\pi_i^{y_i}(1-\pi_i)^{n_i - y_i}, & \text{if } y_i > 0. \end{cases} \tag{1}$$

Here, ω_i is the zero-inflation parameter, and π_i is the intensity parameter representing the probability of success, both modeled via logit link functions:

$$\text{logit}(\omega_i) = \mathbf{x}_{i1}^T \gamma, \tag{2}$$

$$\text{logit}(\pi_i) = \mathbf{x}_{i2}^T \beta. \tag{3}$$

In the preceding, $\mathbf{x}_{i1}$ and $\mathbf{x}_{i2}$ are sets of explanatory variables for the corresponding vectors of regression coefficients γ and β. The Expectation Maximization (EM) algorithm or the Newton-Raphson method can be used to obtain the parameter estimates.

2.2. Observation-driven ZIB models

In this section, we introduce an autoregressive model for binomial time series with excess zeros based on an observation-driven approach. We retain the same model structure as that introduced in Section 2.1 to account for the binomial mixture, yet we employ lagged responses as covariates to resolve the temporal correlation. The proposed model can be viewed as an extension of the binomial time series model presented by Kedem and Fokianos [20].

Let y_t denote the binomial count response. Define the information set

$$\mathcal{F}_{t-1} = \sigma\{y_{t-1}, y_{t-2}, \ldots, \mathbf{x}_t\} \tag{4}$$

so as to represent all that is known to the observer at time t about the response and any relevant covariate processes. Thus, the vector $\mathbf{x}_t$ represents a collection of past and possibly present time-dependent covariates that are observed at time $t-1$. In the present setting, $\mathbf{x}_t$ may be viewed as either fixed or random. Conditioning on the information $\mathcal{F}_{t-1}$, the response is assumed to follow a ZIB distribution with probability mass function defined as follows:

$$f_t(y_t|\mathcal{F}_{t-1};\pi_t,\omega_t) = \begin{cases} \omega_t + (1-\omega_t)(1-\pi_t)^{n_t}, & \text{if } y_t = 0, \\ (1-\omega_t)\binom{n_t}{y_t}\pi_t^{y_t}(1-\pi_t)^{n_t-y_t}, & \text{if } y_t > 0. \end{cases} \tag{5}$$

Similarly, ω_t and π_t represent the zero-inflation parameter and the intensity parameter, respectively. Both parameters are modeled via logit link functions. Specifically, we assume that

$$\text{logit}(\omega_t) = \mathbf{x}_{1,t}^T\gamma, \tag{6}$$

$$\text{logit}(\pi_t) = \mathbf{x}_{2,t}^T\beta + \sum_{j=1}^{p}\phi_j y_{t-j}, \tag{7}$$

where $\mathbf{x}_{1,t}$ and $\mathbf{x}_{2,t}$ are sets of time-dependent explanatory variables for the corresponding vectors of regression coefficients γ and β, and $\boldsymbol{\phi}=[\phi_1,\ldots,\phi_p]^T$ is a vector of autoregressive coefficients corresponding to the past responses $[y_{t-1},\ldots,y_{t-p}]^T$. For simplicity, we treat the zero-inflation parameter ω_t as a constant that does not vary over time. In the observation-driven ZIB model, serial correlation is accommodated by introducing lagged values of the response to the linear predictor.

The partial data likelihood of the observed series is

$$\text{PL}(\boldsymbol{\theta}) = \prod_{t=1}^{n} f_t(y_t|\mathcal{F}_{t-1}), \tag{8}$$

where $\boldsymbol{\theta}=[\boldsymbol{\beta},\boldsymbol{\phi},\boldsymbol{\gamma}]^T$ is the vector of unknown parameters. The partial likelihood does not require the derivation of the joint distribution of the response and the covariates, and is largely simplified relative to the full likelihood. This approach facilitates conditional inference for a fairly large class of transitional processes where the response depends on its past values.

The log-likelihood for the observation-driven ZIB model is

$$\log \text{PL}(\boldsymbol{\theta}) = \sum_{t=1}^{n} \log\left\{\omega_t I_{(y_t=0)} + (1-\omega_t)\binom{n_t}{y_t}\pi_t^{y_t}(1-\pi_t)^{n_t-y_t}\right\}. \tag{9}$$

The vector $\hat{\theta}$ obtained by maximizing the partial likelihood is called the maximum partial likelihood estimator (MPLE).

Similar to Section 2.1, we can apply the EM algorithm or the Newton–Raphson method to obtain the MPLE. This estimation process can be conveniently conducted in practice using standard software tools available for fitting classical ZIB models. In SAS, we can use the finite mixture models (FMM) procedure to fit the observation-driven ZIB model, while we can use function gamlss in the package generalized additive models for location scale and shape (GAMLSS) for model fitting in R. Hypothesis testing for $\boldsymbol{\theta}$ is carried out through the partial likelihood method. The common tests are based on Wald statistics, score statistics, and partial likelihood ratio statistics. All of these tests are conducted based on the framework for classical maximum likelihood inference.

3. Parameter-driven ZIB models

3.1. Model formulation

An alternative approach to describe binomial time series with excess zeros is based on parameter-driven ZIB models. This class of models can be viewed as an analogue of the parameter-driven ZIP models presented by Yang et al. [5].

To account for temporal dynamics in the series, we introduce a latent stationary autoregressive process $\{z_t\}$ of order p (AR(p)):

$$z_t = \sum_{i=1}^{p} \phi_i z_{t-i} + \varepsilon_t. \tag{10}$$

Here, ε_t is a Gaussian white noise process with a mean of 0 and a variance of σ^2. Additionally, ϕ_i explains how the past state z_{t-i} relates to the current state z_t.

Let y_t be the observed count at time t. Given the current state z_t, the positive count response y_t is assumed to follow a ZIB distribution with a probability mass function defined as

$$f_t(y_t|z_t; \pi_t, \omega_t) = \begin{cases} \omega_t + (1-\omega_t)(1-\pi_t)^{n_t}, & \text{if } y_t = 0, \\ (1-\omega_t)\binom{n_t}{y_t}\pi_t^{y_t}(1-\pi_t)^{n_t-y_t}, & \text{if } y_t > 0. \end{cases} \tag{11}$$

Similar to the previous model parameterizations, ω_t and π_t represent the zero-inflation parameter and the intensity parameter, respectively. Both parameters are modeled via logit link functions and could be time-varying. To relate the intensity parameter π_t to the latent component z_t, we use the model

$$\text{logit}(\pi_t) = \mathbf{x}_t^{\mathrm{T}}\beta + z_t, \tag{12}$$

where $\mathbf{x}_t$ is a set of explanatory variables observed at time t, and β is the corresponding vector of regression coefficients. In the present setting, $\mathbf{x}_t$ is assumed fixed. For simplicity, we treat the zero-inflation parameter ω_t as a constant that does not vary over time.

For the parameter-driven ZIB model, the conditional mean and variance of the response variable y_t are given by

$$\text{E}(Y_t|z_t) = (1\text{-}\omega_t)n_t\pi_t, \tag{13}$$

$$\text{Var}(Y_t|z_t) = (1\text{-}\omega_t)n_t\pi_t[1\text{-}\pi_t(1\text{-}\omega_t n_t)]. \tag{14}$$

Obviously, the presence of zero-inflation ($\omega_t > 0$) not only explains the excess zeros in the series, but also introduces overdispersion. Additionally, the correlated random effects z_t contribute to the extra variance.

We can write the parameter-driven ZIB model in the following hierarchical form:

$$\mathbf{s}_t|\mathbf{s}_{t-1} \sim \mathcal{N}_p(\mathbf{\Phi s}_{t-1}, \mathbf{\Sigma}), \tag{15}$$

$$u_t \sim \text{Bernoulli}(\omega), \tag{16}$$

$$y_t|\mathbf{s}_t, u_t \sim \text{Binomial}(n_t, (1-u_t)\pi_t), \tag{17}$$

where $\mathbf{s}_t = [z_t, \ldots, z_{t-p+1}]^T$ is a p-dimensional state vector with z_t being its first element, u_t is an unobservable membership indicator that determines whether the response comes from a degenerate distribution or an ordinary binomial distribution, $\boldsymbol{\Phi}$ is an unknown transition matrix, and $\mathbf{\Sigma}$ is the covariance matrix of the state noise process $\mathbf{s}_t$. The process $\mathbf{s}_t$ is initiated with a normal vector $\mathbf{s}_0$ that has mean $\boldsymbol{\mu}_0$ and covariance matrix $\mathbf{\Sigma}_0$. Diffuse priors are often assigned to $\mathbf{s}_0$ in practice. Given the two unobserved latent processes $\mathbf{s}_t$ and u_t, we can conceptualize a sequential update of the response variable y_t.

In Eq. (15), $\boldsymbol{\Phi}$ and $\mathbf{\Sigma}$ are $p \times p$ matrices defined as follows:

$$\boldsymbol{\Phi} = \begin{bmatrix} \phi_1 & \phi_2 & \cdots & \phi_{p-1} & \phi_p \\ 1 & 0 & \cdots & 0 & 0 \\ 0 & 1 & \cdots & 0 & 0 \\ \vdots & \vdots & \ddots & \vdots & \vdots \\ 0 & 0 & \cdots & 1 & 0 \end{bmatrix}, \quad \mathbf{\Sigma} = \begin{bmatrix} \sigma^2 & 0 & \cdots & 0 & 0 \\ 0 & 0 & \cdots & 0 & 0 \\ \vdots & \vdots & \ddots & \vdots & \vdots \\ 0 & 0 & \cdots & 0 & 0 \\ 0 & 0 & \cdots & 0 & 0 \end{bmatrix}. \tag{18}$$

The transition matrix $\boldsymbol{\Phi}$ governs the generation of the state vector $\mathbf{s}_t$ from the past state $\mathbf{s}_{t-1}$ for time points $t = 1, \ldots, n$. Note that the covariance matrix $\mathbf{\Sigma}$ in Eq. (18) is not positive definite. This is both legitimate and common in the state-space modeling approach.

3.2. Parameter estimation via MCEM algorithm

3.2.1. Model fitting

To fit the parameter-driven ZIB model, in principle, one would first obtain the marginal likelihood of the observed data $y_1, \ldots, y_n$ by integrating out unobserved components. However, because of the presence of correlated random effects and the non-Gaussian nature of the response, these integrals are not analytically tractable. Therefore, approximations or numerical solutions for the maximum likelihood estimates (MLEs) are necessary. Instead of obtaining the MLEs based on the marginal likelihood, we propose an EM algorithm [23], which relies on the complete-data likelihood to estimate the parameters.

Let $y_{1:t} = [y_1, y_2, \ldots, y_t]^T$ denote the vector of observed data from time point 1 through t. In a similar fashion, let $\mathbf{s}_{0:t} = [\mathbf{s}_0, \mathbf{s}_1, \ldots, \mathbf{s}_t]^T$ and $u_{1:t} = [u_1, u_2, \ldots, u_t]^T$ denote the vectors of two latent processes, respectively, over the same time frame. Let $\boldsymbol{\theta} = [\omega, \beta^T, \phi^T, \sigma]^T$ denote the vector of unknown parameters.

To develop an EM algorithm for parameter estimation of the mixture model, Eqs. (15)–(17), we begin by formulating the complete-data likelihood; i.e., the joint density of $\mathbf{s}_{0:n}$, $u_{1:n}$, and $y_{1:n}$. The two latent processes $\mathbf{s}_{0:n}$ and $u_{1:n}$ are considered missing. Based on the state-space representation, the complete-data likelihood may be orthogonally decomposed as follows:

$$\begin{aligned} L_c(\boldsymbol{\theta}) &= f\left(\mathbf{s}_{0:n}, u_{1:n}, y_{1:n}\right) \\ &= f(\mathbf{s}_{0:n}, u_{1:n}) f\left(y_{1:n} | \mathbf{s}_{0:n}, u_{1:n}\right) \\ &= f(\mathbf{s}_{0:n}) f(u_{1:n}) f\left(y_{1:n} | \mathbf{s}_{0:n}, u_{1:n}\right) \\ &= f(\mathbf{s}_0) \prod_{t=1}^{n} f(\mathbf{s}_t | \mathbf{s}_{t-1}) \prod_{t=1}^{n} f(u_t) \prod_{t=1}^{n} f\left(y_t | \mathbf{s}_t, u_t\right). \end{aligned} \tag{19}$$

Here, the initial state vector $\mathbf{s}_0$ is assumed to be normally distributed with mean vector μ_0 and covariance matrix $\boldsymbol{\Sigma}_0$. In implementing the algorithm, we set $\boldsymbol{\mu}_0 = 0$ and $\boldsymbol{\Sigma}_0 = \mathbf{I}_p$, as the effect of the starting values of $\boldsymbol{\mu}_0$ and $\boldsymbol{\Sigma}_0$ on the estimated parameters $\boldsymbol{\theta}$ is negligible.

Up to an additive constant, the complete-data log-likelihood is given by

$$\begin{aligned} l_c(\boldsymbol{\theta}) = &-\frac{n}{2} \log \sigma^2 - \frac{1}{2\sigma^2} \sum_{t=1}^{n} \left(z_t - \phi^T \mathbf{s}_{t-1}\right)^2 \\ &+ \sum_{t=1}^{n} \{u_t \log \omega + (1 - u_t) \log (1 - \omega)\} \\ &+ \sum_{t=1}^{n} (1 - u_t) \left\{y_t \mathbf{x}_t^T \beta - n_t \log \left(1 + \exp \left(\mathbf{x}_t^T \beta + z_t\right)\right)\right\}. \end{aligned} \tag{20}$$

The complete-data log-likelihood can be described as the sum of three functionally independent parameter forms, such that $l_c(\boldsymbol{\theta}) = l(\phi, \sigma \mid \mathbf{s}_t) + l(\omega \mid u_t) + l(\beta \mid \mathbf{s}_t, u_t)$, resulting in ease of the maximization in the M-step for each set of parameters.

With the implementation of the EM algorithm, we need to compute the conditional expectation of $l_c(\boldsymbol{\theta})$ given the observed data $y_{1:n}$. Deriving an analytical form for the conditional expectation is not feasible due to the nonlinear forms in the latent variables and the response, as well as the non-Gaussian distributions of the response and the latent indicators. There are many numerical methods available to approximate the conditional expectation, such as the Markov chain Monte Carlo (MCMC) algorithm [24], the MCEM algorithm [7, 25], the penalized quasi-likelihood (PQL) method [2], and integrated nested Laplace approximations (INLA) [26]. Following Yang et al. [5], we develop an MCEM algorithm to approximate the conditional expectation.

To simplify the notation, we let $\mathbf{A}_t^{(j)}$, $\mathbf{b}_t^{(j)}$, $c_t^{(j)}$, $d_t^{(j)}$, $e_t^{(j)}$, and $f_t^{(j)}$ denote the conditional expectations of $\mathbf{s}_{t-1}\mathbf{s}_{t-1}^T$, $z_t\mathbf{s}_{t-1}$, z_t^2, u_t, $(1 - u_t) \log \left(1 + \exp \left(\mathbf{x}_t^T \beta + z_t\right)\right)$, and $(1 - u_t)\exp \left(\mathbf{x}_t^T \beta + z_t\right) / \left(1 + \exp \left(\mathbf{x}_t^T \beta + z_t\right)\right)$ evaluated at $\boldsymbol{\theta}^{(j)}$, respectively. In the Monte Carlo E-step of the algorithm, we first compute the conditional expectation of $l_c(\boldsymbol{\theta})$:

$$\begin{aligned} Q\left(\boldsymbol{\theta}|\boldsymbol{\theta}^{(j)}\right) &= E\left\{l_c(\boldsymbol{\theta})|y_{1:n}, \boldsymbol{\theta}^{(j)}\right\} \\ &= -\frac{n}{2}\log\sigma^2 - \frac{1}{2\sigma^2}\sum_{t=1}^{n}\left(c_t^{(j)} - 2\phi^T\mathbf{b}_t^{(j)} + \phi^T\mathbf{A}_t^{(j)}\phi\right) \\ &+ \sum_{t=1}^{n}\left\{d_t^{(j)}\log\omega + \left(1 - d_t^{(j)}\right)\log(1-\omega)\right\} \\ &+ \sum_{t=1}^{n}\left\{\left(1 - d_t^{(j)}\right)y_t\mathbf{x}_t^T\beta - n_t e_t^{(j)}\right\}, \end{aligned} \tag{21}$$

where particle filtering and smoothing techniques are used to approximate the conditional expectations. The details of the particle methods for the parameter-driven ZIB model are presented in Section 3.3.

The following partial derivatives are applied to maximize $Q(\boldsymbol{\theta} \mid \boldsymbol{\theta}^{(j)})$ in the M-step:

$$\frac{\partial Q}{\partial\omega} = \frac{1}{\omega}\sum_{t=1}^{n}d_t^{(j)} - \frac{1}{1-\omega}\sum_{t=1}^{n}\left(1 - d_t^{(j)}\right), \tag{22}$$

$$\frac{\partial Q}{\partial\phi} = \frac{1}{\sigma^2}\sum_{t=1}^{n}\left(\mathbf{b}_t^{(j)} - \mathbf{A}_t^{(j)}\phi\right), \tag{23}$$

$$\frac{\partial Q}{\partial\sigma} = -\frac{n}{\sigma} + \frac{1}{\sigma^3}\sum_{t=1}^{n}\left(c_t^{(j)} - 2\phi^T\mathbf{b}_t^{(j)} + \phi^T\mathbf{A}_t^{(j)}\phi\right), \tag{24}$$

$$\begin{aligned} \frac{\partial Q}{\partial\beta} &= \frac{\partial E\left\{l_c(\boldsymbol{\theta})|y_{1:n}, \boldsymbol{\theta}^{(j)}\right\}}{\partial\beta} \\ &= E\left(\frac{\partial l_c(\boldsymbol{\theta})}{\partial\beta}|y_{1:n}, \boldsymbol{\theta}^{(j)}\right) \\ &= E\left(\sum_{t=1}^{n}\left\{(1-u_t)y_t - n_t(1-u_t)\frac{\exp\left(\mathbf{x}_t^T\beta + z_t\right)}{1+\exp\left(\mathbf{x}_t^T\beta + z_t\right)}\right\}\mathbf{x}_t|y_{1:n}, \boldsymbol{\theta}^{(j)}\right) \\ &= \sum_{t=1}^{n}\left\{\left(1 - d_t^{(j)}\right)y_t - n_t f_t^{(j)}\right\}\mathbf{x}_t. \end{aligned} \tag{25}$$

At the jth iteration, we obtain the following closed-form solutions for $\omega^{(j+1)}$, $\phi^{(j+1)}$, and $\sigma^{(j+1)}$:

$$\omega^{(j+1)} = \frac{1}{n}\sum_{t=1}^{n}d_t^{(j)}, \tag{26}$$

$$\phi^{(j+1)} = \left(\sum_{t=1}^{n}\mathbf{A}_t^{(j)}\right)^{-1}\sum_{t=1}^{n}\mathbf{b}_t^{(j)}, \tag{27}$$

$$\sigma^{(j+1)} = \sqrt{\frac{1}{n}\left\{\sum_{t=1}^{n} a_t^{(j)} - \left(\sum_{t=1}^{n} \mathbf{b}_t^{(j)}\right)^T \left(\sum_{t=1}^{n} \mathbf{A}_t^{(j)}\right)^{-1} \sum_{t=1}^{n} \mathbf{b}_t^{(j)}\right\}}. \quad (28)$$

In addition, we can easily compute $\beta^{(j+1)}$ through iterative algorithms such as Broyden-Fletcher-Goldfarb-Shanno (BFGS). Once we acquire the particle smoothers from the smoothing step, we can obtain the MCEM estimates by plugging in the sample means of the functions of particle smoothers for the conditional expectations.

To offset the slow convergence and to reduce the computational cost of the EM algorithm, starting with good initial parameters is essential. For the proposed parameter-driven ZIB model, we suggest using the estimates of the parameters from a classical ZIB model or from the observation-driven ZIB model discussed in Section 2.2.

3.2.2. Standard errors

Standard errors of the parameter estimators can be obtained either by using the inverse of the observed information to approximate the variance/covariance matrix, or by employing a collection of replicated bootstrapped parameter estimates. Given the computational cost of the MCEM algorithm, we pursue the first approach by applying Louis's formula [27] to compute the observed information matrix $\mathbf{I}_o(\boldsymbol{\theta})$. Based on the missing information principle, we have

$$\mathbf{I}_o(\boldsymbol{\theta}) = \mathbf{I}_c(\boldsymbol{\theta}) - \mathbf{I}_m(\boldsymbol{\theta}), \quad (29)$$

where $\mathbf{I}_c(\boldsymbol{\theta})$ and $\mathbf{I}_m(\boldsymbol{\theta})$ are defined as follows:

$$\mathbf{I}_c(\boldsymbol{\theta}) = E\left(-\frac{\partial^2 l_c}{\partial\boldsymbol{\theta}\partial\boldsymbol{\theta}^T}|y_{1:n}\right), \quad (30)$$

$$\mathbf{I}_m(\boldsymbol{\theta}) = E\left(\frac{\partial l_c}{\partial\boldsymbol{\theta}}\frac{\partial l_c}{\partial\boldsymbol{\theta}^T}|y_{1:n}\right) - E\left(\frac{\partial l_c}{\partial\boldsymbol{\theta}}|y_{1:n}\right)E\left(\frac{\partial l_c}{\partial\boldsymbol{\theta}^T}|y_{1:n}\right). \quad (31)$$

The first-order derivatives of $l_c(\boldsymbol{\theta})$ are given by

$$\frac{\partial l_c}{\partial\omega} = \frac{1}{\omega}\sum_{t=1}^{n} u_t - \frac{1}{1-\omega}\sum_{t=1}^{n}(1-u_t), \quad (32)$$

$$\frac{\partial l_c}{\partial\beta} = \sum_{t=1}^{n}(1-u_t)\left\{y_t - n_t\frac{\exp\left(\mathbf{x}_t^T\beta + z_t\right)}{1+\exp\left(\mathbf{x}_t^T\beta + z_t\right)}\right\}\mathbf{x}_t, \quad (33)$$

$$\frac{\partial l_c}{\partial\phi} = \frac{1}{\sigma^2}\sum_{t=1}^{n}\left(z_t - \phi^T\mathbf{s}_{t-1}\right)\mathbf{s}_{t-1}, \quad (34)$$

$$\frac{\partial l_c}{\partial \sigma} = -\frac{n}{\sigma} + \frac{1}{\sigma^3}\sum_{t=1}^{n}\left(z_t - \phi^T \mathbf{s}_{t-1}\right)^2. \tag{35}$$

The second-order derivatives of $l_c(\theta)$ are given by

$$\frac{\partial^2 l_c}{\partial \omega \partial \omega} = -\frac{1}{\omega^2}\sum_{t=1}^{n} u_t - \frac{1}{(1-\omega)^2}\sum_{t=1}^{n}(1-u_t), \tag{36}$$

$$\frac{\partial^2 l_c}{\partial \beta \partial \beta^T} = -\sum_{t=1}^{n}(1-u_t)n_t \frac{\exp\left(\mathbf{x}_t^T\beta + z_t\right)}{\left[1+\exp\left(\mathbf{x}_t^T\beta + z_t\right)\right]^2}\mathbf{x}_t\mathbf{x}_t^T, \tag{37}$$

$$\frac{\partial^2 l_c}{\partial \phi \partial \phi^T} = -\frac{1}{\sigma^2}\sum_{t=1}^{n}\mathbf{s}_{t-1}\mathbf{s}_{t-1}^T, \tag{38}$$

$$\frac{\partial^2 l_c}{\partial \sigma \partial \sigma} = \frac{n}{\sigma^2} - \frac{3}{\sigma^4}\sum_{t=1}^{n}\left(z_t - \phi^T \mathbf{s}_{t-1}\right)^2, \tag{39}$$

$$\frac{\partial^2 l_c}{\partial \phi \partial \sigma} = -\frac{2}{\sigma^3}\sum_{t=1}^{n}\left(z_t - \phi^T \mathbf{s}_{t-1}\right)\mathbf{s}_{t-1}. \tag{40}$$

Again, particle filtering and smoothing techniques are used to approximate the conditional expectations in $\mathbf{I}_c(\boldsymbol{\theta})$ and $\mathbf{I}_m(\boldsymbol{\theta})$.

In principle, the variance/covariance matrix can be approximated by taking the inverse of the observed information matrix. However, the computation of the inverse is often problematic. As indicated by Kim and Stoffer [25], the observed information matrix is not guaranteed to be numerically positive definite. To address this problem, we slightly modify Louis's formula by introducing a slack variable ξ, such that

$$\mathbf{I}_o(\boldsymbol{\theta}) = \mathbf{I}_c(\boldsymbol{\theta}) - (1-\xi)\mathbf{I}_m(\boldsymbol{\theta}), \tag{41}$$

where ξ is a non-negative variable ranging from 0 to 1. In practice, we can iteratively increase this value until the observed information matrix can be inverted.

3.3. Particle methods

Particle filtering [21] and particle smoothing [22] belong to the class of sequential Monte Carlo (SMC) methods [28]. These particle methods can be viewed as the non-linear and non-Gaussian extensions of the popular Kalman filtering and smoothing algorithms for traditional state-space models. Rather than yielding a single estimate for the filter or the smoother, as computed through conventional Kalman filtering and smoothing, particle methods provide a set of particles with associated weights to approximate the conditional densities governing the filters and smoothers. Implemented via sequential importance sampling (SIS), in the E-step of the EM algorithm, particle methods provide approximate solutions to the intractable integrals corresponding to the conditional expectations of functions of the latent components given the observed data. However, sample degeneracy is a typical problem for SIS methods. In particular, degeneracy occurs when particles have small weights or even negative weights, rendering their contributions to the conditional density negligible. Resampling (e.g., bootstrapping) offers a recourse for eliminating particles with negligible effects. Kim [29] provides an elegant treatment of particle filtering and smoothing for state-space models.

Particle filtering

For the parameter-driven ZIB model, we implement particle filtering by first generating $\mathbf{s}_{0|0}^{(i)} \sim \mathcal{N}_p(\boldsymbol{\mu}_0, \boldsymbol{\Sigma}_0)$. Then for $t = 1, \ldots, n$:

(F.1) Generate $\mathbf{s}_{t|t-1}^{(i)} \sim \mathcal{N}_p\left(\boldsymbol{\Phi}\mathbf{s}_{t-1|t-1}^{(i)}, \boldsymbol{\Sigma}\right)$ and $u_{t|t-1}^{(i)} \sim \text{Bernoulli}(\omega)$.

(F.2) Compute the filtering weights

$$q_{t|t-1}^{(i)} \propto \binom{n_t}{y_t}\left(\left(1-u_{t|t-1}^{(i)}\right)\pi_{t|t-1}^{(i)}\right)^{y_t}\left(1-\left(1-u_{t|t-1}^{(i)}\right)\pi_{t|t-1}^{(i)}\right)^{n_t-y_t}, \tag{42}$$

where $\text{logit}\left(\pi_{t|t-1}^{(i)}\right) = \mathrm{x}_t^{\mathrm{T}}\beta + z_{t|t-1}^{(i)}$ and $z_{t|t-1}^{(i)}$ is the first element of $\mathbf{s}_{t|t-1}^{(i)}$.

(F.3) Generate $\left(\mathbf{s}_{t|t}^{(i)}, u_{t|t}^{(i)}\right)$ by resampling $\left(\mathbf{s}_{t|t-1}^{(i)}, u_{t|t-1}^{(i)}\right)$ with replacement based on the preceding filtering weights.

As a byproduct of the particle filtering, the observed-data log-likelihood can be approximated by

$$\sum_{t=1}^{n} \log\left(\frac{1}{N}\sum_{i=1}^{N} q_{t|t-1}^{(i)}\right), \tag{43}$$

where N is the number of particles in the filtering step.

Particle smoothing

Next, we employ the particle smoothing algorithm proposed by Godsill et al. [22] to obtain the conditional expectations of the functions of the latent variables given the complete set of observed data. In this step, we first choose $\left(\mathbf{s}_{n|n}^{(r)}, u_{n|n}^{(r)}\right) = \left(\mathbf{s}_{n|n}^{(i)}, u_{n|n}^{(i)}\right)$ with probability $q_{n|n-1}^{(i)}$. Then for $t = n-1, \ldots, 1$:

(S.1) Calculate the smoothing weights

$$q_{t|n}^{(i)} \propto q_{t|t-1}^{(i)} \exp\left\{-\frac{1}{2\sigma^2}\left(z_{t+1|n}^{(i)} - \phi^T\mathbf{s}_{t|t}^{(i)}\right)^2\right\}\omega^{u_{t+1|n}^{(i)}}(1-\omega)^{1-u_{t+1|n}^{(i)}}. \tag{44}$$

(S.2) Choose $\left(\mathbf{s}_{t|n}^{(r)}, u_{t|n}^{(r)}\right) = \left(\mathbf{s}_{t|t}^{(i)}, u_{t|t}^{(i)}\right)$ with probability $q_{t|n}^{(i)}$.

We obtain independent realizations by repeating the preceding process for $r = 1, \ldots, R$.

4. Simulation studies

In this section, we investigate through simulation two salient issues pertaining to the proposed modeling frameworks. In the first part, we explore the convergence of the MCEM algorithm through simulated examples, and investigate the finite sample distributional properties of the parameter estimators through a comprehensive simulation study. In the second part, we present a simulation study to compare the performance of the proposed ZIB models to their counterpart ZIP models in characterizing zero-inflated count time series.

4.1. Evaluation of the MCEM algorithm

We consider time series data simulated from four different parameter-driven models: ZIB + AR (2), binomial + AR(2), ZIB + AR(1), and binomial + AR(1). The sample size is set to 300 and the number of cases n_t for each time point is set to 30. All of the models feature the following linear predictor:

$$\text{logit}(\pi_t) = \beta_0 + \beta_1 x_{1,t} + z_t, \tag{45}$$

where $x_{1,t}$ is a covariate series generated from a standard uniform distribution. The true parameters for the most complicated model ZIB + AR(2) are as follows:

$$\omega = 0.3, \beta_0 = 2, \beta_1 = -3, \phi_1 = 0.8, \phi_2 = -0.6, \text{and } \sigma = 0.5. \tag{46}$$

For the rest of the models considered, the corresponding parameters are set to 0 if no such a form is included. Autoregressive (AR) coefficients are chosen to assure stationarity of the series. In fitting the models, the number of particle filters (N) is set to 500 and the number of particle smoothers (R) is set to 300. We stop the MCEM algorithm after 300 iterations. **Table 1** presents the parameter estimates for the simulated data corresponding to the four parameter-driven models.

Figure 1 shows the trace plots of the log-likelihood for the four fitted parameter-driven models. Note that the log-likelihood of the MCEM algorithm is not strictly increasing at each iteration due to the introduction of Monte Carlo errors. However, the log-likelihood stabilizes after a few dozen iterations with slight fluctuations around the maximal value. **Figure 2** shows the trace plots for the parameter estimates from the most complex fitted model, ZIB + AR(2). The plots indicate that the parameter estimates converge to the MLEs quickly with negligible

	ω	β_0	β_1	ϕ_1	ϕ_2	σ
True	0.300	2.000	−3.000	0.800	−0.600	0.500
Binomial + AR(1)		1.984	−2.968	0.800		0.540
ZIB + AR(1)	0.283	2.124	−2.930	0.781		0.563
Binomial + AR(2)		1.989	−3.012	0.852	−0.620	0.499
ZIB + AR(2)	0.293	1.992	−2.872	0.831	−0.576	0.506

Table 1. True and estimated parameters for the simulated examples.

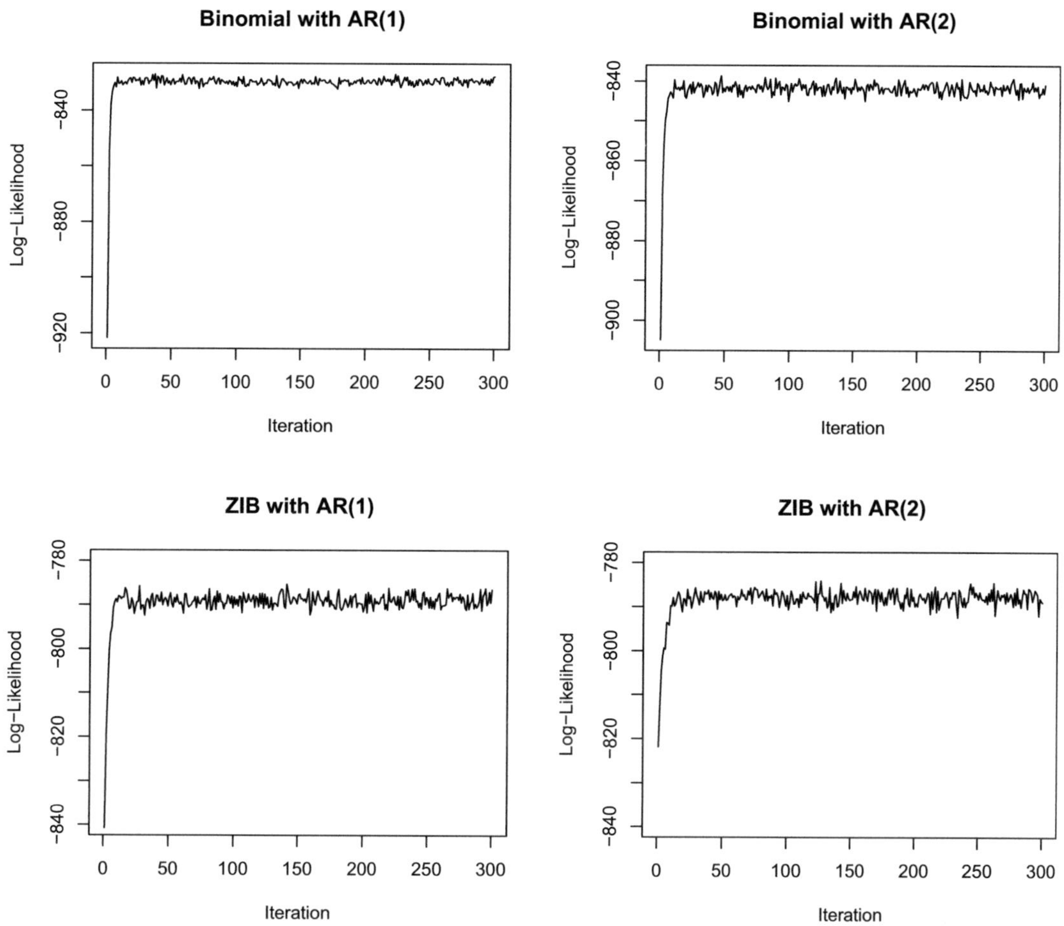

Figure 1. Trace plots of the log-likelihood for fitted parameter-driven models based on simulated data.

fluctuations. The trace plots of the parameter estimates for the other three models exhibit similar patterns (results not shown). In practice, we recommend always checking the trace plots of the estimates to assess convergence of the MCEM algorithm.

We next investigate the finite sample distributional properties of the parameter estimators from the MCEM algorithm. We consider the same parameter-driven models presented in the preceding simulated example. For each model structure, 500 replications are generated based on sample sizes of 200 and 500. We employ the proposed MCEM algorithm to fit models based on these replications, and record the subsequent parameter estimates and their standard errors. As the MECM algorithm is computationally expensive, we set the number of particles for both filters and smoothers to 200, and the stopping iteration for the MCEM algorithm at 100. In **Tables 2–3**, we provide the simulation results based on the most complex model, ZIB + AR(2).

In general, the mean and median of the estimates converge to the true parameters, with a minor degree of negative bias associated with the estimation of the AR coefficients. The empirical

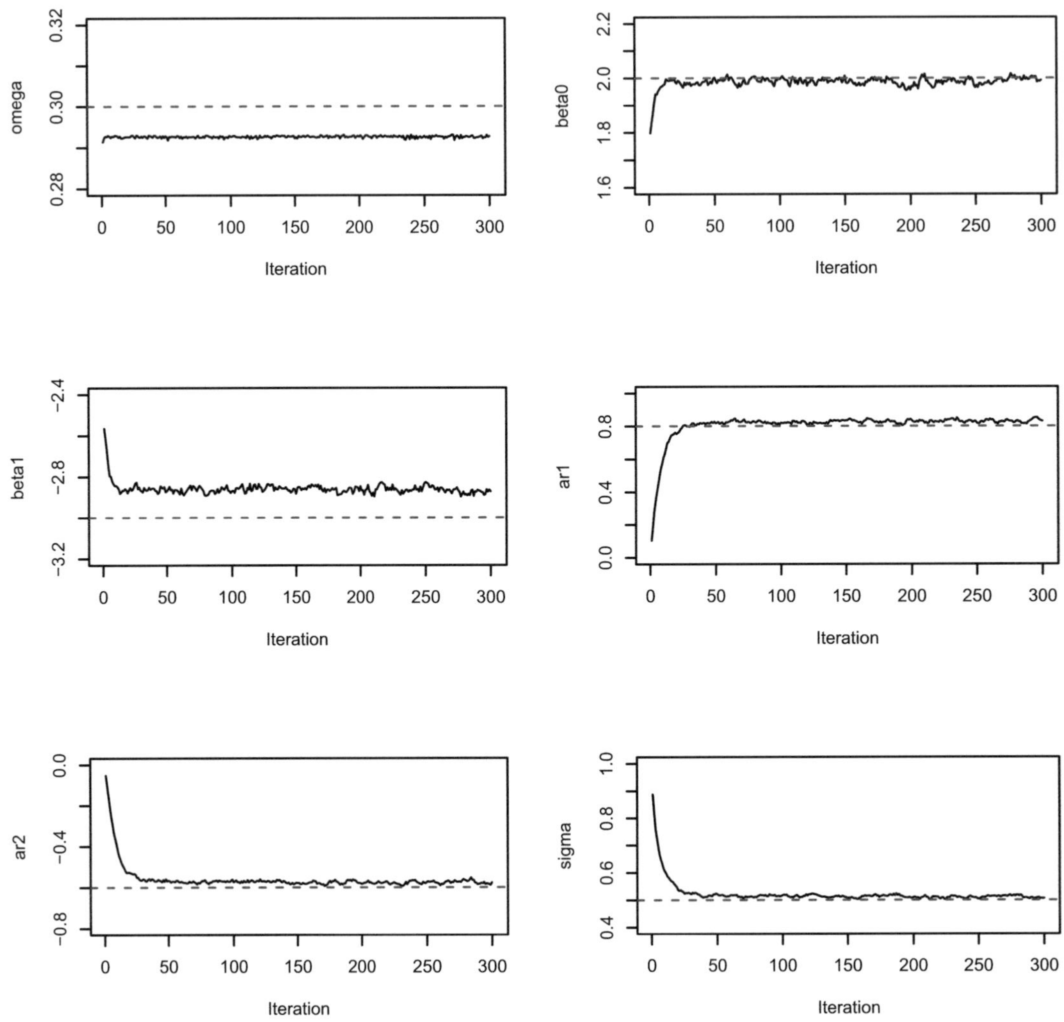

Figure 2. Trace plots of the estimated parameters for the fitted ZIB + AR(2) model.

standard deviations (ESDs) are reasonably close to the average asymptotic standard errors (ASEs). Therefore, the standard errors calculated by Louis's method prove to be sufficient. As the sample size increases from 200 to 500, the bias for the estimation of the AR coefficients attenuates, and the standard errors tend to diminish. The two behaviors indicate that weak convergence holds. The results for the other three parameter-driven models are analogous to those presented in **Tables 2–3**. **Tables 4–9** show the simulation results for the binomial + AR(2) model, ZIB + AR(1) model, and binomial + AR(1) model, respectively.

The normality of the parameter estimators is assessed by Q-Q plots based on the sets of replicated estimates (figures not shown). For the most complex ZIB + AR(2) model, approximate normality holds for the finite sample distribution of the parameter estimators, with

	True	Mean	Median	ESD	ASE
ω	0.300	0.299	0.295	0.032	0.032
β_0	2.000	1.999	1.992	0.139	0.166
β_1	−3.000	−2.992	−2.980	0.235	0.224
ϕ_1	0.800	0.743	0.757	0.120	0.165
ϕ_2	−0.600	−0.563	−0.572	0.104	0.145
σ	0.500	0.504	0.508	0.063	0.098

Table 2. Summary statistics for replicated parameter estimates from fitted ZIB + AR(2) models with sample size 200.

	True	Mean	Median	ESD	ASE
ω	0.300	0.300	0.299	0.020	0.020
β_0	2.000	2.002	2.002	0.081	0.104
β_1	−3.000	−3.006	−3.007	0.138	0.139
ϕ_1	0.800	0.754	0.754	0.076	0.095
ϕ_2	−0.600	−0.566	−0.573	0.067	0.086
σ	0.500	0.509	0.510	0.039	0.057

Table 3. Summary statistics for replicated parameter estimates from fitted ZIB + AR(2) models with sample size 500.

	True	Mean	Median	ESD	ASE
β_0	2.000	1.998	2.003	0.108	0.167
β_1	−3.000	−3.002	−3.010	0.179	0.174
ϕ_1	0.800	0.783	0.783	0.087	0.101
ϕ_2	−0.600	−0.593	−0.596	0.080	0.094
σ	0.500	0.496	0.494	0.052	0.062

Table 4. Summary statistics for replicated parameter estimates from fitted binomial + AR(2) models with sample size 200.

	True	Mean	Median	ESD	ASE
β_0	2.000	1.995	1.989	0.070	0.101
β_1	−3.000	−2.994	−2.995	0.113	0.108
ϕ_1	0.800	0.791	0.791	0.057	0.063
ϕ_2	−0.600	−0.593	−0.595	0.053	0.059
σ	0.500	0.498	0.496	0.032	0.038

Table 5. Summary statistics for replicated parameter estimates from fitted binomial + AR(2) models with sample size 500.

	True	Mean	Median	ESD	ASE
ω	0.300	0.299	0.299	0.031	0.032
β_0	2.000	1.971	1.971	0.208	0.251
β_1	−3.000	−2.982	−2.969	0.199	0.210
ϕ_1	0.800	0.763	0.770	0.073	0.067
σ	0.500	0.500	0.502	0.056	0.063

Table 6. Summary statistics for replicated parameter estimates from fitted ZIB + AR(1) models with sample size 200.

	True	Mean	Median	ESD	ASE
ω	0.300	0.299	0.299	0.020	0.021
β_0	2.000	1.984	1.989	0.135	0.168
β_1	−3.000	−2.992	−2.991	0.133	0.132
ϕ_1	0.800	0.781	0.785	0.041	0.040
σ	0.500	0.500	0.499	0.035	0.040

Table 7. Summary statistics for replicated parameter estimates from fitted ZIB + AR(1) models with sample size 500.

	True	Mean	Median	ESD	ASE
β_0	2.000	2.006	2.024	0.192	0.233
β_1	−3.000	−2.987	−2.988	0.165	0.167
ϕ_1	0.800	0.782	0.788	0.054	0.056
σ	0.500	0.497	0.496	0.051	0.052

Table 8. Summary statistics for replicated parameter estimates from fitted binomial + AR(1) models with sample size 200.

	True	Mean	Median	ESD	ASE
β_0	2.000	1.997	1.996	0.125	0.168
β_1	−3.000	−2.997	−2.994	0.106	0.106
ϕ_1	0.800	0.787	0.789	0.035	0.035
σ	0.500	0.499	0.499	0.030	0.033

Table 9. Summary statistics for replicated parameter estimates from fitted binomial + AR(1) models with sample size 500.

slightly non-normal tail behavior (thick or thin) evident for the estimated AR coefficients. As the sample size is increased from 200 to 500, this non-normal behavior is attenuated. Similar patterns are observed for the other three parameter-driven models.

4.2. Model comparison

As previously mentioned, based on a Poisson mixture distribution, extensive methodology has been published to deal with count time series with excess zeros. In addition, the Poisson distribution provides an accurate approximation to the binomial distribution when the sample size is large and the success probability is small. Therefore, one may question whether Poisson-type models are sufficient for approximating binomial-type models when data are generated from a binomial mixture distribution. In this section, we try to address this question through a simulation study.

Two different types of ZIB models are proposed in this work: the parameter-driven ZIB model, and the observation-driven ZIB model. To evaluate the propriety of the binomial-type models, we consider two corresponding Poisson-type counterparts: the parameter-driven ZIP model, and the observation-driven ZIP model. We assess the performance of the four models under two scenarios: first, where data are generated from the parameter-driven ZIB model, and second, where data are generated from the observation-driven ZIB model.

To denote the parameter-driven ZIB/ZIP model with an AR(p) latent process, we use PDZIB(p)/PDZIP(p). Similarly, we use ODZIB(p)/ODZIP(p) to denote the observation-driven ZIB/ZIP model with p lagged responses employed as covariates.

In the first scenario, data are generated from a PDZIB(2) model having the same form as that provided in Section 4.1. To reduce the computational burden associated with fitting the models, 100 replicated series of length 200 are generated. We fit four different zero-inflated models to each of the series. For the two parameter-driven models, we specify a latent autoregressive process of order two, and employ the MECM algorithm to fit the models. For the two observation-driven models, we incorporate the lagged responses y_{t-1} and y_{t-2} to account for the temporal correlation, and employ the Newton–Raphson algorithm to fit the models.

In the second scenario, data are generated from an ODZIB(2) model featuring the following structures:

$$\text{logit}(\pi_t) = \beta_0 + \beta_1 x_{1,t} + \phi_1 y_{t-1} + \phi_2 y_{t-2}, \text{ and } \text{logit}(\omega) = \gamma_0. \tag{47}$$

Here, $x_{1,t}$ is a covariate series generated from a standard uniform distribution, and ϕ_1 and ϕ_2 are the autoregressive coefficients for the lagged responses y_{t-1} and y_{t-2}, respectively. The values of the true parameters are the same as those for the parameter-driven model.

Again, we generate 100 replications of length 200 based on the preceding model. The same four zero-inflated models are fit to each of the replications. The Akaike information criterion (AIC) [30] is used to guide the selection of an optimal model in both scenarios. To evaluate the magnitude of the absolute difference in AIC values, Burnham and Anderson [31] provide the following guidelines (**Table 10**).

Thus, a difference in AIC values of two or more is considered meaningful, and a difference of 10 or more is considered pronounced.

Difference in AIC	Level of empirical support for model with larger AIC
0–2	Substantial
4–7	Considerably less
>10	Essentially none

Table 10. Guidelines for assessing AIC differences.

Figure 3 illustrates the performance of the four zero-inflated models, in terms of AIC differences, when data are generated from a PDZIB(2) model. The PDZIB(2) model serves as the reference for model comparison. Each point represents the difference in the AIC value between the target model and the reference model. As evident from the figure, the PDZIB(2) model markedly outperforms the other three models for all 100 replications, with AIC differences over 50. Although vastly inferior to the PDZIB(2) model, the PDZIP(2) model performs better than the two observation-driven models. The ODZIB(2) performs the worst among the four models considered. Parameter-driven models clearly exhibit a substantial advantage over observation-driven models when the underlying data arise via a parameter-driven approach.

Figure 4 shows the performance of the four zero-inflated models, in terms of AIC differences, when data are generated from an ODZIB(2) model. Similarly, the ODZIB(2) model serves as

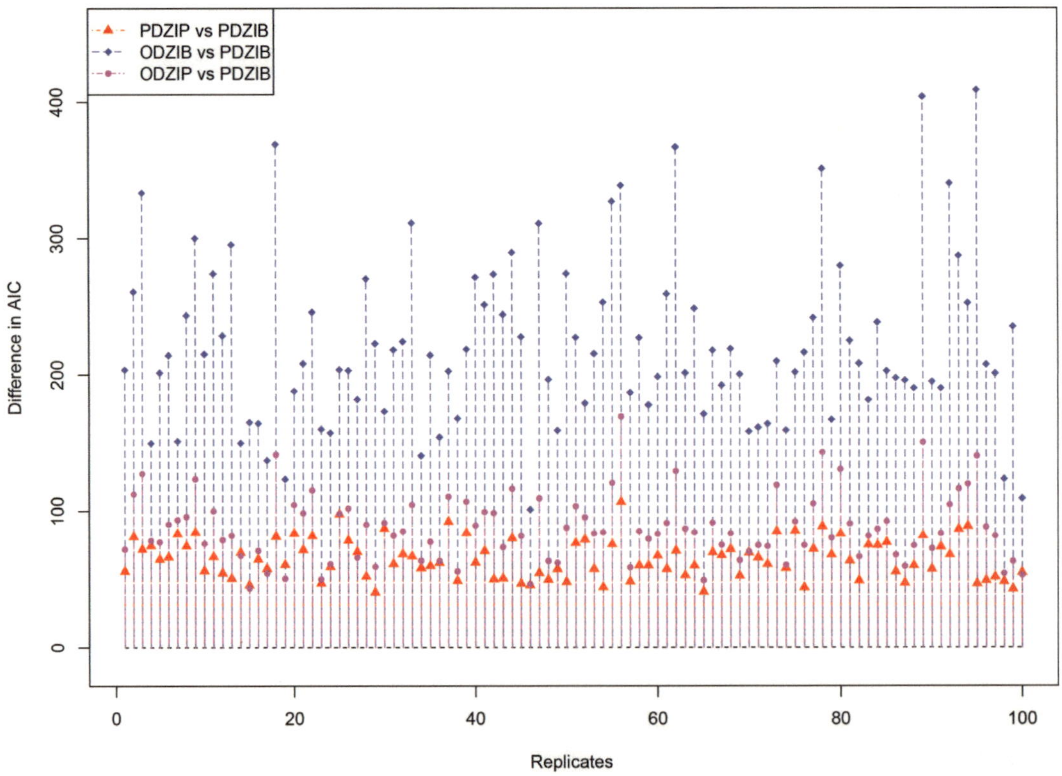

Figure 3. AIC differences of zero-inflated fitted models relative to parameter-driven ZIB fitted models.

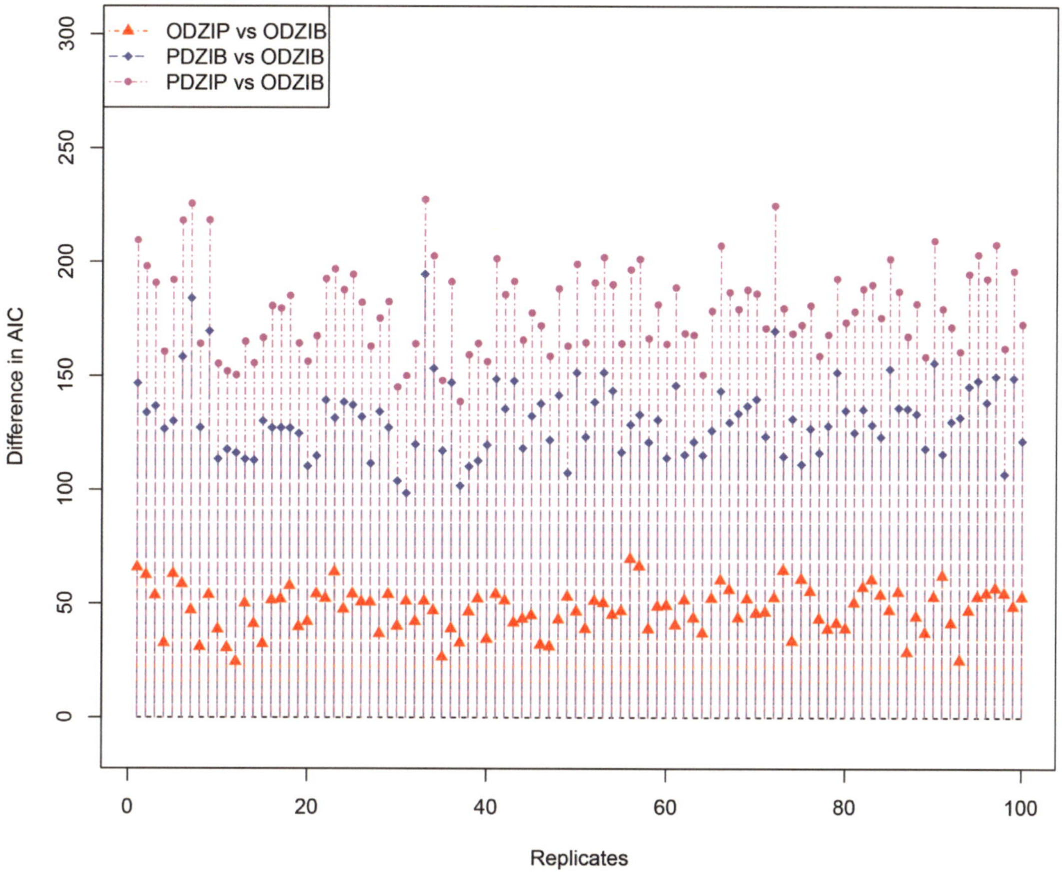

Figure 4. AIC differences of zero-inflated fitted models relative to observation-driven ZIB fitted models.

the reference. The ODZIB(2) model easily performs the best among all four models for all 100 replications, reflecting a substantial improvement in model fit over the other three models based on AIC differences (>20). Compared to the two parameter-driven models, the ODZIP(2) model accommodates the data much more appropriately. Between the two parameter-driven models, the PDZIB(2) model is substantially favored over the PDZIP(2) model. Thus, observation-driven models markedly outperform parameter-driven models when the underlying data arise via an observation-driven approach.

We close this section with a brief discussion of issues germane to model selection. These issues are relevant not only in evaluating the results of the preceding simulations, but also in facilitating the choice of a model in practice.

First, one may question which class of models should be considered when coping with binomial time series data with excess zeros. In the simulation sets, the fitted parameter-driven models markedly outperform the fitted observation-driven models when data are generated via a parameter-driven approach. Although parameter-driven models are computationally expensive to fit, observation-driven models do not appear to provide an adequate characterization of the data in such settings. Additionally, unlike observation-driven models, parameter-driven models provide a description of the underlying latent processes that govern the temporal correlation and zero inflation. Observation-driven models, in contrast, outperform parameter-driven models when the underlying data are generated via an observation-driven approach. In general, the selection of the class of models depends on the conceptualization of the model structure and the perceived value of recovering and investigating the underlying latent processes. However, in the context of zero-inflated count time series, since an understanding of the phenomenon that gives rise to the data will rarely inform the practitioner as to whether the parameter-driven or observation-driven conceptualization is more appropriate, we recommend the use of AIC or an alternate likelihood-based selection criterion in choosing between these two model classes.

Second, one may question which distribution should be used when dealing with count time series with excess zeros. The Poisson-type model with an offset is often considered an appropriate approximating model for a binomial-type model when the sample size is large and the success probability is low. However, in the presence of zero inflation, our simulation results indicate the necessity of using binomial-type models over their Poisson counterparts when the underlying distribution is actually a binomial mixture. In practice, if the dynamics of the phenomenon that gives rise to the data do not inform the underlying data generating distribution, we again recommend the use of AIC or another likelihood-based criterion in choosing an appropriate distribution.

5. Application

In this section, to illustrate our proposed methodology, we consider an application pertaining to the diagnosis coding of a severe disease, Kaposi's sarcoma (KS). The application concerns the assessment of a particular level change for a primary KS diagnosis. The data used are extracted from the Healthcare Cost and Utilization Project (HCUP) database. We identify all hospitalizations during the period from January 1998 through December 2011 during which a primary or secondary diagnosis of KS is received. For case ascertainment, we use the International Classification of Diseases, 9th Revision, Clinical Modification (ICD-9-CM), code 176. We then aggregate all cases of KS by month to produce a national sample of the monthly KS hospitalizations. The data consist of monthly counts of both primary and overall KS hospitalizations from January 1998 to December 2011. The sample size for both KS series is 168. **Figure 5** shows both the primary KS count time series and the overall KS count time series. In the latter, the overall KS count serves as the denominator for the binomial-type model and the offset for the Poisson-type model.

A coding change was implemented in early 2008, during which many hospitals may have modified the coding convention by switching the primary code to secondary, as this modification may lead to an increase in hospital reimbursements. During the study period, a large number of zero counts is observed and data among adjacent points seem to be highly correlated. Since the primary KS count series exhibits a relatively large degree of zero-inflation (appropriately 25% of the values are zero), we apply our proposed ZIB models to characterize the data.

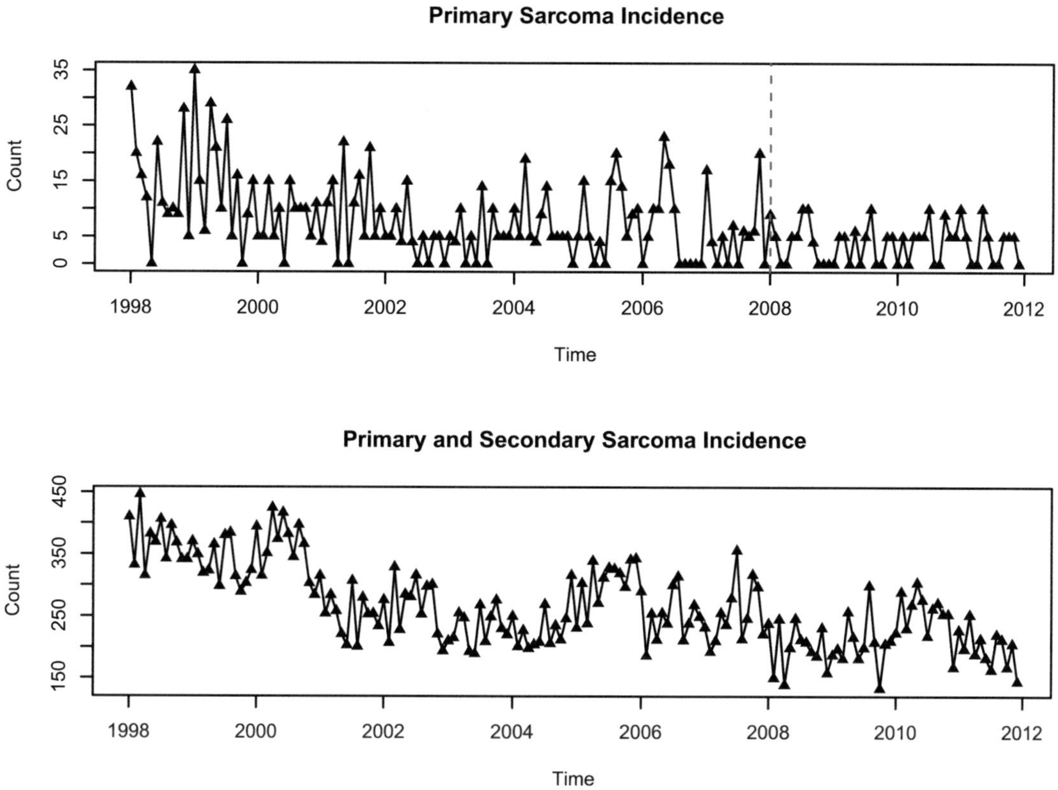

Figure 5. Monthly time series plots of primary KS hospitalizations (top panel) and overall KS hospitalizations (bottom panel) from January 1998 to December 2011.

Our analysis focuses on two objectives. First, we aim to model the dynamic pattern of the primary KS series; in particular, we are interested in determining the appropriate order of the autoregressive process embedded in the series, and evaluate whether there is a significant level change at January 2008. Second, we aim to compare the performance of our proposed ODZIB (p) and PDZIB(p) models to their counterpart ODZIP(p) and PDZIP(p) models.

For potential autocorrelation structures, we let p be either 1 or 2. As a result, we consider eight candidate models in total. Each of the models features an indicator to represent an intervention in January 2008, which allows us to test whether there is significant level change at this time period.

Specifically, for the two PDZIB(p) models, we employ the following linear predictor:

$$\text{logit}(\pi_t) = \beta_0 + \beta_1 x_t + z_t, \tag{48}$$

$$z_t = \sum_{i=1}^{p} \phi_i z_{t-i} + \varepsilon_t, \tag{49}$$

where t is a discrete time index, and $x_t = I_{(t>2008)}$ is a dummy variable indicating whether the index t is greater than the predefined change point (January 2008). Thus, β_1 reflects the level

Model	AIC	ω	β_0	β_1	ϕ_1	ϕ_2	σ
PDZIB(1)	922.98	0.248	−3.349	−0.249	−0.223		0.430
		(0.034)	(0.051)	(0.120)	(0.160)		(0.044)
PDZIP(1)	923.31	0.248	−3.389	−0.242	−0.241		0.410
		(0.034)	(0.051)	(0.116)	(0.166)		(0.043)
ODZIB(1)	1039.80	0.341	−3.184	−0.319	−0.007		
		(0.061)	(0.024)	(0.086)	(0.002)		
ODZIP(1)	1030.04	0.341	−3.224	−0.309	−0.007		
		(0.061)	(0.046)	(0.084)	(0.004)		
PDZIB(2)	922.98	0.248	−3.359	−0.237	−0.120	0.264	0.426
		(0.034)	(0.054)	(0.126)	(0.166)	(0.153)	(0.046)
PDZIP(2)	924.09	0.248	−3.395	−0.230	−0.119	0.263	0.402
		(0.034)	(0.052)	(0.118)	(0.178)	(0.158)	(0.045)
ODZIB(2)	1038.11	0.341	−3.250	−0.275	−0.008	0.007	
		(0.061)	(0.033)	(0.088)	(0.002)	(0.002)	
ODZIP(2)	1028.49	0.341	−3.288	−0.266	−0.007	0.007	
		(0.061)	(0.058)	(0.087)	(0.004)	(0.004)	

Table 11. Model fitting results for eight different zero-inflated models.

change in KS counts due to the coding practice, and the ϕ_i denote the coefficients for the autoregressive process.

For the two ODZIB(p) models, we employ the following linear predictor:

$$\text{logit}\,(\pi_t) = \beta_0 + \beta_1 x_t + \sum_{i=1}^{p} \phi_i y_{t-i}, \tag{50}$$

where β_1 and ϕ_i reflect parameters analogous to those defined for the parameter-driven setting.

In addition, we consider four comparable Poisson-type models based on the work by Yang et al. [5, 7]. For the two PDZIP(p) models, we employ the linear predictor

$$\log\left(\mu_t\right) = \log\left(n_t\right) + \beta_0 + \beta_1 x_t + z_t, \tag{51}$$

$$z_t = \sum_{i=1}^{p} \phi_i z_{t-i} + \varepsilon_t. \tag{52}$$

For the two ODZIP(p) models, we employ the linear predictor

$$\log\left(\mu_t\right) = \log\left(n_t\right) + \beta_0 + \beta_1 x_t + \sum_{i=1}^{p} \phi_i y_{t-i}. \tag{53}$$

Here, n_t serves as an offset variable representing the overall number of KS diagnoses. AIC is used to guide the selection of the optimal model.

Table 11 features results for the eight fitted candidate models. The parameter estimates along with their standard errors are presented. All eight models indicate a significant level change for the primary KS series after the introduction of the potential coding change practice ($\beta_1 < 0$). Among the first four models, which feature an autocorrelation structure of order one, parameter-driven models are deemed superior to observation-driven models, with AIC differences over 100. The PDZIB(1) model is slightly favored over the PDZIP(1) in terms of the AIC value. We observe similar patterns in the last four models, which feature an autocorrelation structure of order two. Among the parameter-driven models, adding a second order to the autocorrelation offers little improvement in model fit, since the increase in goodness-of-fit is offset by a decrease in parsimony. Therefore, the best model appears to be PDZIB(1).

6. Conclusion

Count time series featuring a preponderance of zeros are commonly encountered in a variety of scientific applications. In characterizing such series, modeling frameworks that assume a Poisson mixture distribution have been extensively studied. However, minimal work has been focused on modeling frameworks that assume a binomial mixture distribution. When data are more naturally assumed to arise from the latter, a Poisson-type model with an offset is often employed; however, the propriety of such an approximation is unclear.

We propose two general classes of models to effectively characterize a count time series that arises from a zero-inflated binomial mixture distribution. The observation-driven ZIB model, formulated in the partial likelihood framework, is fit using the Newton–Raphson algorithm. The parameter-driven ZIB model, formulated in the state-space framework, is fit using the MCEM algorithm. When data are generated from a binomial mixture, our proposed ZIB models outperform their Poisson-type counterparts. We illustrate our methodology with an application that assesses a particular level change for a diagnosis code.

Future work involves extending the current frameworks to the zero-inflated beta-binomial (ZIBB) model. Both observation-driven and parameter-driven ZIBB models can be formulated and fit based on methodological developments similar to those presented in this work. However, weak identifiability could arise as a potentially problematic issue in fitting the parameter-driven ZIBB model, as not only the overdispersion explicitly induced by the beta distribution but also the correlated random effects account for any excess variability in the data [5]. In addition, we could consider more complicated correlation structures by incorporating moving average components in the linear predictors for parameter-driven models. Such an extension necessitates non-trivial revisions to the state-space model formulation and the complete-data likelihood, which warrant further investigation.

Author details

Fan Tang[1] and Joseph E. Cavanaugh[2*]

*Address all correspondence to: joe-cavanaugh@uiowa.edu

1 Genentech Inc., South San Francisco, CA, USA

2 Department of Biostatistics, College of Public Health, University of Iowa, Iowa City, IA, USA

References

[1] Lambert D. Zero-inflated Poisson regression, with an application to defects in manufacturing. Technometrics. 1992;**34**:1-14

[2] Yau KKW, Lee AH. Zero-inflated Poisson regression with random effects to evaluate an occupational injury prevention programme. Statistics in Medicine. 2001;**20**:2907-2920

[3] Min Y, Agresti A. Random effect models for repeated measures of zero-inflated count data. Statistical Modeling. 2005;**5**:1-19

[4] Yau KKW, Lee AH, Carrivick PJW. Modeling zero-inflated count series with application to occupational health. Computer Methods and Programs in Biomedicine. 2004;**74**:47-52

[5] Yang M, Zamba GKD, Cavanaugh JE. State-space models for count time series with excess zeros. Statistical Modeling. 2015;**15**:70-90

[6] Hall DB. Zero-inflated Poisson and binomial regression with random effects: A case study. Biometrics. 2000;**56**:1030-1039

[7] Yang M, Zamba GKD, Cavanaugh JE. Markov regression models for count time series with excess zeros: A partial likelihood approach. Statistical Methodology. 2013;**14**:26-38

[8] Cox DR. Statistical analysis of time series: Some recent developments. Scandinavian Journal of Statistics. 1981;**8**:93-115

[9] Zeger SL, Qaqish B. Markov regression models for time series: A quasi-likelihood approach. Biometrics. 1988;**44**:1019-1031

[10] Slud E, Kedem B. Partial likelihood analysis of logistic regression and autoregression. Statistica Sinica. 1994;**4**:89-106

[11] Davis RA, Dunsmuir WTM, Streett SB. Observation-driven models for Poisson counts. Biometrika. 2003;**90**:777-790

[12] Freeland RK, McCabe BPM. Analysis of low count time series data by Poisson autoregression. Journal of Time Series Analysis. 2004;**25**:701-722

[13] Fokianos K, Kedem B. Partial likelihood inference for time series following generalized linear models. Journal of Time Series Analysis. 2004;**25**:173-197

[14] Hudecoa Š. Structural changes in autoregressive models for binary time series. Journal of Statistical Planning and Inference. 2013;**143**:1744-1752

[15] Zeger SL. A regression model for time series of counts. Biometrika. 1988;**75**:621-629

[16] Chan KS, Ledolter J. Monte Carlo EM estimation for time series models involving counts. Journal of the American Statistical Association. 1995;**90**:242-252

[17] Nelson KP, Leroux BG. Statistical models for autocorrelated count data. Statistics in Medicine. 2006;**25**:1413-1430

[18] Klingenberg B. Regression models for binary time series with gaps. Computational Statistics and Data Analysis. 2008;**52**:4076-4090

[19] Wu R, Cui Y. A parameter-driven logit regression model for binary time series. Journal of Time Series Analysis. 2014;**35**:462-477

[20] Kedem B, Fokianos K. Regression Models for Time Series Analysis. New Jersey: Wiley; 2002. p. 49-59

[21] Gordon NJ, Salmond DJ, Smith AFM. Novel approach to nonlinear/non-Gaussian Bayesian state estimation. IEE Proceedings-F, Radar and Signal Processing. 1993;**140**:107-113

[22] Godsill SJ, Doucet A, West M. Monte Carlo smoothing for nonlinear time series. Journal of the American Statistical Association. 2004;**99**:156-168

[23] Dempster AP, Laird NM, Rubin DB. Maximum likelihood estimation from incomplete data via the EM algorithm. Journal of the Royal Statistical Society, Series B. 1977;**39**:1-39

[24] Liu SI. Bayesian model determination for binary-time-series data with applications. Computational Statistics and Data Analysis. 2001;**36**:461-473

[25] Kim J, Stoffer DS. Fitting stochastic volatility models in the presence of irregular sampling via particle methods and the EM algorithm. Journal of Time Series Analysis. 2008;**29**:811-833

[26] Rue H, Martino S, Chopin N. Approximate Bayesian inference for latent Gaussian models by using integrated nested Laplace approximations (with discussion). Journal of the Royal Statistical Society, Series B. 2009;**71**:319-392

[27] Louis TA. Finding the observed information matrix when using the EM algorithm. Journal of the Royal Statistical Society Series B. 1982;**44**:226-233

[28] Doucet A, Freitas ND, Gordon N. Sequential Monte Carlo Methods in Practice. New York: Springer; 2001

[29] Kim J. Parameter estimation in stochastic volatility models with missing data using particle methods and the EM algorithm. PhD Thesis. Pittsburgh, PA: University of Pittsburgh; 2005. p. 10-27

[30] Akaike H. A new look at the statistical model identification. IEEE Transactions on Automatic Control. 1974;**19**:716-723

[31] Burnham KP, Anderson DR. Model Selection and Multimodel Inference: A Practical Information-Theoretic Approach. 2nd ed. New York: Springer; 2002. p. 70

Chapter 10

Ensemble Prediction of Stream Flows Enhanced by Harmony Search Optimization

Milan Cisty and Veronika Soldanova

Additional information is available at the end of the chapter

http://dx.doi.org/10.5772/intechopen.71192

Abstract

This work presents the application of a data-driven model for streamflow predictions, which can be one of the possibilities for the preventive protection of a population and its property. A new methodology was investigated in which ensemble modeling by data-driven models was applied and in which harmony search was used to optimize the ensemble structure. The diversity of the individual basic learners which form the ensemble is achieved through the application of different learning algorithms. In the proposed ensemble modeling of river flow predictions, powerful algorithms with good performances were used as ensemble constituents (gradient boosting machines, support vector machines, random forests, etc.). The proposed ensemble provides a better degree of precision in the prediction task, which was evaluated as a case study in comparison with the ensemble components, although they were powerful algorithms themselves. For this reason, the proposed methodology could be considered as a potential tool in flood predictions and prediction tasks in general.

Keywords: time series of river flows, ensemble prediction, optimisation, harmony search, data-driven methods

1. Introduction

Effective water resources management is one of the most crucial environmental challenges of our time. The inundation and flooding of landscapes and urban areas are serious problems, which cause immense damage to infrastructures and human lives in various parts of the world (e.g., recently in Australia, South America, Pakistan, West Africa and China, just to mention a few). Flood prevention requires various management tools, among which flow prediction models occupy an important place. Flood warnings several days in advance could provide civil protection authorities and the public with the necessary preparation time and could reduce the socio-economic impacts of flooding [1].

This work presents the application of a data-driven model for streamflow predictions, which can be one of the possibilities for the preventive protection of a population and its property. There are various types of models for flow predictions: physically based, conceptual and data-driven models are among the most well known. While physically based models mainly depend on our knowledge of the physical laws in a watershed and on the corresponding geographical database, which serve as an information background for the application of the physical laws, data-driven models extract knowledge only from the monitored data describing the inputs and outputs of the watershed, e.g., time series of precipitation, temperatures, river flows, etc. For this reason, data-driven models are much more suitable for this task. It is not possible operatively to update all the detailed information about a watershed and its stated variables on a day-to-day or even hour-to-hour basis, which is necessary in the case of the application of physically based models.

The authors of this paper have focused on the application of a supervised learning methodology for flow prediction, namely, on a proposed ensemble approach, with the aim of refining the precision of the results of such modeling. In a typical supervised learning scheme, a set of input data instances, also referred to as a training set, is given. The output values of these data in the training set are known, and the goal is to construct a model in order to compute the outputs for the new instances (where the outputs are unknown).

Various models frequently show different capacities to maintain certain aspects of the hydrological processes [2], so the application of a single model often leads to predictions that could be more precise in some part of the problem domain but are less suitable in others [3].

The recognition of this fact has led to the application of an ensemble or committee of models being simultaneously considered. Many researchers have shown that by combining the output of many predictors, more accurate predictions can be produced than what could be obtained from any of the individual predictors [4–6]. Individual predictors should be accurate enough and also different from each other [7–9]. Sampling different training datasets, using different learning architectures and using different subsets of variables are the most popular approaches used to achieve such diversity [5, 10] in the application of the data-driven modeling approach. For example, in bagging [4], each classifier is trained using a different training set sampled from all the available training data. Boosting algorithms are different and powerful ensemble learners, which implement forward stagewise additive modeling, where in each stage the data are reweighted: the examples that produced the worst predictions gain weight and the examples that produced precise results lose weight. Thus, the next basic learner is focused more on examples that were previously incorrectly predicted. Stacking, another type of ensemble learner concept, tries to learn which base models are more reliable than others by using a meta data-driven algorithm, the task of which is to discover how to best combine the output of the base models to achieve the final results.

In the field of streamflow forecasting, various papers have been published [3] in which the data-driven ensemble modeling approach has been studied, but they are usually focused on climate inputs obtained by ensemble modeling of weather, which is not the subject of this paper. Selection of existing works from the focus of this article follows.

The application of a modular approach that uses different neural network rainfall-runoff models according to the hydrologic situation in a catchment was presented in Ref. [11]. A specific model from a set of trained models is proposed here to apply to particular input data. This work proposes that the model used for particular inputs is chosen on the basis of the most similar hydrological and meteorological conditions used to train the selected model. A clustering technique based on self-organizing maps was applied to manage the model's selection. A boosting application is presented in Ref. [12], where the authors demonstrated the advantages of an improved version of boosting, namely, AdaBoost.RT, which is compared to other learning methods for several benchmarking problems, and two problems involving river flow forecasting. In a recent study [13], the authors investigated the potential usage of bagging and boosting in building classification and regression tree ensembles to refine the accuracy of streamflow predictions. They report that the bagged model performs slightly better than the boosted model in the testing phase. An ensemble neural network (ENN) designed to monthly inflows forecasting was applied in Ref. [14] to prediction of inflows into the Daecheong Dam in Korea. The ENN combined the outputs of the members of a neural network employing the bagging method. The overall results showed that the ENN outperformed a simple artificial neural network (ANN) among the three rainfall-runoff models. Cannon and Whitfield [15] studied the use of ensemble neural network modeling in streamflow forecasting. Boucher et al. [16] used bagged multi-layer perceptrons for the purpose of a 1-day ahead streamflow forecasting on three watersheds.

In general, the ensemble methods as described in the published theoretical and application papers are usually composed of weak predictors, e.g., decision trees or neural networks commonly used as base predictors while building ensemble machine learning models. On the other hand, there are only a few works in which the ensemble is formed by a fusion of strong learners. The authors of the present paper assume that it is also important to examine ensembles based on nonweak learners, such as support vector machines, random forests or various other types of strong models, which are in some cases eventually ensembles themselves (composed of weak learners, e.g., various types of boosting methods).

A major goal of the analysis in this study is to precisely evaluate ensembles composed of various strong machine learning algorithms in comparison with the results achieved by individual learners. The final prediction by the proposed ensemble is accomplished by weighted summation of the results of the individual learners. The specification of these weights is a particularly important step in ensemble model building and is proposed to be solved with the help of the harmony search optimization methodology [17]. The harmony search methodol ogy has been successfully applied to various optimization tasks and also in the area of hydrology and water resources management, e.g. [18, 19].

In Section 2, the methods of the particular machine learning algorithms involved in this study are briefly explained, together with the ensemble methodologies used. Then, the data acquisition and preparation is presented. In Section 3, the settings of the experimental computations are described and the results are evaluated. Finally, Section 4 summarizes the main achievements and conclusions of the work and proposes ideas for future work in this area.

2. Materials and methods

2.1. Description of case study and preparation of data

Ensemble modeling by data-driven methods was applied for the 2-day ahead prediction of flows on the Hron River in Slovakia. The watershed of this river is a sub-basin of the Danube River. This task was accomplished by using data observed in the period from 01-01-1984 to 31-12-2000. Specifically, the average daily flow [$m^3 s^{-1}$], the average daily temperatures [°C] and the daily rainfall depths [mm] were used.

The prediction of flows at the Banska Bystrica gauging station (**Figure 1**) serves as the case study in this paper. Each row in the input file for this task includes the date of the predicted flow, the predicted flow itself (two days' ahead—these are the modeled data, but their values are necessary for the training and testing mechanism), the input data of the flows from the three measuring stations, the temperatures from five meteorological stations, and the precipitation from 51 stations. All the input data were included in the input dataset from 1, 2, 3 and 4 days before the date of the predicted flow. This means that a summary of 238 variables is in each data row. Because daily data were used from 01-01-1984 to 31-12-2000, 6209 rows are in the dataset.

Some data preprocessing procedures had to be accomplished: cleansing the data, formatting it, inputting the missing data and normalizing it. These operations are not described here, because they are common procedures in data mining. A few words will follow about the division of the data and the sampling, which were important from the point of view of this paper.

The correct prediction of high flows is the most important task for flood predictions. The period from 1996 to 2000 includes many situations with high flows and floods, which was the reason for its selection as the testing period. The rest of the years (1984–1996) were used for the training (**Table 1**).

A sampling of the data was also accomplished to obtain a balanced training dataset and dataset that led to less demanding requirements from the point of view of the hardware and

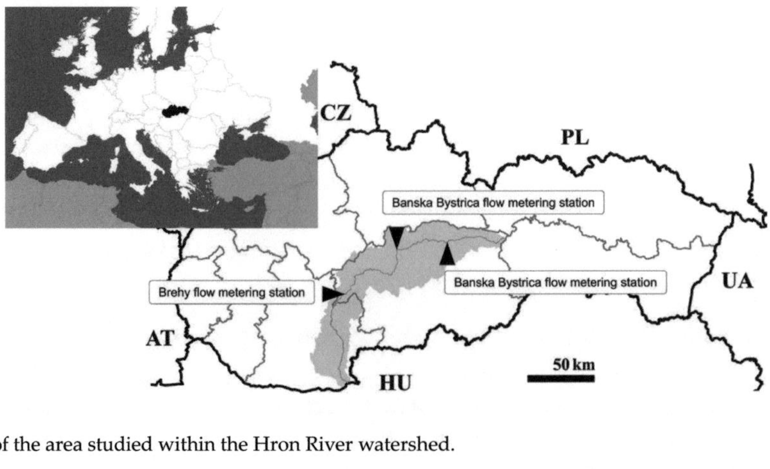

Figure 1. Map of the area studied within the Hron River watershed.

	Flows in Banská Bystrica [m³ s⁻¹]			Average temperatures—all 5 stations [°C]			Average precipitation—all 51 stations [mm]		
Data	All data	Training (84–96)	Testing (96–00)	All data	Training (84–96)	Testing (96–00)	All data	Training (84–96)	Testing (96–00)
Min	5.18	5.18	5.29	−27.0	−27.0	−21.7	0.0	0.0	0.0
Max	219.20	219.20	157.90	27.6	27.3	27.6	123.6	123.6	93.5
Avg.	23.04	22.94	23.23	7.75	7.67	7.98	1.99	1.98	2.07

Table 1. Statistics of the data.

CPU time. Because of these computer power demands, sampling as a form of data reduction is a particularly important procedure in ensemble modeling, because in such modeling many runs of many algorithms are necessary, and computer demands rise with the amount of data used for training. A proper sampling methodology should be chosen in relation to the properties of the data and the problem studied. In streamflow predictions, a high amount of relatively low flows is usually available (also in the case studied), which led to the authors' decision to filter out some of them. On the contrary, high flows are somewhat rare. Because high flows are the most important data in flood predictions, the decision was made to filter out the data nonuniformly and leave all the input rows with this rare and large flow data in the final training dataset. Exactly, the same sampling of the same data was described in the previous work of the authors of the present paper [20], in which more details can be found.

2.2. Methodology

The goal of the proposed ensemble methodology is to combine the predictions of several models in order to improve the robustness/generalizability that could be obtained from any of the constituent models. The proposed ensemble methodology for predicting the river flows is divided into four equally important steps (**Figure 2**). The preparation of the data was described in a previous part of this chapter. This section follows two subsections: in the first, members of the ensemble are described, whereas the second subsection contains a description of each model's weight optimization by the harmony search methodology. The final model is predicted using the weighted average of the base learners in which these weights are used.

2.2.1. Selection and training of ensemble members

In contrast to the usual approach when ensemble consists of less powerful algorithms, the authors' intention was to evaluate the use of strong algorithms for members of the ensemble. The choice of "strong" algorithms is based on some papers, which evaluate existing data mining algorithms [21, 22].

A grid search combined with a repeated cross-validation methodology was used for finding the parameters of all the models included in the ensemble [6, 7]. In this approach, a set of each model's parameters from a predetermined grid is sent to the parameter-evaluating algorithm. A 5-times repeated 10-fold cross validation was used to find best parameters for the final

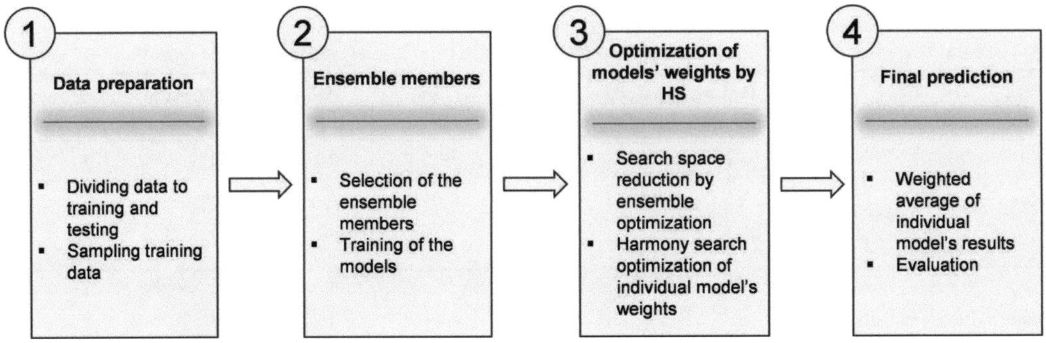

Figure 2. Proposed steps for the development of ensemble predictions of river flows.

models. Sampling of the data (as mentioned in the data preparation part of this chapter) was used in this process, because each basic algorithm runs in such a strategy many times.

Only a sketch of the algorithms is provided hereinafter, because in this work, a number of algorithms are used, and it is neither possible nor useful in this paper to go into a more thorough explanation. In the case of interest, the authors have indicated links to the relevant literature for detailed information.

2.2.1.1. Support vector machines (SVM)

A support vector machine (SVM) [23] is very effective, supervised, machine learning method for various machine learning tasks. It is specific by using kernel trick-nonlinear mapping used to transform the original training data of a nonlinear problem (which is also our case) into a higher dimension. Herein, SVM learn a nonlinear function indirectly and easier: they learn a linear function in the space induced by the particular kernel, which matches to a nonlinear function in the original space.

The next important concept in SVM methodology is to fully ignore small errors. In SVM, bounds for regression are set by defining the loss function that ignores errors, which are situated within the distance ε of the true value. This type of function is called epsilon insensitive loss function. As a consequence, good generalization of SVM is gained, because not all the input vectors of data are used, but only the so-called support vectors, which are training samples that lie outside of the boundary of the ε-tube.

In this chapter, the ε-SVM model was created by: (1) choosing a radial basis kernel with parameter sigma = 0.0005; (2) specifying the ε parameter to be equal to 0.1 and (3) specifying the capacity $C = 10.5$. All parameters were found by a grid search.

Multilayer perceptron (MLP).

Artificial neural networks (ANNs) are the most popular and well-known data-driven methodology; it has been described and is available in various literature sources, e.g. [24]. Briefly summarized, a multilayer perceptron, the most commonly used type of neural network, which was used also in this work, consists of input, hidden and output layers, all of which contain some processing elements or neurons. Input and output layer contains as many neurons as the model has input, respectively output variables. The so-called learning involves determination of number, types and particular properties of neurons in hidden layer. This layer is used for the transformation of the inputs to the outputs. A type of ANN known as a multi-layer perceptron (MLP), which uses a back propagation training algorithm, was used for generating the flow predictions in this study. The number of neurons in a hidden layer was found by a grid search and is equal to 6. Neurons with a logistic activation function were used in the hidden layer and with the linear activation function in the output layer.

2.2.1.2. *Random forest (RF)*

Random forests (RF) [25] are formed by a set of trees, which can either be classification or regression trees, depending on the problem being addressed. An RF prediction is an average of many trees (weak learners) grown on a bootstrap sample of the training data. The user chooses the number of trees in the forest (ensemble). Each tree is trained using a different bootstrap sample, which causes that different trees are obtained. For the regression task, the values predicted by each tree are averaged to obtain the final random forest prediction. In this work, a number of variables randomly sampled as candidates at each tree split were optimized with the help of a grid search, with the final value equal to 123. The minimum size of the terminal nodes is set at 5 and the number of trees at 500.

2.2.1.3. *Multiple linear regression (MLR)*

Multiple linear regression (MLR) analysis is generally used to find the relevant coefficients (*a, b, c,…, intercept*) in the following model:

$$Y = aX_1 + bX_2 + cX_3 + \ldots + intercept \tag{1}$$

This is a simple, well-known methodology, which the authors included in this paper mainly for the purposes of comparison with other, more powerful, methods.

2.2.1.4. *Generalized linear model with an elastic-net (GLMNET)*

Also in this method, as in previous case, a linear model is applied for flows prediction. Additional improvement in comparison to the basic multiple linear model is usage of regularization technique while searching parameters *a, b, c,…* from Eq. (1).

Regularization introduces additional criterion (or penalty) to the objective functions of optimization problems in order to prevent overfitting and for obtaining a more general model. In this case, least squares method for linear regression is meant as optimization problem. Various types of regularization exist. Ridge regression uses penalty, which limits the size of the coefficients in Eq. (1). Lasso uses a type of penalty which is trying to set some coefficients to be equal to zero. Elastic-net is a compromise between these two techniques and is used in this work. In work presented in this paper software provided by the authors of this regularization method was used [26].

2.2.1.5. *Multivariate adaptive regression splines (MARS)*

MARS [27] construct regression relations from a set of coefficients β and linear basis functions h that are determined from the training data. The general MARS model equation is given as:

$$y = f(X) = \beta_o + \sum_{m=1}^{M} \beta_m h_m(X) \tag{2}$$

The basis function $h(x)$ takes one of the following three forms:

1. A constant (the intercept).
2. A function of the form $max(0, x - const)$ or $max(0, const - x)$. MARS selects the values of *const* for the knots of this function. These breakpoints define the region of application for a particular linear equation.
3. A product of two or more of the above-mentioned functions. The model interactions between two or more variables are modeled in this case.

The best parameters of multivariate adaptive regression splines were found by a grid search procedure; the maximum degree of interaction is equal to 1, and the maximum number of terms (including the intercept) in the pruned model was found as 31.

In recent years, boosting has developed into one of the most important techniques for fitting regression models in high-dimensional data settings. So, the authors decided to include the proposed ensemble in the three boosting models described below. Boosting, or additive models [28], express the searched function as a weighted sum of the basis functions as follows:

$$f(x) = \sum\nolimits_m \beta_m fm(x) = \sum\nolimits_m \beta_m b(x; \gamma_m) \tag{3}$$

The basis functions b are dependent on the type of boosting method, and the parameters (β_m and γ_m) are assessed by minimizing a loss function (e.g. a mean square error) over the training data. Forward stagewise fitting is used for estimating β_m and γ_m sequentially from $m = 1$ to n. For example, for boosted trees with a squared error loss, we fit a least-squares regression tree to the residuals of the previous iteration.

2.2.1.6. *Boosted linear models (B_GLM)*

In this case, a linear model is fitted using gradient boosting, where the component-wise linear models are utilized as base learners. The methodology is described in Ref. [29]. In this work, the R package mboost and glmboost function with a default setting were used for this methodology [30, 31]. The number of initial boosting iterations was found by grid search and is equal to 150; shrinkage parameter was set to 0.1.

2.2.1.7. *Gradient Boosting with Smooth Components (B_GAM)*

A (generalized) additive model is fitted in this case using a boosting algorithm based on component-wise univariate base learners (where only one variable is updated in each iteration of the algorithm) in combination with the L_2 loss function. A spline, which is a sufficiently smooth polynomial function that is piecewise-defined, is suitable for this task. It possesses a high degree of smoothness at the places where the polynomial pieces connect (which are known as "knots"). In this study, P-splines with a B-spline basis [32] were used as a base learner. In each iteration of the gradient-boosting algorithm, a base learner is fitted to the negative gradient of the L_2 loss function. The current estimate of the predictor function is then updated with the actual estimate of the negative gradient, which automatically results in an additive model fit. In this work, the gamboost function of the R mboost package [33] was used to fit the flow prediction model. The number of initial boosting iterations was found by grid search and is equal to 100; shrinkage parameter was set to 0.1.

2.2.1.8. Gradient boosting machines (GBM)

Gradient boosting machines (GBM) are one of the most powerful boosting methods. Similarly to the other boosting methods, gradient boosting combines weak learners into a single strong learner. In GBM, decision trees (regression trees in our case) are usually employed. Weak learners are sequentially used with continually modified selection of the data. Moreover, training set is in this stepwise procedure weighted for current iteration according to the accuracy of the previously fitted model. The final prediction is obtained as a weighted average. Gradient boosting used in this work is implemented in the R package gbm [34] and is freely available. The total number of trees to fit is equal to 700 in this work and this parameter was found by a grid search. The shrinkage in GBM is controlled by parameter v, which was set in this work to 0.01 (default value). Also, the maximum depth of the variable interactions was found by a grid search with up to 10-way interactions.

2.2.2. Harmony search (HS)

The harmony search [17] algorithm (HS) was adopted from the musical process of finding "pleasant harmonies" through improvisation. The five fundamental steps of HS could be summarized as follows:

> Step 1. Design the variables and initialization of the algorithm parameters. Initialization of HS search parameters: harmony memory size (HMS), harmony memory consideration rate (HMCR), the pitch adjustment rate (PAR) and the maximum number of improvisations (NI). The definition of the objective function $f(x)$, which has to be minimized (or maximized), is also performed in this step.
>
> Step 2. Initialization of harmony memory. The harmony memory is a memory location (matrix), where the solution vectors (sets of weights) and corresponding objective function values are stored. The initial HS memory consists of different randomly generated solution vectors.
>
> Step 3. The generation of a new harmony inspired by improvisation process in music is performed and accomplished in this step. New harmony represents new solution of given optimisation problem. It consists of three basic procedures: (1) selection of harmony from the memory controlled by parameter HMCR, (2) pitch adjustment (parameter PAR) and (3) a pick a random value with probability 1-HMCR. A more detailed description of these HS operators can be found in existing HS literature, e.g. [18].

Step 4. A new solution's objective function computation. If the new harmony has better value of the objective function than any harmony in the harmony memory, the worst harmony vector in harmony memory is replaced by this new harmony vector.

Step 5. Repeat from Step 3 to Step 5 until termination criterion is satisfied. In this work, the harmony search stops if there is no improvement in an objective function during the last 500 iterations or if the total (predefined) number of iterations is reached.

3. Results and discussion

In this section, the computation procedures, which are necessary for obtaining the ensemble model, are described. The ensemble model is proposed to have the following structure:

$$P^j_{ensemble} = \sum_{n}^{i=1} \beta_i * P^j_i \tag{4}$$

where β_i are the weights of the individual learners and P^t_i is a vector of predicted flows by model i for day j. The harmony search method was used to determine the corresponding weights of individual models. Application of this method for 2-day ahead prediction of flows follows in the subsequent paragraphs.

One harmony consists of n members, where n is the number of models. In the case of this work, there are nine models present in the ensemble. All values of the weights β_i are restricted to the interval $\langle 0, 1 \rangle$.

The problem solved should be defined by the objective function, which is proposed in this paper to have the following form:

$$O_f = 1 - \left(1 - \frac{\sum_{i=1}^{N} (O_i - P_i)^2}{\sum_{i=1}^{N} (O_i - \bar{O})^2}\right) + \left|\alpha - \sum_{i=1}^{n} \beta_i\right| \tag{5}$$

$$0 \le \beta_i \le 1, \tag{6}$$

where P_i and O_i are computed and observed flows, N is the number of days and $\bar{O}$ is average value of observed flows. Expression in the rounded parentheses is the Nash-Sutcliffe model efficiency coefficient (NSE). It was used in this study for evaluation of models efficiency because it is most often used to assess the predictive power of hydrological models. The NSE ranges from $-\infty$ up to 1, where NSE = 1 means a perfect agreement between the observed and simulated data, i.e. closer the model efficiency is to 1, the more accurate the model is. The last component of the objective function (as an absolute value) forces the sum of the ensemble members' weights β_i to be equal to α, which is a regularization constant, by default equal to 1. Only rarely in cases when the models are systematically underestimating or overestimating, the regulation constant could have a slightly different values (maximum ±0.05). In this work, the authors only used the default value 1, because a relatively good prediction could be expected from the state-of-the-art models used as the ensemble members. This objective function is proposed to be minimized. In the case of an ideal model, the value of the objective function is zero.

Harmony search algorithm parameters were set as follow: *HMS* (memory size) was set to 10; *HMCR* (the harmony memory's consideration rate) was set to 0.91 and *PAR*, i.e., the pitch adjustment rate, was set to 0.1. The maximum number of improvisations $NI = 500{,}000$.

One of the main issues which must be carefully considered is what exactly has to be data P_i, which will serve as inputs to the harmony search optimization objective function (5). As was previously stated, these are basically the computed values of the predicted flows by each model. While performing these computations, we are in a model building phase, and that is why only training data can be used. There are two possibilities evaluated in this study as to how to obtain such data. The first possibility is achieved using the following steps:

1. The training data and repeated cross validation are used for finding the proper parameters of each model.
2. Every model (ensemble member) is trained with the values, which were found in step 1 with all training data.
3. The values of the predicted flows are computed by the models from step 2 from all the training data for each ensemble member. The number of rows of resulted input matrix for HS $P_{R,C}$ is equal to the number of the rows of training data (535 in this study) and the number of columns $C = n + 1$ (n is the number of models, and one extra column is the observed data). In this work, $n = 9$.

The problem of obtaining data $P_{R,C}$ by this methodology, if it is used for calculating ensemble weights, is that in this approach there is no mechanism that avoids overfitting of the final ensemble. Overfitting or a lack of generalization means that the weights of the models obtained could work well on the training data, but poorly on the testing set. Due to this problem, the authors also proposed a second option, which will be compared to the previous one:

1. The training data and cross validation are used for finding the proper parameters of each model.
2. When these parameters are obtained, the $k - 1$ folds (in the case of a k-fold cross validation) are used for training with the best parameters, and 1 fold is computed by the model obtained as a test.
3. This is repeated k times for every model included in the ensemble.
4. Because the r-repeated cross-validation was proposed in this work, steps 2 and 3 are repeated r times.
5. The computed values from all such testing folds from the cross-validation are used as the input matrix for the optimization by HS, which is proposed for searching the weights of each model in the final ensemble.
6. Consequently, the inputs to the HS are de facto testing data, although from the training set (the results from the testing folds in the cross-validation). When n is the number of models in the ensemble, N is the number of data in the training set and r is the number of repeats of

the cross-validation, the number of rows of this input matrix $P_{R,C}$ is $R = N^*r$ and the number of columns $C = n + 1$ (one column is the observed data). In this work, $n = 9$, $k = 10$, $N = 535$ (the data were reduced by the sampling!) and $r = 5$.

The ensemble models obtained from these two approaches are hereinafter identified as EHS1 for the first case and EHS2 for the second.

The process of assessing the performance of a hydrologic model involves making some estimates of the "closeness" of the simulated behavior of the model to observations (in our case, the streamflow). The most basic approach for assessing a model's performance is through a visual inspection of the simulated and observed hydrographs (**Figure 4**). An objective assessment requires the use of a mathematical estimate of the error between the simulated and observed hydrological variables. The predictive accuracy of the ensemble and its members was evaluated using the Nash-Sutcliffe coefficient of efficiency (NSE), the root mean square error (RMSE) and the correlation coefficient (r).

In **Table 2**, the root mean square error, correlation coefficient and Nash-Sutcliffe efficiency are evaluated for the ensemble members and the proposed ensembles. The identification of the models from their abbreviations in the heading of this table is possible. Two ensemble optimization approaches, which are identified as EHS1 and EHS2, are evaluated in **Table 2** and were described hereinbefore.

The selection of the appropriate settings for the ensemble members evaluated in **Table 2** is described in Section 2.2. A grid search was mostly used for the tuning; in some cases, the settings recommended in the scientific literature were applied. Regarding ensembles EHS1 and EHS2, it can be clearly seen that the hypothesis about the poor performance of the above-mentioned first proposition for obtaining matrix $P_{R,C}$ was confirmed. Ensemble model EHS1 performed well on the training data (with an NSE equal to 0.82, when an NSE of 0.79 was achieved by the best ensemble component, which was the GBM model), but on the testing set, which is evaluated in **Table 2**, the ensemble EHS1 gives worst results than most of the ensemble members. The ensemble approach to modeling is worth applying only in a case where the ensemble performs better than any of its members. If one considers the weights of the multilayer perceptron in ensemble EHS1, it is presumably inappropriately high (MLP are generally less precise

	GBM	B_GLM	RF	MLP	MARS	MLR	SVM	B_GAM	GLMNET	EHS1	EHS2
NSE	0.806	0.783	0.808	0.676	0.593	0.376	0.800	0.787	0.782	0.759	0.825
r	0.898	0.885	0.900	0.832	0.802	0.724	0.896	0.888	0.884	0.874	0.909
RMSE	13.575	14.371	13.519	17.548	19.661	24.355	13.788	14.219	14.410	9.684	8.247
Weights EHS1	0.128	0.011	0.190	0.549	0.021	0.022	0.032	0.003	0.045		
Weights EHS2	0.134	0.056	0.379	0.034	0.083	0.021	0.218	0.029	0.046		

Table 2. Evaluation of the computations by r and NSE and the final values of the model weights in the ensembles.

models), which means that this model is overfitted and that the poor generalization is a consequence of the approach used for the development of the EHS1 model. To the contrary, according to **Table 2**, in which the testing data are evaluated, the results with a good generalization were achieved by ensemble EHS2. From now on, we will only speak about this second model.

Column nine of **Table 2** with the evaluation of the ensemble members could also be seen as a case study of the evaluation of these models. The models are ordered from best to worst, so they can be ranked and compared with each other. As could be expected for such a complicated process as the flow formation in a river is, this process was described more successfully by nonlinear models, especially by the recently developed boosting types of algorithms. However, when the weights of the models for the EHS2 ensemble in **Table 2** are considered, it can be seen that this order does not imply that the weights will also be ordered in the same way as precision. An efficient ensemble should consist of predictors that are not only sufficiently precise, but also diverse, i.e. ones that if make wrong predictions they make them at different parts of the input space, e.g. which are not highly correlated. The correlation of the models is evaluated in **Figure 3**.

From the conjoint consideration of **Table 2** (weights of models for the EHS2) and **Figure 3**, it can be seen that, after optimization of the weights, the best three models, the GBM, RF, and SVM, are included in the proposed ensemble with the highest contribution (their weights are the highest). But the next best model, the boosted GAM (B_GAM), is included in the ensemble with a relatively small weight. That is because this model is highly correlated with the three best models mentioned and also with the GLMNET model. A similar case could also be observed with some other members of the ensemble. From this phenomenon, it could be evaluated that the optimization procedure, which was proposed in this paper, is searching for the best weights not only from the point of view of the best performance of the models but also is considering the diversity of the models as well, which is, as was mentioned,

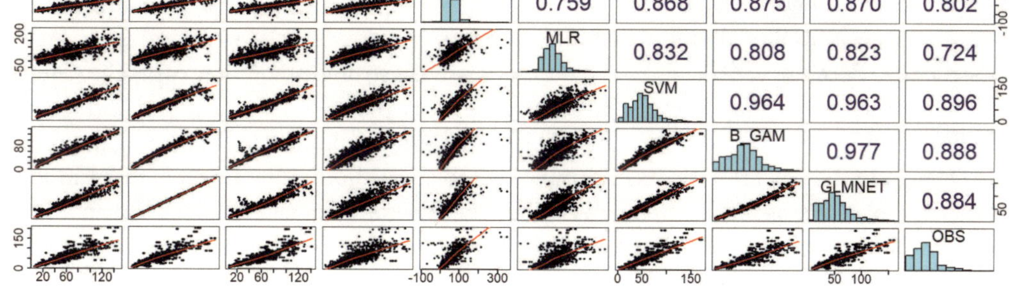

Figure 3. Correlation between the simulated results obtained by the ensemble members and with the observed data.

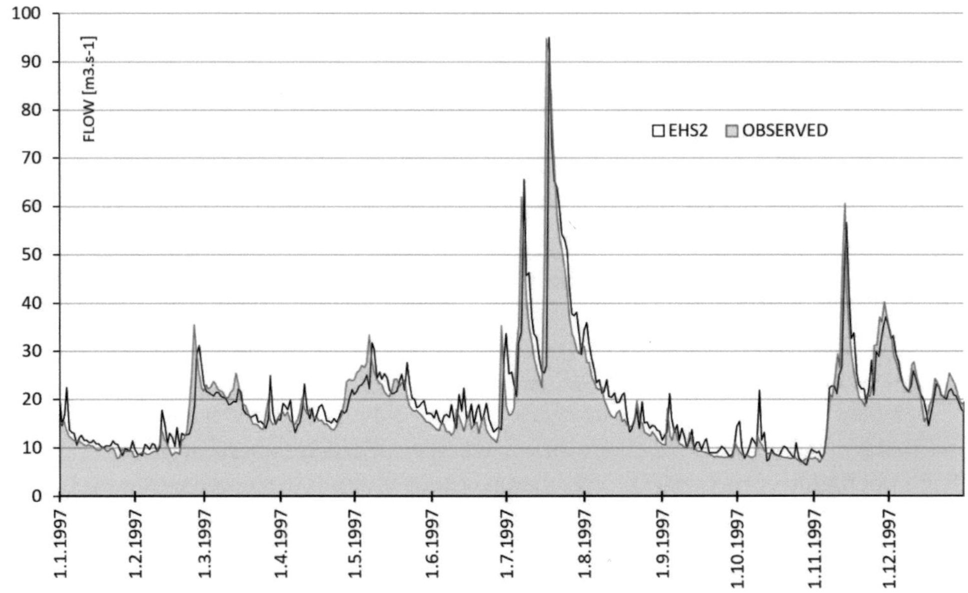

Figure 4. Time series of the testing dataset of the observed flows and the same flows simulated by the proposed ensemble model in the year 1997.

not less important. The authors assume that this is mainly due to the procedure by which matrix $P_{R,C}$ was obtained for model EHS2. As could be expected, the smallest contribution to the EHS2 ensemble has its least precise member: the multiple linear regression (MLR).

In **Figure 4**, a time series graph of the testing dataset with the observed flows and the flows simulated by the proposed ensemble model is seen. As can be seen, the predicted flows follow the real values with a high degree of precision, and the proposed ensemble approach could be used as an innovative alternative for flow predictions.

4. Conclusion

In this work, the authors deal with an investigation of the possible improvement of the river flow predictions. A new methodology was investigated in which ensemble modeling by data-driven models was applied and in which the harmony search was used to optimize the ensemble's structure. Because various data-driven models with strong prediction capability already exist, the authors were trying to evaluate in the case study presented in this paper (2-day ahead prediction of river flows), whether an ensemble paradigm would also bring some gain in cases when strong algorithms are used as ensemble members. Although the improvement in precision was not relatively as high as in the case when the ensemble consists of weak learners, it was proved that the ensemble model worked better than any of its constituents. These results mean, of course, that the proposed ensemble also works better than the ensembles with weak learners which are usually applied, because these were actually among the members of the proposed ensemble.

The authors' intention was to emphasize one important detail: how the input data for a harmony search optimization of weights should be properly computed. In the authors' investigation, it was verified that using the results of testing folds from cross-validation is the best option. This procedure is described in Section 3.

The authors like to emphasize the following practical aspect about ensemble modeling at the end of this paper. It is well known that for different datasets various algorithms may suit as best choice for prediction and it is never certain in advance, which one of these algorithms will perform with best results. This is known as "no free lunch" theorem. Because of this uncertainty, more algorithms must be usually trained, tested and evaluated during data mining process. These three activities (training, testing and evaluation) together with data preparation are quite laborious and computationally intensive. When this work is already done, instead of choosing only one of these algorithms for obtaining final results, it is wiser to use all already tuned algorithms for ensemble prediction of unknown variable (or subset of these algorithms). Updating prediction using ensemble paradigm almost always brings an improvement in precision as was also confirmed in the case study presented (the results are in **Table 2**). It does not mean a lot of extra work because tuned algorithms for a given task are already available. Gain will be different for different datasets, but as was confirmed also in this study it is surely worth to try this for such a little effort.

Acknowledgements

This work was supported by the Slovak Research and Development Agency under Contract No. APVV-15-0489 and by the Scientific Grant Agency of the Ministry of Education of the Slovak Republic and the Slovak Academy of Sciences, Grant No. 1/0665/15 and 1/0625/15.

Author details

Milan Cisty* and Veronika Soldanova

*Address all correspondence to: milan.cisty@stuba.sk

Department of Land and Water Resources Management, Faculty of Civil Engineering, Slovak University of Technology in Bratislava, Bratislava, Slovak Republic

References

[1] Thielen J, Bartholmes J, Pappenberger F. Application of ensembles in flood forecasting. In: ECMWF Workshop on Ensemble Predictions; 7-9 November 2007; UK: Reading

[2] Cloke H, Pappenberger F. Ensemble flood forecasting: A review. Journal of Hydrology. 2009;**375**(3-4):613-626

[3] Duan Q, Ajami NK, Gao X, Sorooshian S. Multi-model ensemble hydrologic prediction using Bayesian model averaging. Advance in Water Resources. 2007;**30**(5):1371-1386

[4] Breiman L. Bagging predictors. Machine Learning. 1996;**24**(2):123-140

[5] Wheway V. Variance reduction trends on 'boosted' classifiers. Journal of Applied Mathematics and Decision Sciences. 2004;**8**(3):141-154

[6] Hastie TJ, Tibshirani RJ, Friedman JH, The Elements of Statistical Learning: Data Mining, Inference, and Prediction, Springer series in statistics. Springer: New York; 2009

[7] Krogh JV. Neural network ensembles, cross validation, and active learning. In: Tesauro G, Touretzky DS, Leen TK, editors. Advances in Neural Information Processing Systems; Cambridge, MA: MIT Press; 1995. p. 231-238

[8] Bacauskiene M, Verikas A. Selecting salient features for classification based on neural network committees. Pattern Recognition Letters. 2004;**25**(16):1879-1891

[9] Kuncheva LI, Whitaker CJ. Measures of diversity in classifier ensembles and their relationship with the ensemble accuracy. Machine Learning. 2003;**51**(2):181-207

[10] Bacauskiene M, Verikas A, Gelzinis A, Valincius D. A feature selection technique for generation of classification committees and its application to categorization of laryngeal images. Pattern Recognition. 2009;**42**(5):645-654

[11] Toth E. Classification of hydro-meteorological conditions and multiple artificial neural networks for streamflow forecasting. Hydrology and Earth System Sciences. 2009; **13**(9):1555-1566

[12] Shrestha DL, Solomatine DP. Experiments with AdaBoostRT, an improved boosting scheme for regression. Neural Computing. 2006;**18**(7):1678-1710

[13] Erdal IH, Karakurt O. Advancing monthly streamflow prediction accuracy of CART models using ensemble learning paradigms. Journal of Hydrology. 2013;**477**:119-128

[14] Jeong DI, Kim Y-O. Rainfall-runoff models using artificial neural networks for ensemble streamflow prediction. Hydrological Processes. 2005;**19**(19):3819-3835

[15] Cannon AJ, Whitfield PH. Downscaling recent streamflow conditions in British Columbia, Canada using ensemble neural network models. Journal of Hydrology. 2002; **259**(1):136-151

[16] Boucher MA, Laliberté JP, Anctil F. An experiment on the evolution of an ensemble of neural networks for streamflow forecasting. Hydrology and Earth Systems Science. 2010;**14**(3):603-612

[17] Geem ZW, Kim JH, Loganathan GV. A new heuristic optimization algorithm: Harmony search. Simulation. 2001;**76**(2):60-68

[18] Geem ZW, Tseng CL, Williams JC. Harmony search algorithms for water and environmental systems. In: Music-Inspired Harmony Search Algorithm. Berlin Heidelberg: Springer; 2009. p. 113-127

[19] Karahan H, Gurarslan G, Geem ZW. Parameter estimation of the nonlinear Muskingum flood routing model using a hybrid harmony search algorithm. Journal of Hydrologic Engineering. 2012;**18**(3):352-360

[20] Cisty M, Bezak J, Bajtek Z. Evaluation of the impact of the pre-processing of data on the effectiveness and accuracy of SVM. In: 13th International Multidisciplinary Scientific GeoConference SGEM. 2013;**2**

[21] Rich C, Niculescu-Mizil A. An empirical comparison of supervised learning algorithms. Proceedings of the 23rd International Conference on Machine Learning. ACM. 2006, Pittsburgh, USA. pp. 161-168

[22] Rich C, Karampatziakis N, Yessenalina A. An empirical evaluation of supervised learning in high dimensions. Proceedings of the 25th International Conference on Machine Learning. ACM. 2008; New York, USA. pp. 96-103

[23] Vapnik V. The nature of statistical learning theory, Springer-Verlag: New York; 1995

[24] Haykin SS. Neural Networks: A Comprehensive Foundation. Prentice Hall: Englewood Cliffs, NJ; 2007

[25] Breiman L. Random forests. Machine Learning. 2001;**45**(1):5-32

[26] Friedman J, Hastie T, Tibshirani R. Regularization paths for generalized linear models via coordinate descent. Journal of Statistical Software. 2010;**33**(1):1-22

[27] Friedman J. Multivariate adaptive regression splines (with discussion). Annals of Statistics. 1991:1-141

[28] De'ath G. Boosted trees for ecological modeling and prediction. Ecology. 2007;**88**(1): 243-251

[29] Buehlmann P. Boosting for high-dimensional linear models. The Annals of Statistics. 2006;**34**(2):559-583

[30] Hofner B, Mayr A, Robinzonov N, Schmid M. Model-based boosting in R: A hands-on tutorial using the R package mboost. Department of Statistics, Technical Report No. 120. 2012

[31] Buehlmann P, Hothorn T. Boosting algorithms: Regularization, prediction and model fitting. Statistical Science. 2007;**22**(4):477-505

[32] Schmid M, Hothorn T. Boosting additive models using component-wise P-splines as base-learners. Computational Statistics & Data Analysis. 2008;**53**(2):298-311

[33] Torsten H, Bühlmann P, Kneib T, Schmid M, Hofner B. Model-based boosting 2.0. The Journal of Machine Learning Research. 2010;**11**:2109-2113

[34] Ridgeway G. Generalized boosted models: A guide to the gbm package. Update 1.1. 2007